Leaving the
Adventist Ministry

**Recent Titles in
Religion in the Age of Transformation**

Leaving the Adventist Ministry

A Study of the Process of Exiting

Peter H. Ballis

Religion in the Age of Transformation
Anson Shupe, Series Adviser

PRAEGER

Westport, Connecticut
London

Library of Congress Cataloging-in-Publication Data

Ballis, Peter H. (Peter Harry)
    Leaving the adventist ministry : a study of the process of exiting
/ Peter H. Ballis.
      p.   cm.—(Religion in the age of transformation, ISSN
1087–2388)
    Includes bibliographical references and index.
    ISBN 0–275–96229–6 (alk. paper)
    1. Ex-clergy. 2. Seventh-Day Adventists—Clergy. I. Title.
II. Series.
BV672.5.B29 1999
262'.1467—dc21   98–33607

British Library Cataloguing in Publication Data is available.

Library of Congress Catalog Card Number: 98–33607
ISBN: 0–275–96229–6
ISSN: 1087–2388

First published in 1999

Praeger Publishers, 88 Post Road West, Westport, CT 06881
An imprint of Greenwood Publishing Group, Inc.

Printed in the United States of America

The paper used in this book complies with the
Permanent Paper Standard issued by the National
Information Standards Organization (Z39.48–1984).

10 9 8 7 6 5 4 3 2 1

For Chris, Sarah, and Peter

Contents

Tables and Figures

TABLES

FIGURES

Acknowledgments

This study of exiting from the Seventh-day Adventist ministry was written *in situ*, and would not have been completed without the support of a great number of people. The insights it contains, the experiences that shaped it, the provision for everyday practicalities and motivation to endure, testify to the collaboration of colleagues, friends and family. I am grateful to the forty-three expastors and twelve wives for their willingness to open heart and soul and to share with a relative stranger painful memories and intimate details. For the most part they did this not with a spirit of malice toward the institution but in the hope that their combined stories might effect both understanding and change.

I am indebted to Rowan Ireland and David Hickman, under whose supervision the original research for this study was conducted, for their unfailing encouragement, comment and critical evaluation that enabled me to make sense of the experiences of others as well as my own. A number of colleagues at the Gippsland campus of Monash University also contributed to the study, including Ian Hamilton, who assisted with the analysis of the questionnaire data, and Marion Collis, who read and commented on the chapter on wives.

I am particularly grateful to James T. Richardson, Helen Rose Ebaugh and Michael Hill, who recommended the publication of my work.

Sue and Charles Duncan, Ross Jones, and the members of the Hawke's Bay Outreach Trust under the chairmanship of Peter Young encouraged me to pursue my academic interests and provided initial financial support for the research. Gaylene and Lyle Heise, Pam and Max Brinsmead, Keryn and Laurie Byrne, the late Joan and George Sorbello, Mum (Maggie) Ballis, Debbie and Glen Ballis, Theminy and Craig Bates, Vassily and Robert Skinner, and Margaret and Colin Flinn provided food, shelter, and transport (in some instances for many days at a time) to enable me to conduct the interviews. Winston Kent rescued my computer when it failed under the strain of the data. Evan Willis inspired me to persevere with the research and facilitated my personal transition from pastor to academic.

Last, but not least, I must acknowledge the support of Chris, Sarah, and Peter, who accompanied me along the path of exit and supported, tolerated, and loved me throughout the research. Chris challenged my theoretical assumptions, gave precision to the interpretation, and commented on the writing. The final work is symbolic of a joint journey.

Chapter 1

Radical Departures

This book is about Seventh-day Adventist expastors. At one level it records the career crises and exits of ministers from a sectarian religious community; at a different level it is about failed expectations, loss of commitment, and the erosion of faith. The focus of the study is on the social processes that culminate with exit from the Adventist ministry, but indirectly it is also about a religious organization as depicted by former pastors whose lives have been radically transformed by it. The study endeavors to contribute to an understanding of what happened in the Adventist community that brought about the crises among its pastors by discussing how exit occurs, the social processes that mobilize action and bring about change, and the language expastors use to account for past action.

Leaving and membership loss are common experiences to most people in contemporary society—people leave home, shift neighborhoods, change jobs and marital partners. Exiting has become such a regular feature of everyday life that we think very little about what processes are involved. Some exits are routinely undertaken and thus are not pathological, like promotion at work and going on holiday. In other instances problems arise when individuals fail to undertake the anticipated exits, as with some youth who refuse to leave home when they reach adulthood, or hospital patients who become accustomed to the "sick role." The present study focuses on a different kind of exit, what Levine (1984) terms "radical departures."

Exits of this sort, like the collapse of a business, the ending of a close relationship, and exit from a high commitment status or even a voluntary association, may be accompanied by dramatic transformations and radical shifts in personal and social identity. These exits are more difficult to negotiate, are usually quite painful, and call for explanation and justification. While exiting the ministry of a religious minority is unusual, I have come to understand that the processes involved are not. For this reason the study of expastors may be viewed as illustrating the social dynamics and complexity of processes associated with a wider category of exits.

The Adventist ministry and the sectarian community represent a unique setting in which to study the process of exiting. Leaving any kind of job involves some degree of agonizing, social relocation, abandonment of previous social networks and adoption of new ones, changes in occupational and social identity, and the construction of a narrative to account for and justify past action. Ministry as an occupation and the sectarian context make exit even more painful than it usually is. For most expastors, becoming an Adventist pastor involved years of anticipatory socialisation and role modelling and the adoption of a lifestyle that regulated every aspect of their lives, including family relationships and choice of marital partners and friends. For these reasons, processes that normally are obscure or pushed to the background are amplified and dramatized. The process of leaving the Adventist ministry thus enables us to broaden our understanding of exiting and to review theoretical assumptions about exit as a sociological phenomenon.

The primary purpose of this study is to examine the process whereby ministers from a conservative sectarian community began to entertain doubts concerning the sectarian cause, questioned their occupational "calling," and turned their backs on ministry. Using the data gathered from semi-structured focused interviews with forty-three expastors and twelve expastors' wives, detailed case study profiles are developed which highlight the ministry careers of former pastors, from initial interest in becoming ministers, through theological training, experiences in ministry, and finally, the actual process of separation from ministry. The aim throughout is to identify and discuss the types of personal experiences, organizational processes, and social relationships that generated the momentum for exit. The chronicling of the collapse of expastors' careers is used to highlight the fragility of commitment to sect values and the sectarian worldview.

CRISIS IN ADVENTISM

The Seventh-day Adventist movement in Australia attracted extensive media attention during the 1980s with the disappearance of baby Azaria, whose father, Michael Chamberlain was a pastor (Anti-Discrimination Board 1984:196). At the same time the Chamberlain case[1] was arousing extraordinary emotions in the public giving rise to wild speculations about the movement as a cult that practiced bizarre rituals involving humans (*Weekend Australian*, 21–22 February 1981; *Sun-Herald*, 7 February 1982), the Adventist Church was experiencing an internal schism that had potential to destroy it. The controversy during the 1970s provoked by the teaching and preaching of Des Ford, the Adventist scholar and former chairman of the Theology Department at Avondale College, the single training institution for Adventist ministers in Australia, came to a head in 1980 with his heresy trial and dismissal. Ford questioned the legitimacy of some cherished Adventist beliefs, including Ellen White's inspiration and "canonical" status and the Adventist interpretation of the Old and New Testament prophecies. Church leaders saw in Ford's attempts to bring the movement's theology closer to its Protestant origins a threat to the very existence of Adventist sectarianism. They reacted swiftly and violently. A large number of pastors left the Adventist ministry in the aftermath of Ford's dismissal, a falling away greater than at any other time in the movement's 150-year history.

In the introduction to his book on Seventh-day Adventist fringe movements, Tarling informed his readers that his account covered the breadth of Adventist history up to Ford's heresy trial. Tarling explains:

[At] this point I can leave Seventh-day Adventist at the cross-roads—the point at which the movement can choose to proceed as if nothing has happened, or else it can change direction. Undoubtedly some members will change, and others will not. But the fate of the movement as a whole cannot be easily speculated upon. Ten years may reveal a much different church to the one which people now identify as Seventh-day Adventism. Or ten years may produce two separate churches, both claiming to be the heirs of William Miller, Ellen and James White, Joseph Bates, John Nevins Andrews and Uriah Smith. (Tarling 1981:7)

Tarling saw the dismissal of the Australian scholar as a turning point in Adventist history and one where the movement's future directions were being decided. He reasoned that a ten-year interval would suffice for one to assess the full impact of the Ford dismissal on Adventism, and he outlined two contrasting futures in his prognosis: the church may adopt a business-as-usual approach to the Ford issues, a position Tarling views as a victory for the authorities and a crushing defeat of the revisionists; or alternatively, the revisionists may secede, leading to the commencement of a separate Adventist community which would share the same family roots but move out of the traditional family home. Tarling anticipated the latter outcome.

The secession of an entire Adventist church in San Diego and the establishment of *Evangelica*, a new periodical devoted to promoting the evangelical cause, along with the exit by February 1981 of eight Australian ministers, was interpreted by Tarling (1981:230) as pointing in the direction of schism. Adventist authorities favored the first option and belittled the idea of schism as "hogwash." In a report in Melbourne's *Sun-Herald* (8 February 1981), Pastor Alf Jorgenson, the South Pacific Division's field secretary, made light of the early exits from ministry by asking, "But what are three [probationary Adventist ministers] among hundreds?" Neither Tarling nor Jorgenson anticipated what did eventuate: no new Adventist church formed, although dozens of Adventist churches throughout Australia and New Zealand struggle to remain in operation as a result of unprecedented membership losses. Neither anticipated the full extent of the fallout from the Adventist ministry.

The present study focuses on Adventist pastors in Australia and New Zealand who left during the ten-year interval identified by Tarling. This is not to ignore the fact that numerous Adventist pastors exited in previous decades and since, or to imply that the issues were place-specific and confined to the Australian continent. However, the controversy among Adventists in the South Pacific Division was more intense and the fallout from the ministry greater than in any other area of Adventist presence, and it is the extent of the fallout that gives a sense of urgency to the present study.

Church members and sect officials attribute the exits to the influence of Des Ford. Interviews with expastors (and my own impressions from my familiarity with the personal histories of some of the leavers) indicate that many expastors were variously enabled by the Ford dismissal to act on their own hurts and disappointments in ministry. But as the full testimonies show, the enabling/ legitimating place of the Des Ford affair and its surrounding theological controversies also belie the official administration account of the spate of exits: that it was provoked solely by the baleful influence of a heretic on pastors who were weak in understanding and commitment to the truths of Seventh-day Adventism. This contradiction of official story and expastors' testimony provides the intellectual challenge of the study.

BIOGRAPHICAL CONTEXT

It is not uncommon for social researchers to acknowledge that their autobiographies have played a role in the construction of their research. As Atkinson and Shakespeare note, "personal histories are germane to the conduct of research and construction of knowledge" (1993:8). In some instances the researcher's biography shapes the whole research enterprise, from choice and area of study, to the experience of fieldwork, through analysis and writing (Okely 1992:1). This book similarly embodies a personal history. The time-frame of the study corresponds with my fifteen-year ministry as a Seventh-day Adventist pastor in New Zealand and Australia.

My initial interest in knowing more about Adventist expastors was generated by a genuine puzzlement over why anyone would want to leave work I had recently entered and to which I intended to commit myself for life. Some of my preoccupation with the murkier aspects of the Adventist past commenced while researching the history of Adventism in New Zealand (Ballis 1985). I was surprised to discover in the denomination's official minutes and publications scores of references to apostates and "heretics." During my fifteen-year ministry I heard numerous pastors at formal and informal gatherings recount narratives of apostasy and anecdotes about ministers who questioned the faith and the tragedies that befell them because they left. Implicit in these references to leavers was the belief that some familiarity with the circumstances and views of former pastors may have the positive outcome of inoculating potential "deviants" against similar failings. Recalling the darker side of ministry was intended to discourage independent thinking and caution pastors to remain loyal. A number of factors, however, led me to shift my interest from wanting to learn more about the *personal troubles* of expastors to thinking about *denominational processes* that generate exit.

Almost every Adventist pastor, at least in the South Pacific Division, was in one way or another affected by the 1980 heresy trial and defrocking of Des Ford. The dismissal of the former theology lecturer, whom I respected as a teacher and admired as a kind Christian gentleman, affected me also, although it was not so much his theology as the church's treatment of him and its response to the issues he raised that jolted my confidence in the Adventist establishment. My perceptions of the way administrators and academics responded to theological issues in general troubled me for some time, but their reactions to Ford raised questions in my mind concerning some in leadership.

I was affected by the sheer number of Adventist pastors leaving. It may have been possible in previous generations to explain away the one or two exits from ministry each year by pointing to individual factors and personal failings. However, the annual loss of between twenty and twenty-five ministers at a time during the 1980s of a work force totalling less than four hundred was more difficult to justify. I was not alone in wondering about the extent of the fallout. In the course of the present research I came across two Adventist academics and one church pastor who kept lists of ministers who left. At formal ministers' meetings and other church gatherings I recall discussing with groups of pastors the most recent departures and wondering who would be next to leave.

Many were surprised by the magnitude of the fallout and shocked by the church's apparent disregard of the phenomenon of pastor loss. In small groups pastors deplored the fact that church authorities appeared unconcerned and often welcomed the departure of some pastors. At ministers' meetings church officials and visiting speakers would remind pastors, citing Ellen White, that "in the last days there would be a falling away from the truth" but that a remnant will remain steadfast and not be shaken. It was quite apparent during private discussions, however, that the confidence of pastors had been shaken.

Many who left I knew personally and viewed as honest and sincere men who loved the church and were committed to the work of ministry. Some were close friends whom I got to know while studying for ministry, and others I worked with in the same Conference. Each dismissal or resignation of a minister friend or colleague affected me also. During one camp meeting the Conference president informed a gathering of pastors that "there were many dedicated literature evangelists[2] in the Conference ready and willing to take the place of ministers who resign." I was one of the pastors who left that meeting convinced the Adventist Church did not value its ministers. It was difficult to remain detached from the exits of fellow pastors and unable to transpose the departures of friends and colleagues into "object lessons" for the edification of those who remained.

It is possible for lay members to continue in the Adventist community as "cultural Adventists" while remaining ambivalent toward the organization (Neff and Neff 1985:152). This is more difficult for the pastors to achieve. Eventually it becomes pointless to continue in ministry when one feels insecure in one's work and unable to discuss problems with those in authority. I feared that anything I shared with the authorities in confidence would in time be used to condemn me in the same way former pastor friends were condemned. It was the compounding effect of these factors—the administration's attitude to Ford, the number of exits, my personal knowledge of leavers and empathy with their concerns—that compelled me to reconsider my future in ministry.

Exit was not something that I entertained during the early 1980s, although the confused political and theological climate in the Adventist Church following the dismissal of Des Ford did influence my decision to return to university. It was not until my appointment as a tutor in sociology that the possibility of exit became a reality. My experience of exit was in all likelihood shaped by the academic discipline I have taken on: becoming an expastor was bound up with becoming a sociologist.

I began this study as an "insider"—an ordained Seventh-day Adventist pastor having been granted study leave for the purpose of undertaking a doctoral program. In this respect I was an active participant in the life and ministry of the Adventist church. I brought to the study an insider's perspective on the idiosyncrasies and distinctive character of the Adventist minority—a familiarity with its "atmosphere," "ethos," "collective response," and "expressive culture" (B. Wilson 1982:24) as well as with the politics and conflicts over theology. More important, I had first hand knowledge of the work of the pastor and the variety of pressures Adventist ministers have to endure. My insider status was a key factor enabling me to survey continuing pastors and to gain access to official church records—a privilege afforded to few, and rarely to "outsiders." Church administrators and pastors had an expectation that I would produce a work that would protect the organization and defend its public image. This attitude is reflected in the unsolicited comments from church pastors on returned questionnaires. Four pastors wished me "God's blessing" for the research, two expressed an interest in the results, two others responded to the task of filling out the questionnaire as a "spreading of Jesus's love" and a ministry to "the fallen." My insider status thus facilitated the study in ways that would not have been possible as an outsider.

At the same time, however, the fact that I was studying at a "secular" university and devoted time and energy to the narratives of leavers meant that others regarded me with suspicion or viewed me as an expastor. Two Adventist scholars who kept records of pastors who left the ministry had my name on their lists. At the conclusion of their interviews seven expastors insisted that in exchange I tell them about myself and discuss my own future in ministry. Three explained that they viewed me as an expastor even though I had not formally resigned from ministry. If being an Adventist pastor gave me "sympathetic understanding" and "privileged access" (Merton 1988: ix) to the organization, university study facilitated the relationship with expastors who looked upon me as "one of them."

In the preface to her book *Becoming an Ex*, which contains glimpses of autobiography, Ebaugh writes:

In the course of analyzing data, I became one of my own statistics. I left the [religious] order to become an ex-nun. How much my decision was influenced by what I was studying is hard to unravel. What is clear is that I gained enormous insight into the process of exiting from my own experience. In fact, there are nuances and depths of meaning that probably cannot be learned any other way. I lived what I had been studying. I too became one of the subjects in the course of the study. (1988a: xvi)

I officially resigned from the Adventist ministry in 1992—like Ebaugh, after the material for the study had been collected and while analyzing the data. In the words of Merton (1988:ix), I found myself "collecting data as an insider and analyzing it as an outsider." My firsthand knowledge of Adventist ministry, familiarity with many of the leavers, and insights derived from my own experience of leaving are pivotal to the research. The insights derived as insider inform both the interpretation of the data and my theorizing about exit.

OVERVIEW

The study begins by locating the exits into a recurring pattern of exit from the Adventist ministry and explores the magnitude of the most recent minister fallout relative to other denominations. A profile of the expastor is developed in Chapter 3 by comparing popular typification of leavers in the light of key demographic characteristics of respondents. The chapter highlights the limitation of the preoccupation with background factors predisposing pastors to leave and draws attention to the need to better understand expastors' retrospective accounts of their exits. The different versions of leaving the Adventist ministry that can be heard in expastors' accounts are identified and examined in Chapter 4.

Chapters 5, 6, and 7 are parallel chapters and focus on social experiences and organizational processes. Expastors trace the genesis of their disillusionment with ministry to a host of similar experiences that compelled them to reevaluate their futures in ministry. Chapter 5 outlines the links between loss of idealism and exit. Chapter 6 examines the sources on which the former pastors drew for inspiration while in ministry to identify key organizational processes contributing to decisions to leave ministry.

The interviews abound with references to church administrators, close minister friends and other expastors. References to other people led me to explore which groups are featured in exit narratives and thus contributed most to the exit process. Chapter 7 discusses the possibility that exit from ministry was a group phenomenon as well as an individual experience.

Turning from the social and organizational dimensions of exiting, Chapters 8 and 9 focus on the contributions of significant others to exit. As already pointed out, the person of Des Ford looms large in the present study. Chapter 8 draws on the testimonies of expastors to show in what ways the Ford issues impacted on their thinking. It was not my intention to interview wives because I thought the inclusion of another set of narratives might distract from the focus on expastors, a belief reinforced by the fact that studies of clergy exit without exception focused exclusively on the clergy themselves. At the conclusion of one of the interviews, the expastor's wife present during her husband's interview suggested that I interview wives, arguing that a study based solely on the testimony of husbands would be incomplete and one-sided. In response to this suggestion, twelve expastors' wives were interviewed, and Chapter 9 outlines their versions of exit.

Chapter 10 details the actual separation. Exit is presented not as an orderly progression of predictable steps but as the culmination of a host of painful experiences, and contradictory thoughts and emotions. In each of the chapters that trace the sequence and interaction of factors in the process of exit, a variety of theories employed by academics and the parties involved to explain exit are tested. But the aim of the testing of theory is always to elucidate process; it is not the quest for a prime cause of exit. Finally, Chapter 11 thus outlines the typical process of pastor exit and major variations on this typical process.

NOTES

1. On the night of 17 August 1980, nine-week old Azaria Chamberlain disappeared from her parents' tent while camping at Ayers Rock in central Australia. Her mother Lindy Chamberlain, claimed that a dingo had taken the sleeping child. The unusual circumstances of the baby's disappearance generated "months of innuendoes, suspicion and probably the most malicious gossip in this country" (Anti-Discrimination Board 1984:196). Although neither body nor motive were found, Lindy Chamberlain was convicted of murder and was sentenced to life imprisonment. In response to a groundswell of legal support for her innocence, a Royal Commission found serious deficiencies in the forensic evidence used to convict her, and Mrs Chamberlain was pardoned (Young 1989). The conviction was quashed eight years after the disappearance, with the discovery of children's clothing which was identified as belonging to Azaria. The trial of Lindy and Michael Chamberlain has become a *cause celebre* in Australia's criminal history. The New South Wales Anti-Discrimination Board referred to this case as a "notable instance of prejudicial reporting." A report in Melbourne's *Sun Herald* (7 March 1982) on "The Chamberlains' Church," linked the Chamberlain case with the theological divisions in the Adventist Church following Des Ford's dismissal.

2. A literature evangelist is "an SDA who regularly sells from house to house denominational books and magazines to the public" (Neufeld and Neuffer 1996:705). "If there is one work more important than another," wrote Ellen White, "it is that of getting our publications before the public, thus leading them to search the Scriptures" (1948, vol. 5:389, 390). Since the 1880s, literature evangelism has proved "one of the most effective ways of introducing Adventism to a new locality" (R. W. Schwarz 1979:348) and was a strategy adopted for the establishment of Adventist presence in Australia and New Zealand (Goldstone 1980). Although few literature evangelists receive formal training in theology and ministry, their work is considered "a sacred one" (Neufeld and Neuffer 1996:706).

Chapter 2 _____

Adventism and Exiting

Resignations and dismissals of pastors are recurring themes in Adventist discourse. Disproportionate amounts of time and money have been invested over the years by the movement to combat the enemy "from within." The falling away of Seventh-day Adventist pastors during the 1980s is one more expression of a phenomenon that has troubled the sectarian community from its beginning, although, as will become evident in the course of the study, the most recent wave of exits differs from similar previous occurrences in magnitude and consequences for the organization. This chapter outlines the extent of minister loss in the Adventist community relative to other denominations and introduces the theoretical framework of the study.

ADVENTIST CONTEXT

The Seventh-day Adventist Church is one of a number of minority religious groups operating on the fringes of Australian and New Zealand societies. Adventists are best known by their sabbatarianism, vegetarianism, and their stand as conscientious objectors. While in census reports 0.3 percent of Australians and New Zealanders identify with the movement, Seventh-day Adventists remain relatively unknown in these societies and therefore are either poorly understood or misunderstood.

Bloom (1993:154) describes Seventh-day Adventism as "an American religion of health, crossed with the postapocalyptic dream of an end-time never to be." The description identifies four characteristics of the movement. First, Adventism is an "American religion." It is one of a number of religious minority groups that traces its origins to the social and religious ferment affecting America in the first half of the nineteenth century (Kapitzke 1995). The moral awakening and millennial speculation that overwhelmed the eastern states of North America during the early nineteenth century form the matrix of the Adventist worldview and "the womb from which was born the modern child" (Spalding 1961:23). Whereas a majority of Millerite adventists[1] admitted their incorrect chronology following the nonoccurrence of the return of Christ predicted to occur on October 22, 1844, a handful of followers reinterpreted the prophecies and arrived at an explanation. The "hard core" who survived the stigma of disappointment (Boyer 1992:92) and refused to admit their "mistake" (Linden 1978:80) concluded that the date was right but that the geographical location of "the event" was wrong and announced that the "cleansing of the sanctuary" mentioned in the Old Testament Book of Daniel referred to something that transpired in heaven and not on earth. Emerging out of the cognitive dissonance of the "Great Disappointment" (Festinger, Riecken and Schachter 1956:14) and armed with "a new understanding" of the prophecies (Damsteegt 1977:295), a "remnant" had arisen free of doubting and despondency. Thus the second characteristic of the movement noted by Bloom is that Adventism is a religion "crossed with the postapocalyptic dream."

The new movement was dedicated to warning the world that the cleansing of the heavenly sanctuary or "investigative judgement" which will decide who will spend eternity with God and who will be banished to damnation commenced in 1844 and that at the conclusion of an *unspecified* but brief period of time Christ would return (Spalding 1961:97–113). For the next decade and a half, under the supervisory role of Ellen White's visions (Damsteegt 1977:164), the advent followers discarded some of their more extreme views (Linden 1982), and consolidated their doctrinal beliefs (Damsteegt 1977:103–164). In May 1863 the "remnant" that had also turned sabbatarian was formally organized into the Seventh-day Adventist Church.

During the mid-1870s the fledgling church, which for more than thirty years had confined its activities to North America, lifted its sights to evangelizing the world (Damsteegt 1977:271–293). The transformation from an all-American movement to a worldwide organization took place at breathtaking pace (Schantz 1983; Oosterwal 1980:5). By the turn of the century, and with barely four decades of organisational history, Adventism had grown from a small community of about 4,000 followers when it organized in 1863 to an international body of 75,000. By 1885 Adventist missionaries had established a presence in Australia (Goldstone 1980; Clapham 1985) and New Zealand (Ballis 1985). At the time of Ellen White's death in 1915, church membership had grown to 125,000 scattered throughout the world. By the 1980s, the period covered by the present study, Adventism had become "the most widespread Protestant denomination" (Land 1986:vii), with almost 4 million members, even though "the power base" of the church continued to reside with the 15 percent of members in America (Pearson 1990:7).

Clark (1949:25) contends that "Adventism is the typical cult of the disinherited and suffering poor." However, there is considerable evidence to show that from its beginnings Seventh-day Adventism flourished among the "occupationally independent" (Graybill 1979:31–32; Goldschmidt 1959:348–355; Anders 1973:287). Adventist converts in New Zealand and Australia, for example, have been disproportionately drawn from the upper side of the socioeconomic spectrum (Ballis 1992:45–60). A more accurate summation of the class disposition of Adventists is implied by G. Schwartz (1970:218), who believes Seventh-day Adventism is a modern equivalent of Weber's Protestant ethic.

A third characteristic noted by Bloom is the minority's institutional focus: Adventism is a "religion of health." It is paradoxical that a movement ostensibly dedicated to proclaiming the end of the world and the imminent return of Christ simultaneously has a this-worldly focus that belies its other-worldly orientation. In view of the enormous range of educational, medical, welfare, and evangelistic activities operated by the Adventist minority, Gaustad's (1976:151) jibe that "while expecting a kingdom from the heavens, [Adventists] work diligently for one on earth" seems appropriate. Large sums of money have been invested erecting and keeping in operation a range of Adventist health and education institutions. In 1981, in addition to 22,357 churches, the movement was operating 4,834 schools, 78 secondary colleges, 2 universities, 41 schools of nursing, 166 hospitals, 269 dispensaries and clinics, 23 food factories, 86 retirement homes, and 50 publishing houses. The active work force of the organization totalled 94,891, including 9,889 active pastors.

Schwartz (1970) believes the institutional focus of Adventism is an expression of a work ethic that promotes upward mobility. Theobald (1979) contends that institutionalization is a response to a perceived need to modernize and adapt the movement to a changing social environment. According to B. Wilson (1975:34–43), the process signals Adventism's drift from sectarian hostility to the world to an accommodation akin to that of the established churches.

Early Sabbatarian Adventists held tenaciously to the belief that the "moment" a church is organized, it "becomes Babylon" (R. W. Schwarz 1979:86). However, over a period of seventy years, and with considerable debate and conflict (Anderson 1986:36–65; R. W. Schwarz 1979:151–165, 373–392), the membership arrived at an organisational structure that is not unlike that of other denominational competitors. The system of church government, which Adventists commonly describe as representative, has characteristics of several systems: "the congregational, with its emphasis on local church authority; the presbyterian, which provides for government by elected representatives; and in some points the Methodist (in Australia, the Uniting Church), in that it has conferences (or synods) as organizational units and that the conference assigns ministers to the local churches" (Neufeld and Neuffer 1996:929). At the same time, however, a dominant feature is its hierarchical structure modelled, in part, on the traditional structure of the Catholic Church. The organization structure of local Conferences that are grouped into Unions and Divisions, according to G. Schwartz, "fits [Adventism's] predilection for orderly, predictable, and rational allocation of religious energies and economic resources" (1970:187).

Notwithstanding the movement's dramatic expansion and institutional growth, in doctrine and lifestyle Seventh-day Adventism remains "ultra-conservative" (Froom 1953:378). "[The] Seventh-day Adventist Church is in many ways similar to the strict Protestant sects of the 1800s, strongly emphasising what Max Weber called inner worldly asceticism" (Borhek 1960:9). Darroch (1984) locates Adventists midway between evangelical Protestantism and what he terms "sects" on the grounds that while holding to the core of Protestant beliefs, it also maintains teachings at variance with it, including the teachings of Saturday as Sabbath, conditional mortality, the investigative judgement, and belief in the inspiration of Ellen White. Alongside its simplified ethical system (Pearson 1990), the movement advocates a lifestyle and values that reflect its nineteenth-century ethos, with prohibitions against the consumption of alcohol, coffee, condiments and meat (especially pork), the use of tobacco, wearing immodest jewellery, card-playing, the theatre, and other forms of "worldly" entertainment (Numbers 1992). Butler argues that Adventism survives in the twentieth century as "a Victorian Protestant subculture sustaining itself long after the large host society has disappeared." The culture and values of Adventism, according to Ahlstrom (1972:1021), bear unmistakable evidence of the movement's American ethos.

Seventh-day Adventism is not isolationist in the strict sense of the term, nor does the movement require members to withdraw completely from the wider society. However, it is "totalist" in the sense that it maintains definitive social boundaries and demands wholehearted commitment from its members. According to Ebaugh, "Totalist organisations that aim to imbue every member with a prevailing ideology create boundary-maintenance structures to achieve this goal. Boundaries are those structures—physical, social, behavioral, cultural, and psychological—which define the group, set it off from its environment, and give the group a clear, coherent reason for existence, thereby facilitating commitment on the part of members" (1977:41). This description of Catholic orders can be applied also to the Adventist movement. Seventh-day Adventism demands a high degree of commitment from its members, insists on some degree of separation from the larger society, and endeavors to maintain undisputed social and ideological boundaries that define who is *in* and who is *out*. The observance of Saturday as the Sabbath, the Adventist health emphasis and lifestyle (no smoking, drinking alcohol, etc.), and the sophisticated parochial school system together serve to differentiate those who belong to the movement from those who do not (B. Wilson 1975). The most extreme measure aimed at keeping the faith pure and maintaining continuity with the past has been the marginalization and expulsion of members who deviate from traditional Adventist norms.

Bloom's fourth item, that Seventh-day Adventism is a religion preoccupied with an "end-time never to be," highlights the precariousness of a community proclaiming the "soon coming of Christ" while simultaneously coming to terms with and legitimating its "delay." Ford (1980a) rightly points out that the Adventist interpretation of the prophecies has been pivotal in the multitude of controversies, heresy trials, and apostasies that have plagued the movement throughout its 150-year history. Seventh-day Adventist historical records abound with the names of some well known and a host of lesser known persons who were dismissed, resigned, or just turned their backs on sectarianism. In the mid-1880s Dudley M. Canright, a convert to Adventism, terminated his twenty-year ministry disillusioned with Adventist apocalyptic and Ellen White's visions, which he ridiculed as the "imaginings of her own mind" (Schwarz 1979:469). At the turn of the century, Albion Fox Ballenger, the son of an Adventist minister was dismissed for heresy for promoting a contrary interpretation of the prophecies concerning the sanctuary (Adams 1993). A. T. Jones and E. J. Waggoner left the ministry during the first decade of the twentieth century and were labelled heretics for their pantheism (G. R. Knight 1987; McMahon 1979). Whereas the above leavers confined their operations to the United States, Louis R. Conradi's fifty-year ministry centered in Europe. According to Schwarz (1979:475), Conradi adopted divergent views concerning Christ's work in the heavenly sanctuary and the inspiration of Ellen White. From Tarling's (1981) study of the "edges" of Seventh-day Adventism one may generalize that heresy, apostasy, and separatism are ubiquitous to Adventist sectarianism and that the movement has been far more fissiparous than researchers have heretofore acknowledged.

Australia also has had its share of "heretics" and deviants in ministry. Some of the best known include W. W. Fletcher, who resigned in 1932 (Tarling 1981:178–179), Louis Were, who was ousted in the 1940s, and Robert Greive, who was dismissed in 1956 (Tarling 1981:180–185). Three themes dominate Adventist controversies both past and present: the role and authority of Ellen White, the Adventist interpretation of the prophecies, and conflict with administration.

According to Schwartz (1970:93), Ellen White endowed "traditional Adventist beliefs with divine legitimacy," and her inspired interventionism has kept the membership "back from the edge of intellectual chaos." But as Pearson (1990:8) and J. M. Butler (1992) observe, boasting a prophet from the Victorian era heightens Adventism's displacement in contemporary society. Some of the strongest criticisms of Ellen White have come not from "outsiders" but from third and fourth generation Adventists who attribute her visions to psychopathology (Numbers 1992:202–227). The Adventist interpretation of prophecy and the teaching of the investigative judgement—the movement's distinct contribution to Christendom (Paxton 1978:147)—are recurring themes in Adventist internal polemics. The same issues were the focus of the controversy that culminated with the defrocking of Australian Adventist scholar Des Ford.

Officials consistently point to personal failings and individual factors (Schwarz 1979:195, 449, 475) to explain these crises. According to one official church statement, the problems have been "brought on by our inexcusable delinquency in failing to adopt God's plan for finishing the work" (Annual Council 1976). An alternative explanation is provided by Ford (1980a), who notes that the conflicts have a common theological foundation. According to Ford, Adventist heretics of one generation build on the questioning of their predecessors, and issues unresolved in that generation become amplified with time and pose an even greater threat to the next. Theology has consistently featured in exits, although it would be both incorrect and simplistic to attribute the fallout exclusively to one set of theological issues or to assume that the conflicts occurred in a social vacuum.

At the time of his retirement as General Conference president, Robert H. Pierson (1978) issued "An Earnest Appeal" to denominational leaders, admonishing them to maintain the vitality of the sect and resist the ossification of the church. In his appeal Pierson noted that in time sects become institutionalized and take on the characteristics of the mainline churches from which they separated. He thus warns church leaders that "this must . . . not happen to the Seventh-day Adventist Church" because Adventism "is not just another church—it is God's remnant." The General Conference president's appeal reveals a leader not only aware of the forces generating change within the church, but calling on loyal Adventists to be on guard against the forces threatening the movement and where necessary to take action to preserve its sectarian properties. It will become evident in the course of this study that the central administration, a bureaucracy Magnusson (1991:22–23) likens to a "hierarchical episcopacy" that is largely self-appointed and has the power both to regulate innovation and stifle change, is a key factor that explains at least the most recent occurrences of exit from ministry.

RESEARCH ON ADVENTIST EXPASTORS

Studies focusing specifically on Seventh-day Adventist clergy are few and in general make only passing reference to the subject of exit. Schoun's *Helping Pastors Cope: A Psycho-social Support System for Pastors* (1982) does not address loss of pastors, although his discussion of career adjustment and job satisfaction has a ring of urgency that suggests all is not well in the Seventh-day Adventist ministry. Dudley and Cummings' "Factors Related to Pastoral Morale in the Seventh-day Adventist Church" (1982) is the only sociological study of Adventist clergy. Dudley and Cummings surveyed 172 Adventist pastors in the United States and Canada and found that a "substantial minority" experience low morale for a variety of reasons, including theological dissonance, conflict with spouse and with the administration, and frustration with the administrative minutiae of running a church. The authors report that 21 percent of the pastors surveyed expressed interest in transferring to administrative or teaching work, while 35 percent had discussed with their spouses the possibility of transferring to another type of ministry. Significantly more than one out of every four Adventist pastors they surveyed (28 percent) had contemplated leaving the pastoral ministry altogether. The authors concluded from their survey that Seventh-day Adventist ministers in the United States were relatively contented and secure in their work. However, a different picture emerges of Adventist pastors in the South Pacific Division.

From his 1983 survey of pastors in Australia and New Zealand, Winter (1983) reports that 27.2 percent of his respondents had seriously considered leaving the Adventist ministry, a figure that approximates that reported by Dudley and Cummings. Winter notes that if pastors in the "maybe" category are included with those who have contemplated exit, the percentage of discontented Adventist pastors in his survey rises to 43.1 percent. Winter contends that his findings depict an organization in trouble and admonishes Adventist authorities to interpret the results as forewarning an impending crisis. Figures on the actual number of Adventist pastors who resigned or were dismissed during the 1980s are not available, although official statistical reports *hint* that the attrition rate among the Seventh-day Adventist pastors in Australia and New Zealand has reached alarming proportions.

EXTENT OF FALLOUT

Figures on the actual number who left the Adventist ministry during the period under review are hard to come by; officials have deliberately avoided publishing this information. Requests directed to the South Pacific Division for more accurate statistics proved unfruitful. The ministerial secretary, for instance, acknowledged the importance of this study, adding that "the morale of [pastors] is very precious to us and no doubt some of the material you obtain would be most helpful to us in learning how to do better," but the question of how many ministers left during the 1980s remained unanswered.

In order to obtain some estimate of the number of ministers who left, a letter was sent to each of the eleven Conference secretaries in this Division requesting the number of ministers who had resigned or were dismissed between 1970 and 1985. Only four of the eleven Conference secretaries responded, and the figures they provided were at best conservative. According to these four responses, seventeen pastors were dismissed or had resigned between 1980 and 1985. In the course of the research I collected the names of twenty-eight expastors who left these Conferences during the same interval. It would appear that the figures provided by Conference secretaries were either deliberately kept low to minimize the extent of the problems affecting the church or selective as to who they included among the leavers.

The South Pacific Division publishes an annual *Statistical Report* which records among other things the numerical strength of the various Conferences and Unions and the number of ministerial licensees, ordained ministers, and pastors holding honorary ministerial credentials. The published figures are inconsistent and at times inaccurate; however, while they do not disclose the exact number of ministers who have exited, they allude to the problems affecting Australasian Adventism. Figure 2.1 records the number of Adventist pastors in Australia and New Zealand between 1972 and 1981. The distinction between "licensed ministers" and "ordained pastors" is an important one and requires explanation.

The Seventh-day Adventist Church issues licenses to its employees according to job status and duties performed. Ordination is considered the highest calling and is conferred on Adventist males following "careful, unhurried and prayerful examination." The revised May 1983 statement of the *Working Policy of the South Pacific Division* (1986:113) additionally states that "the proofs of a man's divine call must be clearly evident before the church sets him apart by ordination." These "proofs" of one's calling to ministry include some "evidence of being divinely called" and a sense of being "set apart" evident in the individual's "personal spirituality, personality, home and family life, handling of personal finances, success in soul-winning," and, most important, harmony with the fundamental beliefs of the movement. Ordination is preceded by a period of between four and six years of probationary service as a licensed minister. Most often ordination is dependent on the two factors of evangelistic success and overt commitment to the Adventist doctrines.

By contrast, ministerial licenses are granted "to those who are engaged in ministerial work and who would be expected to be ordained in due course" (*Working Policy* 1986:39). Licensees are new entrants to ministry and subordinates to ordained pastors. Their duties differ from those of ordained pastors in two respects: the latter are additionally authorized to conduct baptisms and marriage services. Ordination carries symbolic value in the Adventist community and signifies that the individual has shown commitment to the Adventist cause and thus has the support of the authorities. It is my view that ordination could be and was used by Conference leaders to reward cooperators by a shorter probation time, and to censure dissenters with postponement.

Figure 2.1
Adventist Ministers in Australia and New Zealand

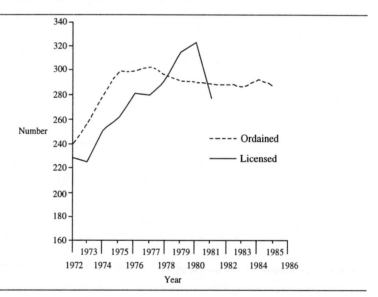

In the light of the distinction between licensed ministers and ordained pastors, Figure 2.1 highlights important trends in the Adventist ministry during the 1970s and 1980s. About half the number of ministers (51) were ordained between 1972 and 1980 relative to the number who entered ministry (95). If the distinction between the two categories of Adventist minister is one of status and power, as suggested above, then the mechanism for passing on the running of the church to the new generation slowed down during the 1970s, as is evident from the gradual stockpiling of licensees and the leveling in numbers of ordained pastors during the same period. The dramatic reduction in the number of licensed ministers from 323 in 1980 to 277 in 1981, a decline of 7 percent, is one indication of the fallout, albeit a conservative one.

A more accurate way to measure the loss is to manually count the annual number of Avondale College theology graduates who trained, entered ministry, and continue to serve the church as pastors. The figures in Table 2.1 are based on Avondale College theology graduates from 1950 to 1982. Table 2.1 reveals that on average only 54 percent of those who graduated and entered ministry were continuing in ministry as of 1990. It additionally shows that the rate of exit from ministry increased steadily during these decades: 40 percent of the graduates who commenced in ministry during the 1950s left by 1990; 44 percent of graduate starters from the 1960s left by 1990; and 53 percent of graduate starters from the 1970s did the same. Indeed, not only has the number of exits increased with each decade, but more ministers now leave over a shorter period of time.

Early estimates of the number of ministers exiting were conservative. Wolfgramm (1983:313–314) noted that fourteen ministers were removed from the Adventist ministry between 1980 and 1982. Winter (1983:3), who was the first to express concern that exit was reaching crisis proportions in this Division, put the figure at "nearly sixty." *Limboline* (10 August 1985), a monthly newsletter issued by a group of former Adventists in California, named one hundred Adventist pastors who had been "fired, pressured to resign, or resigned voluntarily" since 1980, although only twenty-three of these expastors served in Australia or New Zealand. In the course of my research I compiled a list of 182 ministers who left the Adventist ministry between 1980 and 1988. This figure is equivalent to an astonishing 40 percent of the total ministerial work force in Australia and New Zealand—a statistic without precedent in the Adventist Church at any other time or in any other place. The fallout from the Adventist ministry is even more alarming when viewed against the backdrop of exit from other churches by clergy and members of religious orders.

Fichter (1970) notes that between 1966 and 1969 the female population of Roman Catholic religious orders in the United States declined by 7.8 percent. Zelus (1975:6) estimates that between 1965 and 1971 the American Catholic priesthood lost about 12 percent of its active membership through resignation. Jud et al. (1970:58) estimate that only 1 percent of United Council of Churches ministers in the United States resigned during 1968 and thus conclude that "we are not studying a runaway epidemic but a persistent low-grade infection." However, as Fichter (1970) points out, "any profession is in trouble when the input of personnel does not equal the exodus (both by death and resignation), and this becomes more acute as the population that is served by the professions expands." When coupled with declining numbers training for ministry and an increase in the numbers retiring, the exodus from the Adventist ministry is symptomatic of an organization in trouble.

An overview of research on clergy exit may enable us to gain a comparative perspective on the Adventist phenomenon.

Table 2.1
Avondale College Ministry Graduates, 1950–1982

Year	Grads	Non-Start	Women	Teaching	Left Ministry	Continue in Ministry as of 1990
1950	22	1		1	6	14
1951	13				5	8
1952	20	3			11	6
1953	6	1			1	4
1954	13			1	4	8
1955	14		1	1	3	10
1956	8			2	2	4
1957	8			2	2	4
1958	7				4	3
1959	7			1	2	4
1960	5				3	2
1961	9			2		7
1962	4			1	1	2
1963	11				4	7
1964	11				3	8
1965	15			2	7	6
1966	13	2			5	6
1867	10		1		2	7
1968	21	1			13	7
1969	21				8	13
1970	21	1			9	11
1971	11	1			5	5
1972	17				12	5
1973	22				8	14
1974	13				8	5
1975	21		1		11	9
1976	23	2	1	1	7	12
1977	12	1		1	4	6
1978	18	1			11	6
1979	25		1		15	9
1980	10				2	8
1981	11			1	5	5
1982	15	1	1	1	4	9
	457	15	5	16	187	234

THE CLERGY CRISIS

A considerable amount of social research since the 1960s has been devoted to analyzing the changing fortunes of the clergy profession (Campiche and Bovay 1979). Much of this research has been concerned with the displacement of clergy in contemporary society generally, a problem said to be founded on "the anachronistic relationship of religion to a secular society and culture" (Towler 1969). B. Wilson (1966:76), for example, compares today's clergy to "the charcoal-burners or alchemists in an age when the process in which they were engaged had been rendered obsolete, technically or intellectually." Similarly, Towler (1969:448) argues that the social position of clergymen in contemporary society is "comparable to that of the Knight of the Bath, or Earl or Doctor of Letters, each of which was relevant to the structure of an ascription-oriented society, but fundamentally irrelevant to contemporary structure." The dilemma for modern clergy, therefore, is that the profession represents a historical tradition that is discordant with contemporary knowledge and social arrangements (Gustafson 1963). While arguing from different perspectives Berger (1969, 1980), B. Wilson (1966), and Martin (1978) view the ambiguous status of the professional guardians of the sacred as a symptom of the general displacement of religion in public life from center to periphery.

The changing social fortunes of the parish minister have long historical antecedents (Towler and Coxon 1979), although it is in the postwar period that the issue attracted the curiosity of social scientists and the attention of concerned churchmen. The devaluing of the minister's role has been labelled "a problem of plausibility" (Ritti et al. 1974) and a "career crisis" (Klink 1969) signifying the arrival of a wholly new era for religion and religion's place in society. If during earlier generations ministers attracted respect and a degree of authority in secular contexts, this certainly is not the case in the contemporary context.

Ministers are faced with the daunting task of attending to the multiplicity of functions demanded of them. According to Dempsey, a minister is expected to

preach supportive, inspiring and hopefully entertaining sermons, to prove a good leader in the administrative and social life of the church, to be above reproach in his personal behaviour, to maintain all the church's property (including the parsonage) in good repair, to ensure sufficient budget to meet local church commitments, his own stipend and the Connexion's levies, and neither to challenge lay domination of church affairs nor interfere with the prevailing pecking order in the distribution of power in the local church. (1983:110)

Few other occupations carry such diversity of function. The problem of the minister's role is further aggravated by an apparent gulf between lay expectations of the minister's duties and the ministers' own perception of their functions (Fichter 1963). To be effective in any one area of their multifaceted occupation, ministers have had to specialize in their ministries. According to Berger (1969:145), this need to accommodate to "the dynamics of consumer preference" is further evidence of the displacement of religious functionaries in modern times.

Even in those areas previously considered vital functions and unique to this profession the minister is met with competition from a host of para-clerics who have assumed sacerdotal functions. The end result for the clergy is role ambiguity (B. Wilson 1966; Newman 1971; Hadden 1968b), role differentiation (Kelly 1971), and role uncertainty (Potvin 1976). Clergy experience an identity crisis (Bird 1976) which affects both their self-image as individuals (Blizzard 1956b, 1958a) and their morale as church workers (Dudley and Cummings 1982). Whether or not the term "clergy burnout" is an appropriate one to describe the resulting stress (Fichter 1984) is beside the point; what does matter is that the multiplicity of responsibilities has destabilized even further the role of the clergy and added to their occupational dysfunction.

Some ministers have responded by narrowing their social apertures to specifically religious and denominational concerns (Krause 1971; Feeney 1980). A vocal minority has sought to make itself and the church relevant by becoming watchdogs on social issues (Quinley 1974; Bodycomb 1978; Hadden 1968a; Hoge et al. 1981). A large body of literature is devoted to examining the political involvement of the "new breed" of clergy (Campiche and Bovay 1979; Stark and Glock 1968; Quinley 1974). Hadden (1969) sees theological renewal as a form of retreatism and an expression of the changing social status of the clergy and not its solution. The most radical response to the times is transfer to nonparish employment (Hammond and Mitchell 1965) or leaving parish work altogether (Blaikie 1979). Jud et al. (1970:5) argue that those who opt out of the ministry "allowed the radical changes of this world and the radical differences of this age to penetrate their conscious life," and add that

the combined impact of changes in the church, society, family, and faith systems has produced in many ministers a delicate balance of hope and frustration which makes them vulnerable to tipping point exercises, and that out of this situation many have moved to a redefining of self or ministry which leads to career-change decisions. It is our further conviction that this situation is widespread in the ministry today and that *ex-pastors are in many cases not the cast-offs of a stable system, but the bellwethers of massive changes yet to come.* (Jud et al. 1970:91; my emphasis)

When viewed against the backdrop of this larger picture of the social displacement of religion, fallout from ministry becomes "part . . . of a larger cultural tremor" (Schneider and Zurcher 1970). The fact that exit has become a problem for the Seventh-day Adventist movement during the 1980s tells us something about sectarianism. While the sectarian community maintains distance from the wider society and thus is able to delay and minimize the impact of external social influences, it is not altogether exempted from them. Indeed, if clergy loss can be thought of as a way of differentiating "church" from "sect," then the Seventh-day Adventist movement has come of age during the 1980s.

This line of reasoning merely accounts for the phenomenon of loss; it does not tell us much about how ministers exit. The remainder of this chapter focuses on the theorizing about exiting.

PERSPECTIVES ON EXITING

"There is no shortage of conceptual schemes for organising our thoughts" about exiting (Beckford 1985:139). At the same time, however, there is no single body of literature that can easily be identified under the title "exit studies." The literature on exiting is voluminous and draws on a range of studies. Some researchers on exiting draw on studies of social movements for insight (Beckford 1985). Others have found useful the studies of immigrants and how they cope with radically altered self-identities, as well as insights drawn from the study of deviant careers, including those of drug dealers and criminals (Ebaugh 1988a). Wright (1987:5) found the literature on marital separation and divorce useful in analyzing the gradual disengagement of followers from new religious movements.

The research of occupational psychologists and sociologists interested in labor turnover in organizations also features studies on exiting. Some of these include Moberley et al.'s (1979) and Price's (1977) reviews of the process of employee turnover, Becker's (1960) and Kanter's (1968) studies of commitment and the lack of it in organizations, and Hirschman's (1970) exploration of the relationship among exiting, complaint, and commitment in organizations. The works of Mowday (1981) and Mowday et al. (1982), who locate turnover alongside absenteeism as expressions of employee resistance, and Krackhardt and Porter's (1985) examination of the impact of friends' leaving on the attitudes toward work of those who remain proved useful for understanding the exiting of Adventist pastors. Theorizing on exiting, in other words, draws for inspiration on research from a variety of social and organizational settings.

Much of this research, however, is limited in scope in that it focuses on particular aspects of the process of exiting, for example, its impact on organizations or the self-identity of leavers. Examples of attempts to understand the process of exiting itself are few, with the exception of studies in the sociology of religion, where theoretical frameworks have been developed to explain the process of disengaging from religious organizations and roles. It is to this body of literature that I now turn. My intention is to present a brief synopsis of the main theoretical approaches to exiting.

Psychological Explanations

The prevailing view during the early 1960s was to attribute the attrition of parish ministers to spiritual deficiency (Fichter 1961). This view, which may be described as representing an "establishment" perspective on exiting, continues to be endorsed by lay members and management but has not found acceptance among academics. A more popular approach, adopted by psychologists Graham (1985) and Tramonte (1986), focuses on personality factors. According to this view certain personality types lend themselves more readily to apostasy than others. Cryns (1970), for example, argues that former priests and seminarians can be differentiated from active seminarians and priests by their lack of dogmatism and low commitment to the organization's objectives and underlying ideology. Cryns (1970) argues that "religious functionaries who persevere in their respective clerical roles do so, inter alia, as a function of such traits and attitudinal perspectives; those who leave the ministry may do so because of a lack of or underdevelopment of these traits." Schneider and Zurcher (1970:207) similarly attribute exit from the Catholic priesthood to the "emergence of a personality type . . . which would be relatively highly adaptable, change-oriented, and imbued with relatively low emotional commitment to structured social relationships."

Levine (1984) also embraces a psychological framework but views separation from religious groups and exiting as evidence of growing up. From his study of new religious movements over a fifteen-year period, Levine observed that 90 percent of converts leave within two years of joining the movement. Converts, who are usually young, reach adulthood within the context of the religious group, and separation marks their independence and reentry into the mainstream of society. Joining and then leaving new religious movements are "rehearsals" of growing up, according to Levine.

Much research on departure from religious movements is dominated by themes of brainwashing, deprogramming, and coerced exit (A. Robbins and Richardson 1978). Solomon's study of 100 former members of the Unification Church builds on this tradition. Solomon (1981:288) sought to determine whether different types of exits produce different attitudes toward the group and found that anticult sentiments of leavers often are traceable to modes of exit. Leavers who had undergone deprogramming were more likely to hold negative attitudes toward the group as compared with voluntary exiters.

Mauss's (1969:131) eightfold typology is not "psychological" in the strict sense of the term, although it depicts defection as a blending of intellectual, social, and emotional factors. The typology, which was developed from a pilot study of sixty defectors from the Mormon Church, represents an important advancement in the study of exiting because it acknowledges that defection is complex and not easily accounted for by single-cause explanations.

Structural-Organizational Theories

A different approach to exiting is represented by Seidler (1979), who explains the differential rates of exit in American dioceses of the Roman Catholic Church by focusing on organizational factors. Seidler employs the concept of "lazy monopoly" developed by Hirschman (1970) to describe organizations that have singular control over decision-making, are slow to make essential changes, and allow personnel who are critical of the system to leave rather than dealing with their criticisms. Seidler (1979:780) describes the Catholic hierarchy as a "lazy monopoly" in their "unwillingness to face such issues as celibacy." Seidler argues that labor turnover is used by Catholic officials to get rid of priests critical of the organization thus ensuring the continuance of traditional authority structures. The "innovative proposal" (Beckford 1985:138) alerts us to the need to use the same methods to study churches as other work organizations and to employ theoretical frameworks used to explain turnover in other labor organizations.

Dempsey's (1983) longitudinal study of religion in an Australian country town illustrates the ways denominational characteristics are manifest in the patterning of leaving. Dempsey shows that while fallout from the Methodist ministry reflects wider social changes affecting the churches and ministers, the specific circumstances that culminate with exit are due to the denomination's organizational structure. He notes that conflict with lay parishioners was the common denominator among ministers who left the parish he studied. Della Cava's (1975) study of former priests similarly highlights conflict as a precursor to exit, although in the hierarchically structured Catholic Church the conflict is with the bureaucracy over the issue of celibacy. Structural explanations draw attention to the importance of organizational processes overlooked by studies preoccupied with personality types. The structural-organizational focus is useful, as Dempsey's research shows, particularly for highlighting how a group's organization can affect both the manner of exit and the timing. However, explanations that focus on structure have their limitations, and this is poignantly illustrated by Ebaugh's research on former Catholic nuns.

In her 1977 study of the decline of Catholic orders in the United States, Ebaugh adopted a structural perspective to explain the phenomenal loss. Ebaugh reported that orders most receptive of changes introduced by Vatican II experienced the greatest fallout. The crucial factor generating turnover was education, and Ebaugh presents evidence to show that some orders experienced a "brain drain" (Ebaugh and Ritterband 1978:257). Ebaugh explains that in these orders "as education levels rose . . . so did rates of exodus." In a follow-up essay seven years later Ebaugh revisited the interview data on which the 1977 study was based. This time she adopted a radically different approach to exiting. While she reiterates the usefulness of her earlier study for highlighting "general trends" and background factors affecting exit, Ebaugh concedes that she overlooked the "feelings," "personal reflections," and "heart decisions" that accompany exiting which she now sees as critical for understanding the experience. Ebaugh's 1984 essay appropriately focuses on issues of "self-transformation" and "self-identity." Some of these aspects of exiting overlooked by structural models are addressed by researchers who emphasize the importance of relationship issues.

Relationship Models

The relative strengths of social relationships as factors predisposing individuals to seek change occupy a central place in social network models. From their surveys of 1,200 members from new religious movements, Snow, Zurcher, and Ekland-Olson (1980) drew attention to the importance of interpersonal ties to explain why and how individuals align themselves with particular movements. The authors argue that the probability of recruitment to a particular group is conditioned on preexisting friendship relationships and the absence of countervailing networks. The research of Galanter (1983) and Wright (1984) supports these findings. From his study of dropouts from the Unification Church's 1978 induction workshops, Galanter (1983) found that leavers had "greater affiliative ties to people outside the sect." Wright adopts a social-psychological perspective for the study of voluntary defection from new religious movements.

Wright's (1984 and 1987) research focused on the factors that set in motion the processes of exiting. He identified five factors that contribute to the likelihood of defection, including (1) the breakdown in a member's insulation from the outside world; (2) unregulated development of dyadic relationships within the communal context; (3) perceived lack of success in achieving world transformation; (4) failure to meet effective needs of a primary group; and (5) inconsistencies between the actions of leaders and the ideals they symbolically represent (Wright 1984:176). The strength of ties with family members critical of cult membership was most pronounced among the defectors he surveyed. Wright (1984:22) thus argues that "parental disapproval of a son or daughter's involvement was . . . the most important variable in explaining disaffiliation." Friendship with persons outside the group facilitates the breakdown of a member's insulation from the outside world and is the first stage in the process of disengagement, according to Wright.

Whereas Wright's research emphasized the importance of significant others outside the movement, Jacobs's research highlights disillusionment with significant others within the movement. Jacobs argues that in the "patriarchal family structure" of new religious movements "the religious family . . . has replaced the family of origin as the source of primary socio-emotional relationships" and that leaders assume parental responsibilities. In this sense departure from these movements often results from "the failure of yet another familial ideal" (Jacobs 1989:125,126). Disillusionment with the leader who had been "internalized as the idealized patriarchal God" features centrally in Jacobs's theorizing on exit.

The limitations of psychological, structural and relational explanations stem from their preoccupation with "background conditions affecting the decision to leave," according to Beckford (1985:138–139). They describe in broad terms the social profile of leavers and highlight background factors as facilitators of separation (Beckford 1985:139); but as Ebaugh's two sets of studies illustrate, they fail to explain how previously committed members of groups and associations entertain doubts, question earlier convictions, and seek separation. The latter require theoretical tools that are specially sensitive to what Ebaugh (1984) describes as the "heart decisions" of leavers in incremental steps to exit.

Process Models

Beckford (1985:139) uses the phrase "diachronic models" to describe the studies concerned with the dynamics of exiting. The term "process" is preferred because the different approaches are oriented toward the processual aspects of exiting. Brinkerhoff and Burke (1980:52) argue that "religious disaffiliation is a gradual, cumulative social process in which negative labelling may act as a 'catalyst' accelerating the journey of apostasy while giving it form and direction." They discard the static images of earlier studies for an approach that is more sensitive to the "gradual" and "subtle" process of exiting. Brinkerhoff and Burke (1980:43) construct their typology by cross-tabulating the two variables of "religiosity" (the embracing of religious beliefs) and "communality" (a sense of belonging to the group). In the resulting typology leavers are grouped with "apostates" who disavow their beliefs and sever community ties before exiting. They argue that the journey to apostasy may occur in a variety of different ways depending on specific "push-pull" factors like internal organizational politics and clashes with officials, but that in groups with clearly delineated ideological and communal boundaries "negative labelling" may act as a catalyst (Brinkerhoff and Burke 1980:45). In their three-stage model, exit begins with "tagging the heretic," "damning the heretic," and finally "the reaction of the heretic," which serves to reinforce negative labels (Richardson 1975; Richardson et al. 1986). Beckford (1985:140) correctly points out that not all cases of apostasy are attributable to negative labeling. Nor can one assume that "falling from the faith" is a strictly rational process that always begins with questioning one's belief system, as this model suggests. A preoccupation with the rational-ideological dimensions of exiting obscures organizational processes and relational factors that I contend are equally important in the exiting.

Skonovd (1981:6) rejects Brinkerhoff and Burke's two-dimensional model as "incomplete" and develops his own explanation in which defection begins with a crisis of commitment and moves through "review and reflection," "disillusionment," "withdrawal," "emotional transition," and "cognitive reorganization" (Skonovd 1981:179–180). Skonovd presents defection as a sequence of transformation in which the defecting member endeavours at every stage to resolve conflicting emotions and points of view. This preoccupation with cognitive processes and adoption of sequenced stages make the Skonovd model just as limiting by its rigidity.

The most "sensitively and clearly oriented" explanations of disengagement and exiting according to Beckford (1985:141) utilize the concepts of "role passage" (SanGiovanni 1978), "status passage" (Glaser and Strauss 1967), and "role exit" (Ebaugh 1984, 1988a). SanGiovanni (1978) appropriates the concept of "status passage" developed by Glaser and Strauss (1967) to study exit from Catholic orders. Data for the study were gathered from twenty former nuns using a standardized interview schedule. SanGiovanni (1978:17) focused on understanding "the subjectively experienced interplay between the personal and structural factors" evident in the exit process. She depicts the movement of nuns from cloister existence to secular life as "a process of passing between sets of roles and ways of life" (SanGiovanni 1978:11). She employs the term "emergent role-passage" to describe the transformation and gradually evolving self-conceptions of former nuns as they disengage from previous religious lifestyles and adopt lifestyles no longer dominated by convent routines and religious concerns. SanGiovanni identifies three phases in the entire process of role exit: "relinquishment" of past roles, a "transitional" phase of experimentation, and acquiring new roles. The study highlights the "indeterminacy and confused character" (Beckford 1985:142) of the emergent role passage that is "created, discovered and shaped" by leavers in the process of exiting (SanGiovanni 1978:5). Ebaugh uses the parallel concept of "role exit" to discuss "leaving the convent" (1984) and exiting from a variety of occupational and relational "roles" (1988). However, the explanatory model that she develops is more standardized than either Skonovd's or SanGiovanni's.

As was pointed out earlier, Ebaugh's (1984) interest in "the experience of role exit and self-transformation" emerged from a reworking of interviews with former nuns conducted by her for the 1977 study. Ebaugh (1988b:27) observed "very clear-cut patterns" in former nuns' accounts of exiting and concluded that the passage from the religious order to secular life occurred in a "sequence" of six identifiable stages, beginning with "first doubts," followed by "the freedom to decide," "trying out options," "the vacuum" or period of pre-exit anxiety, "the turning point" in which the decision to leave is crystallized, and "creating the ex-role." While changes in role definition and the evolution of new roles are deeply personal and the result of individual decisions, the process of exiting is not. Ebaugh argues that role exit is "a generic social process," is not confined to the religious experience, and has application to a wide range of ex-roles (Ebaugh (1984:15,17). In *Becoming an Ex: The Process of Role Exit* (1988a) the six-stage model is applied to "a variety of career changes . . . people who underwent major changes in family roles . . . and people who exited highly stigmatized roles" (Ebaugh 1988a:xvii).

The concepts of "role exit" and "role passage" have been appropriated by other researchers and applied to a variety of research contexts including marriage breakdown (Hart 1976; Vaughan, 1986), deconversion of women from new religious movements (Jacobs 1984), old age (Blau 1973), the relationships between adults and their parents (De Vaus 1994), and even death (Glaser and Strauss 1965). What is unique about Ebaugh's model is its rigidity. SanGiovanni (1978:147) makes some provision for the possibility that the passage may not occur like clockwork seeing that the "emergent role passage" is "shaped and controlled by the person." Ebaugh makes no such allowances, and the resulting six-stage model depicts exiting as a "smooth" and "programmatic" process (Beckford 1985:142) in which the individual experiences predictable and uniform changes. However, as Hart (1976) notes in her critique, such a model ignores the complex and confused nature of the experience of exiting.

Hart argues that marriage breakdown "is a messy and at best ill-organised affair." Moreover, the experience is not clearly defined, and the boundaries between status lost and gained are blurred. "Changes in the conjugal relationship . . . occur along a number of axes" and to reduce the process to one dimension of the status passage would be to "oversimplify" it. For these reasons Hart (1976:105) deliberately avoids the temptation "to pin down" the more overt features of the status passage, arguing that "the reconstruction of subjective meanings . . . [is] virtually impossible" and that the theoretical construct itself "is critically a subjective process" and something respondents acquire and impose on narratives of past experiences (Hart 1976:126). In light of Hart's critique one may argue that the "step by step" version of status passage either is a framework actors impose on past experience *ex post facto* or that it exists in the mind of the researcher first and is read into the research data.

SUMMARY

The theoretical models discussed in this chapter address fallout of clergy and members of religious orders primarily from mainline denominations. They do not reflect the severity of the experience of exiting encountered by sect ministers. As well, they underestimate the confused and complex process of arriving at decisions to leave. From his research with defectors from the Unification Church, Beckford concluded that

defection was not experienced as an unambiguous transition from one set of roles to another. [Defectors] did not feel that they clearly understood what was happening, although they were certainly under pressure to impose particular interpretations on events. The outcome in most cases was a lengthy period of unsettling confusion and tentative moves to resolve the problem by ad hoc adjustments, trials, and errors . . . [The] passage from being a member of the [Unification Church] to being cast in the role of a defector illustrates unambiguously its complex, subtle, and difficult character in a society lacking an appropriate blueprint or "scenario" for such a change. (1985:142)

Beckford is critical of existing models on three grounds. First, they depict exiting as a tidy process "as if the models were based on the assumption that the actors possessed total rationality and total understanding of their situation," an assumption that Beckford contests. Second, they reflect a narrow range of exits, those in which clinical and therapeutic experts were involved. Third, actors' thoughts and feelings as well as reactions from others are treated separately as if they existed in isolation. The present study builds on Beckford's critique and draws on structural-organizational and relationship models where necessary. While Beckford focused on the retreat of members from new religious movements, and while his theorizing does not address the exit of clergy directly, his approach is a useful one as it is founded on the assumption that exit is more complex, more subtle, and more difficult than researchers have hitherto acknowledged.

The following chapters focus on micro-social process in decisions to exit ministry. They explore how social factors and organizational processes interacted with sectarian beliefs to generate loss of confidence in Adventist bureaucracy, disillusionment with sect ideology, and loss of commitment in ministry, which have contributed to the most rapid and massive exit of Adventist pastors in the movement's 150-year history.

NOTE

1. Seventh-day Adventists trace the beginnings of the present day church to the influence of William Miller, the nineteenth-century farmer and Baptist layman from Low Hampton, New York (Neufeld and Neuffer 1966:787). From his study of the Old Testament prophecies, and specifically the prophecy found in Daniel 8:14—"Unto two thousand and three hundred days; then shall the sanctuary be cleansed" —Miller calculated that Christ would return to earth "about the year

1843." The "Millerite" movement collapsed and splintered into several groups following a series of failed prohecies which culminated in the Great Disappointment of October 22, 1844. The Seventh-day Adventist Church grew from one of these splinter groups.

Adventist Pastors and Expastors

Who are the expastors, and in what ways do they differ from pastors currently serving in the Adventist ministry? Are leavers easily differentiated from stayers by age, success in ministry, and educational achievement, for example? Both in Adventist and some academic discourses leavers are typically younger ministers and converts who neither enjoyed the work of ministry nor experienced success in it. The stereotype is not encoded in writing, but aspects of it can be heard in lay member and official explanations of the fallout from the Adventist ministry. In this chapter this popular stereotype is reviewed and critically examined by comparing the salient characteristics of fifty expastors and sixty-six currently serving Adventist pastors from two Conferences in the South Pacific Division who were surveyed. Continuing pastors are used as a norm to examine the social and demographic profiles of leavers.

AGE FACTORS

While it is not uncommon for successful literature evangelists, "dedicated" schoolteachers, and even persons with a nursing background to find their way into ministry, Adventist pastors are predominantly, although not exclusively, young people who commenced training for ministry upon the completion of their secondary school. The school-to-ministry transition is evident in the median age of starters in ministry. Half of each group of leavers and stayers surveyed commenced training for ministry in their late teens upon completion of high schooling. The comparison of the starting ages indicates that more stayers began training for ministry in their late teens, while a greater number of leavers did so in their early twenties. The most noticeable difference between the surveyed groups is that almost twice as many stayers relative to leavers took the step of training for ministry later in life (30-plus years of age). The evidence outlined in Table 3.1 would seem to suggest that expastors do not come from some especially youthful subgroup among clergy. It would be tempting to conclude that individuals who commence training for ministry later in life are less likely to leave; however, other factors must be considered before we draw such a conclusion.

Table 3.1
Age at Which Leavers and Stayers Commenced Training for Ministry

Age Group	% Leavers (N = 50)	% Stayers (N = 66)
Under 20	50	56
21–25	26	15
26–30	10	7.5
31–35	4	9
36+	8	10.5
No Response	2	1.5
Median Age:	20.5 years	20.5 years

A comparison of the ages of expastors at time of leaving with those of continuing pastors at the time of the survey suggests that there is no particular age at which Adventist pastors are more vulnerable to exit (Table 3.2). While it is true that the median age of leavers (36 years) is lower than that of stayers (40 years) and that there are almost four times as many continuing pastors in the 50-plus age group, this is to be expected. Pastors are not an age-static population, while the age profile of leavers records static age at the point of termination. In other words, there is no firm basis here for the stereotype of the markedly young leaver.

Table 3.2
Age Groupings of Leavers (at Time of Exit) and Stayers

Age Group	Age When Left % Leavers (N = 50)	Present Age % Stayers (N = 66)
Under 30	26	22.5
31–40	44	28.5
41–50	18	19
51+	8	30
No Response	4	-
Median Age:	36 years	40 years

The overwhelming majority of expastors in the present sample (94 percent) left church employment during their first twenty years of ministry. It is noteworthy that approximately one out of every three expastors (32 percent) left during their first five years of ministry. However, this compares favorably with the fact that an approximate number of active pastors (27.3 percent) is in this years of service bracket. In other words, while on first appearances it looks as if leavers are weighted more toward those with shorter (1 to 5 years) ministry careers, the percentages are relative and correspond with that of stayers. Table 3.3 reveals that, contrary to popular claims, leavers are not overwhelmingly recent starters in ministry but that roughly equal thirds are from each of the three categories up to twenty years of service. More than this, the years of service profile of leavers is remarkably similar to the profile of stayers, with some of the differences easily explained in terms of the stayers having had opportunity to accrue more years of service. This evidence belies the stereotype of the leaver as a ministerial youngster. At the very least Table 3.3 indicates that more than half of the expastors were in the middle period of their ministerial careers at time of exit, the period when one would have anticipated some stability in their careers.

Table 3.3
Number of Years in Ministry

Years in Ministry	% Leavers (N = 50)
1–5	32
6–9	30
10–19	32
20–29	2
30+	4

The argument that career change is "age-linked" is an accepted fact in clergy studies (Blaikie 1979:219). Jud et al. (1970:45), for example, argue that "moves out of church employment occur considerably more often among young men than older men" and that exit is particularly more pronounced among those in their twenties. R. A. Schoenherr and Sorensen (1982:28–29) similarly report that the majority of the 3,045 who resigned from the Catholic priesthood in the United States between 1966 and 1973 were under 35 years of age. According to Schoenherr and Sorensen, resignation begins soon after ordination and peaks during the second five-year period in ministry, while priests with ten to nineteen years of seniority experience 40 percent fewer resignations than their younger counterparts. Schoenherr and Sorensen are careful to add, however, that while the influences leading ministers to exit are particularly strong in the first two decades and less so in the third and fourth decades, they are nevertheless felt throughout the ministry career. Similar findings from his survey of career change among clergy in the United States led E. W. Mills (1965:59–60) to argue that disengagement from the ministry "is predominantly neither a young man's nor a mature man's decision but [is] a phenomenon occurring throughout at least the first twenty years of the ministerial career." This also appears to be the case with Adventist expastors.

Nor can one assume that the age at which ministers exit is constant between generations. From their survey of U.S. Catholic clergy fallout between 1966 and 1984 in eighty-six randomly chosen dioceses, R. A. Schoenherr and Young (1990:471–473) observed a gradual increase in the age of leavers compared with the age of those who exited during the 1960s and 1970s, respectively. The age group most at risk during the 1960s was the 31–32 year-olds; by the 1980s it was the 35–39 age group that experienced greatest fallout. Schoenherr and Young (1990:471) thus concluded that "even among younger priests, resignations were decreasing, but the age group most at risk was getting older." The present study does not provide for a conclusion as strong as that. The distribution of leavers among all age categories of active pastors and the facts that former pastors commenced training for ministry at approximately similar ages and were in ministry for almost as long as those who continue in it suggest that the age spread of leavers at time of exit corresponds fairly accurately with that of the present Adventist pastor population. This conclusion parallels Jud et al.'s findings. They observed that

nearly two thirds of the ministers who left for secular employment did so after age 35 when family expenses are heaviest, career advancement possibilities highest, when pension credits have finally begun to amount to something, and when they are at an age where it is difficult to obtain placement and training in another occupation. (1970:45)

The fact that over 70 percent of Adventist expastors made their decision to leave ministry while they were in their thirties, or at an age when change was least beneficial to them professionally and economically, suggests that disengagement is not the easy, almost flippant, reorientation that one associates with the young.

EDUCATION

In the area of education leavers differ from stayers in one major area—level of academic achievement. A cursory reading of Table 3.4 appears to support the popular belief that study is detrimental to ministry. Approximately one out of every three continuing pastors has no academic qualification, whereas a minority of leavers (8 percent) are in this category. A more glaring contrast is that more than two-thirds of leavers have a bachelor's degree (or a licentiate in theology) in contrast to active pastors, of whom just over half (53 percent) completed the four-year ministerial training. Also significant is the fact that 8 percent of leavers hold doctorates; not one of the sixty-six continuing pastors surveyed attained this level of academic achievement. These differences partly reflect the fact that more stayers (21.2 percent) commenced ministry later in life (Table 3.1) than leavers (8 percent). This evidence appears consistent with the findings of research on disaffiliation and clergy loss where education is highlighted as correlating with exit.

Table 3.4
Educational Qualifications of Leavers and Stayers

Academic Qualifications	% Leavers (N = 50)	% Stayers (N = 66)
No Qualifications	8	32
B.A. (Th) or L.Th	70	53
Graduate Diploma	4	3
M.A., M.Div., B.D.	10	12
Ph.D., D.Th	8	-

Jud et al. (1970:44), for example, contend that it is a truism that education facilitates career change as well as career advancement. Researchers thus attribute to education the questioning of traditional values (Burton et al. 1989:355) and the adoption of a "new morality" (Roof and Hadaway 1979:373). While researchers remain divided over whether education is the dependent variable and hence merely a precursor to religious change (Caplovitz and Sharrow 1977:83) and exit (Zelan 1968), the connection between education and exit is not questioned. Bowen and Doyal (1974:311) found that priests employed in secular occupations had four times as many master's, doctorate, and other post graduate degrees as parish priests. In the Jud et al. sample, expastors holding postgraduate degrees outnumber active pastors two to one (1970:174). From studies of Roman Catholic religious orders Ebaugh (1977) and Ebaugh and Ritterband (1978) found that there was a relationship between the education of nuns and the incidence of withdrawal. This theme is echoed also in the limited number of studies that focus on Seventh-day Adventists (J. W. Knight 1977). In an address to a forum of Adventist scholars Bryan Wilson reaffirmed this thesis by forecasting that the Adventist emphasis on having a well-educated and professional ministry ultimately will lead to an increased relativity of religious beliefs. Wilson argues: "To enter into a universe of discourse with outsiders is to begin to share the premises of that discourse, and to accept frameworks for argument and discussion which [do not] belong . . . to the Seventh-day Adventist tradition. This process is likely to lead to reappraisal of one's own teaching, history, assumption and self-identity" (1975:41). With this premise in mind Knight studied a group of Seventh-day Adventist young people in Brisbane in the mid-1970s and found that ex-members had greater exposure to secular university culture and learning. He thus concludes that there is a strong "relationship between university education and loss of sectarian identity" (1977:363). In other words, education bears a problematic relationship not only to the sectarian community but also, and particularly, to the clergy whose task it is to maintain clearly defined boundaries with the outside world.

The simple dichotomy of academic leavers and nonacademic stayers fails to account for the fact that the two groups have much in common, particularly in their attitudes to academia and even in their respective academic achievements. For example, while less than one out of every three leavers (30 percent) had undertaken postgraduate study while in ministry, 39 percent of stayers did so. In other words, in attitudinal terms leavers are no more academically inclined than stayers. Moreover, approximately half of each group reported that they enjoy serious study and writing, yet the same number of leavers and stayers find academic tasks unsatisfying and place less value on this aspect of ministry. When asked whether he read widely, one expastor replied during his interview:

No, but I would love to. I have not been self-disciplined enough to continue studying. I have found it challenging enough just to keep sermons coming out [and] prepare for worships and other things . . . I am not a student. I am not an academic. I struggled through College and passed with the skin of my teeth. . . . I bluffed my way through most of it—maximum mileage out of minimum information (laughs). To me it was a joke that I graduated. I really felt that I did not have any grasp of what [the lecturers] were trying to get across to me, particularly in the areas of systematic and historical theology. I did not have a clue what these things were all about, and still don't. It is just a vague area.

A second explained that he did not enjoy study: "The more I got into theology, the more I got into mind tangles." This expastor preferred "going out and helping people" and preferred the role of pastor to that of scholar. A third "never really saw academic achievement as being a thing of worth." While a high percentage of expastors (48 percent) and a similar number of continuing pastors (49 percent) expressed the desire to further equip themselves academically for ministry and placed "further study" high on their list of priorities for the future, an almost equal number of each group is content with present levels of academic achievement. In other words, it is difficult and even unwise to differentiate leavers and stayers on the basis of education and to draw causal links between education and exit. Conversely, it is equally wrong to assume that education was not a contributing factor to leaving the Adventist ministry. It will become evident in later chapters that it is not education per se that leads to questioning which ultimately leads to exit and/or the collapse of the sectarian worldview, but *a specific kind of education when undertaken at a specific point in their ministries.*

STATUS IN THE ADVENTIST CHURCH

The Seventh-day Adventist Church operates a two-tiered ministry structure: licensed ministers, who are essentially on probation for the first four or five years in ministry, and fully fledged ordained pastors. As was pointed out in the last chapter, however, similarities in the work of licensed ministers and ordained pastors bely the symbolic values attached to each in the Adventist division of labor. The importance of ordination may be gauged from the emotions the former ministers experienced in anticipation. Administrators "dangle [ordination] like a great carrot in front of a guy" to ensure the continued cooperation of licensed ministers, according to one expastor. Four expastors claim that in the Adventist community ordination has also become a ritualized action by means of which a minister's theology is declared kosher; the focus is often more on what the minister thinks than on his suitability for the work. Ordination is experienced in this way particularly by ministers who converted to Adventism. The wife of one expastor did not think it mattered whether one was born an Adventist or converted but was surprised to discover at the ordination of her convert husband its importance for converts:

> I remember Pastors T. and H. came [to talk to us about ordination] and, during our talk around the table, Pastor H. said to [my husband], because you are a new Adventist you were this and that . . . when you came into the work, and only now do I think that you have gone from one side of the pendulum into the middle area where you are accepted fully as a minister. He said that to us. I thought, strike, I didn't think it mattered.

Ordination signals denominational endorsement of one's call to ministry and full acceptance in the Adventist community. It is a ritual of acceptance and a form of legitimation. It relocates converts and laity alike from Adventist periphery to center. A little over half of the leavers (52 percent) compared to two-thirds of stayers (67 percent) were ordained. This difference may be the result of an accelerated ordination program by church leaders during the 1980s to compensate for the number who left. Whether or not this is the case, the fact that more than half of the surveyed leavers had been ordained Adventist pastors cannot be overlooked, suggesting that ordination does not automatically disqualify pastors from leaving the ministry. Adventist ministers exit regardless of whether or not the church has endorsed their calling to ministry.

Authors Brinkerhoff and Burke (1980) develop a typology of disaffiliation by cross-tabulating religiosity with organizational identification and community attachment. Persons are more likely to apostatize, according to these authors, if they reject the group's teachings and spurn their community's fellowship. What is surprising about expastors, and contrary to the above, is that at least up to the time of their leaving expastors were very much ministers of good and regular standing, or "Fervent Followers" (Brinkerhoff and Burke) who identified with the Adventist community and maintained a strong commitment to its belief system.

Nor can one equate leavers with the "institutional powerless" (Bell and Koval 1972:59). It could be argued that in a hierarchically structured bureaucracy like Adventism, all ministers, regardless of background, are located at the base of the pyramid of power dominated by a minority of administrator elites. However, generalizations of this sort are too broad to explain what transpired in the Adventist community during the 1980s. Indeed, if we accept that ordination and positions held by expastors prior to their exit are reliable indicators of a minister's standing in the Adventist community, then leavers as a group were neither marginal to the Adventist community nor located at the bottom of the movement's hierarchy of power. In the course of this study it will be come evident that ministers who are "good at their job," carry status within Adventism, and display an outward persona of compliance may at the same time also be experiencing inner doubts and rebellion.

ADVENTIST BACKGROUND

At one meeting I attended while still in ministry, a Union Conference administrator used Christ's parable of the sower and the soils to address the issue of why Adventist ministers leave. The church leader equated depth of soil with time as an Adventist and argued that ministers with shallow Adventist roots were more likely to exit, while those born in the church and securely established in the Adventist traditions were less likely to leave. He lamented the fact that more Adventist young people did not aspire to enter ministry. Contrary to popular Adventist mythology, a majority of leavers (53 percent) were born and raised Adventists, indeed, about the same proportion as the stayers (56 percent).

The family backgrounds of surveyed stayers and leavers were remarkably similar: 62 percent of stayers and leavers had family members and relatives in the Seventh-day Adventist ministry. A majority also reported that they had family members in ministry: one out of every three stayers and an almost equivalent number of leavers (29 percent) had fathers who were ministers. More than half of each surveyed group had either a brother, son, grandfather, cousin, uncle, or nephew in the ministry. Some were additionally linked to the Adventist ministry through their wives (Table 3.5). The fact that one out of every five expastors is either the son or son-in-law of a minister suggests that despite the many advantages of established kinship ties with ministry, family ties do not automatically preclude exit. If anything, the interviews with expastors reveal pastors' sons turning against their fathers, and sons-in-law turning their backs on the career paths of fathers-in-law and brothers-in-law.

Table 3.5
Relatives of Leavers and Stayers in the Adventist Ministry

Relative	*% Leavers (N = 31)*	*% Stayers (N = 41)*
Father	9	14
Brother	4	10
Uncle	9	7
Nephew	1	3
Cousin	2	-
Grandfather	1	3
Son	1	3
Father-in-law	9	5
Brother-in-law	3	5
Wife's Uncle	7	4
Wife's Grandfather	2	-

SUCCESS AND JOB SATISFACTION

It is more tempting to equate exit with failure in ministry and to argue that success in ministry ensures continuity. Roof and Hadaway (1979) argue that in addition to being more educated and younger, religious disaffiliates may also be differentiated from stayers by their contrasting levels of happiness in their pursuits. If this were the case one would expect expastors to report that they were unhappy in ministry, and had minimal job satisfaction and little or no success. In this sense it is not surprising that job satisfaction and contentment in ministry represent the two areas in which leavers and stayers show significant statistical differences in their survey responses.

Two sets of questions in the questionnaire required respondents to record their attitudes to ministry and to rate their success as pastors. In the first, they were asked to rate three statements from 1 (low) to 6 (high) according to their level of agreement:

I really enjoy(ed) being a pastor.
For the most part I believe I am/was a successful pastor.
I believe I am/was making a contribution to the vitality and mission of the Church.

The first two statements are drawn from Dudley and Cummings's 1981 study of occupational morale, which was based on the responses of 172 Seventh-day Adventist ministers in the North American Division. Expastors' responses to the statements enable us to compare the responses of pastors in Australia and New Zealand with their American counterparts. Dudley and Cummings (1982:128) report that the item "I really enjoy being a pastor" received the second highest percentage of agreement (94 percent) in their survey while 87 percent of respondents rated themselves as successful pastors. The authors therefore concluded that "the overall morale [of Adventist pastors in North America] appears to be better than might have been expected." By contrast, only 73 percent of the continuing pastors surveyed in the South Pacific Division enjoy the work of ministry, and less than three out of every five (59 percent) rate their ministry a success (Table 3.6).

Table 3.6
Occupational Morale of Adventist Pastors in Australia/New Zealand and the United States

	Very Much	
	% A & NZ	*% USA**
Enjoying Ministry	73	94
Successful in Ministry	59	87
Making a Contribution	60	-

* Figures from Dudley & Cummings (1982)

A comparison of these sets of responses suggests that Adventist ministers in the South Pacific Division experience significantly lower levels of satisfaction in ministry than their North American counterparts. A significant proportion of continuing pastors in Australia and New Zealand report that their ministry is not fulfilling or satisfying, and a significant minority (40 percent) report that they do not consider themselves successful in what they are doing or believe they are making a contribution. Overall, in the terms outlined by Dudley and Cummings, the morale of continuing pastors in the South Pacific Division is far from healthy and should be a matter of concern for the authorities. By comparison, about one out of every three leavers state that they did not enjoy the work while in ministry and rate their work during those years in negative terms. Nonetheless, between a third and a half of the leavers state that they both enjoyed pastoral ministry and were successful in it. The caricature of leavers as failures does not sit well with the fact that more than half of the leavers surveyed (57 percent) claim they were successful ministers.

Even more revealing are responses to a second cluster of questions in which ministers were asked to rate their success, stress and job satisfaction in each of their last few years of ministry (maximum of eight years). With these data it was hoped to establish whether the *perceptions* of leavers and stayers had altered over time and to identify in which direction. By deducting their first year's rating from the final year's, a figure was arrived at that recorded the extent of change in expastor outlook. Negative scores record a negative level of success, stress, and job satisfaction; positive scores point to an increase, while a zero score shows that respondents' attitudes had not changed during these years.

Tables 3.7, 3.8, and 3.9 show that there is a consistent pattern in the shift in attitudes of leavers and stayers: in all three areas the outlook of stayers is positive, while for leavers it is consistently the reverse. Expastors rate their success as low, and report an increase in stress and lower levels of job satisfaction by their final years of ministry. Many who began with high expectations ended their ministry disillusioned and disappointed, a point that will be explored in more detail in the next chapter. By contrast the response of stayers is more stable (Table 3.7). However, the differences between the two surveyed groups are not sufficiently large to support the argument that feeling unsuccessful is a causal factor in exit.

Table 3.7
Perceptions of Success in Ministry of Leavers and Stayers

Value	% Leavers (N = 43)	% Stayers (N = 57)
< -1	44	31
0	33	39
> +1	23	30
	100	100
Mean:	-0.33	0.09

Table 3.8
Perceptions of Stress Experienced in Ministry

Value	% Leavers (N = 43)	% Stayers (N = 57)
< -1	21	28
0	16	28
> +1	63	44
	100	100
Mean:	-0.81	0.12

Table 3.9
Expastors' and Continuing Pastors' Levels of Contentment in Ministry

Value	% Leavers (N = 43)	% Stayers (N = 57)
< -1	48	32
0	24	28
> +1	28	40
Mean:	-0.88	0.30

Once again a significant number of individuals in each group deviate from the expected stereotypical response: leavers report greater job satisfaction and success in ministry but lower levels of stress prior to leaving, a proportion that is lower than but not radically different from the responses of stayers. When we combine the categories of success, stress, and job satisfaction, a composite category that I call "contentment" is produced which records the overall tendency of leavers and stayers to ministry (Table 3.9). The difference in mean score for leavers and stayers shows that in retrospect the outlook of leavers to ministry is negative and confirms what we already suspect, that expastors are less content with pastoral ministry.

SUMMARY

The popular image of the expastor as a young, disgruntled convert who had been studying in non-Adventist institutions, and drinking from polluted secular fountains, and who thus had become corrupted and confused by secular thought, fails against the complex portrait that has emerged in this brief overview of expastors. What has been shown in this chapter is that the category of expastor includes young men as well as mature persons in their late fifties; new entrants to ministry with less than ten months of service and pastors with thirty years of experience; some who commenced ministerial training immediately upon completion of secondary schooling and others for whom ministry was a mid-life career choice. The chapter has shown that some among the leavers have no academic qualifications and take little interest in academic matters but that others are highly qualified and continue to enjoy academic pursuits. Ordained pastors and licensed ministers number equally among the leavers, as do expastors who were born Adventists and who, in a number of cases, represented two and three generations of Adventist ministers. As a group expastors reflect fairly accurately the major characteristics of the present Adventist ministerial work force in age, years of service, educational achievements, and status in ministry.

On the basis of the data examined in this chapter one conclusion we may arrive at with confidence is that *every Seventh-day Adventist pastor has the potential of becoming an expastor.* The finding highlights a need to shift our focus of attention from preoccupation with individual demographics and background factors to the social and organizational processes that led committed and successful Adventist pastors to exit. If as a group expastors are not very different from continuing pastors, then there is reason to suspect (a) that exit may have something to do with structural problems in the Adventist church itself rather than with background factors predisposing pastors to exit; and (b) that exit is not so much the unfolding of background characteristics and experiences but emerges processually in the course of a developing ministry. It is to this task of examining exit as a social process that we now turn.

Chapter 4

Narratives of Exiting

In any life story there is an imposed order that goes against the flow of events as they occurred and are remembered. Reflecting on her experience of writing autobiography, New Zealand novelist Janet Frame highlights the artificiality of the remembering process and the contingent nature of recalling and forgetting:

[The] memories do not arrange themselves to be observed and written about, they whirl, propelled by a force beneath, with different memories rising to the surface at different times and thus denying the existence of a "pure" autobiography and confirming, for each moment, a separate story accumulating to a million stories, all different and with some memories forever staying beneath the surface. (Frame 1983:235–236)

Writing about one's past, according to Frame, entails selecting, arranging, and connecting snippets of recollections so as to construct an ordered and coherent narrative. Order is achieved in the autobiographical narrative by superimposing a conceptual framework on what otherwise would appear haphazard recollections. The process of imposing a structure on the stories is not confined solely to the act of producing written accounts. Ordering is part of the everyday stock of methods individuals use for recounting past experience (Middleton and Edwards 1990). This is true also of narratives produced by expastors during interviews. Chapter 3 highlighted the need to examine the *process* of exit. Our starting point for this examination is the stories expastors narrate of leaving ministry.

This chapter introduces the narratives of three expastors. The case studies present an overview of Adventist ministry so as to put exit in context. Expastors narrate a shared story using symbols that are meaningful and make sense to Adventist audiences. Since expastors' own narratives are the basic data on which this study relies, those narratives—both in the summary and edited form presented here and in their raw form—are analyzed for common construction and themes. On the basis of that initial analysis a second inquiry is pursued. Is the common primary focus on a story of cerebral, theological disaffection to be taken at face value? If it is not, what are the grounds for the analyst bringing forward for attention the nontheological social factors involved in exit that are present in expastors' accounts but generally in stories subordinate to the narrative of theological disaffection? In this chapter, consideration of the content and status of expastors' accounts leads to a consideration of the place of theological factors in generalized sociological accounts of exit.

THE STORIES

Hansford, Morton, and Dunmore are actual people, but names and incidental details have been changed to maintain anonymity. The accounts are compressed and edited versions of expastors' retelling to the author, a looking back to a process recognized. Effort has been made to focus on events as reported and as far as possible to preserve the language of expastors.

Philip Hansford

Philip Hansford had been an Adventist minister for less than three years. His exit from the ministry was, as he saw it at the time of interview, the culmination of an extended process of role redefinition which stretched over more than thirteen years. The actual exit was "just a formality . . . just tidying the paperwork." It was not an "existentially problematic moment" in the strict sense of the term but a turning-point experience based on an accumulation of past decisions, a "cumulative epiphany," to use Denzin's (1989:15) term.

Hansford was born into an Adventist family, the oldest of three children. His parents conformed to the ideal typical image of rural Adventists: they were converts, accomplished farmers, and ran a fairly successful business. The Hansfords formed the nucleus of a tightly knit rural Adventist community comprised largely of three extended family networks. The church was all-consuming to them. As well as being their place of spiritual nurturing, it was also the focus of their social world, a visible statement of the things they valued most and a symbol of their hope for the future. Church members "were simple folk [and] had a simplistic belief." They also were conservative and fundamentalist in outlook. Visibly differentiated from the rest of the Christian world by their Saturday-Sabbath, the community was held together by the conviction of the imminence of Christ's second coming. A sense of urgency was imprinted on their minds and motivated their evangelistic zeal. The eschatological motif was a powerful force in the life of the Adventist minority and took hold of the imagination of young Hansford, who was convinced the Adventist Church was at the threshold of "absolutely wonderful things." As a child he was drawn to the "glamour" of the Adventist pastor, who was thought of as being "more important than the policeman and . . . the school teacher" because he played a central role in God's end-time drama. Hansford's childhood ambition was to become an Adventist pastor. As a child he play-acted the role of minister and modelled himself after the local Adventist evangelist. He felt driven by this calling, which developed into a "burning conviction" and which left no room in his mind for alternative career options. When his father decided to sell the farm and train for ministry, Hansford's resolve was well and truly decided. He commenced training for the ministry as his father commenced pastoral duties.

His disillusionment with ministry was a gradual one, beginning with his training, although this was not recognized by him until after he left. He now believes Avondale College was both the realization of his childhood ambition and the beginning of his exit. No one individual stands out in his recall as having impacted on his thinking during training. The "mythical figure" Des Ford was on leave therefore Hansford had been only indirectly exposed to his teaching. But Avondale College was in a state of theological ferment in those years, and Hansford became an active participant in the polemics. He read widely in revisionist literature and took a strong stand on issues of Christology and soteriology. The "new" theological emphasis grew into an obsession that "consumed whatever time I had . . . all my energy went into following the debate . . . obtaining this person's tapes, that person's notes or whatever." Hansford's previous "simplistic" Adventist outlook began to falter.

He became troubled over the delay of Christ's second Advent. He now sees this as "the commencement of [his] ideological change." While the basic framework of Adventist belief remained intact, his understanding of salvation radically changed. He now believed that the church's response to the new theology was the reason for the delay of Christ's return and the key to the future of Adventism. He "firmly believed that the outcome of the debate [on the nature of Christ and righteousness by faith] would be a stepping stone toward . . . the accomplishment of the church's mission and that was very crucial to me." His shift in theology was accompanied by a corresponding shift in attitude toward evangelism, from converting the multitudes to reforming the church. Now his "compelling belief [was] that the big days of Adventism were yet to come." By the end of his third year of training Hansford had become totally enmeshed in the debates. Hoping to distance himself from the theological controversies that were tearing apart the Adventist community in Australia, Hansford resolved to complete his final years of training in the United States; he figured that the change would facilitate a more objective perspective on the doctrinal debates. However, while the change removed him from conflicts dividing Australian Adventists, it simultaneously introduced him to a new set of challenges.

For the first time he came into contact with Adventists from non-Western cultures and non-English backgrounds. He discovered that the version of Seventh-day Adventism he learnt as a child did not reflect the cultural diversity in the wider Adventist community. He discovered that Adventists in other parts of the world were more tolerant of alternative Sabbath-keeping styles, open to evangelical ideas, and not as bound by the proclamations of Ellen White. The new cultural understanding helped unravel the fabric of his sectarian world, and precipitated in him "a very complex and rapid process of change. I never envisaged . . . that environment would have the sort of effect that it had on me. . . . I was surprised . . . just how much I was changing, and I was actually conscious of the change." Hansford's Adventist theological "framework began to come apart" with his questioning of Ellen White. He explained, "Ellen White was . . . my own personal battle that I battled" while overseas. Last ditch efforts to salvage faith in Ellen White's authority proved fruitless against arguments to the contrary put forward by friends he met on his travels. Hansford added, "It really didn't matter what was happening [in Australia any longer]. That really wasn't now all that crucial [to me] because I became unstuck in other ways . . . from other pressures and forces . . . particularly on the Ellen White front." While overseas he married an Adventist woman of non-English background who made it known that she did not aspire to be a minister's wife.

Following a four-year absence Hansford returned to Australia with a theology completely stripped of sectarianism. He rejected Adventist apocalyptic as unbiblical. The Sabbath was stripped of its traditional Adventist connotations and viewed as a cultural symbol. The Adventist emphasis on health he now regarded as an expression of the movement's American cultural roots. He returned to Australia with a "lingering sort of faith" but one in which "the future of Adventism was without Ellen White." The offer to minister in the Adventist Church came as a surprise, but Hansford welcomed it because he was optimistic that the Adventist system could still change and that he would be in a better position to influence change working from within. His wife agreed to give ministry a try "for a couple of years." However, his was to be a ministry radically different from that traditionally accepted by Adventists. "The role I saw [for] myself was as teacher . . . to try and teach [the] local congregation different ways of looking at things and thinking. . . . My particular thing was not to be dramatic but to start chipping away at their conceptions and perceptions of things and to slowly alter their theological views to bring in a broadness of mind and openness." Having by now dispensed with the salient features of Adventist identity, he envisaged a type of ministry free of Adventism's proselytising zeal. "[My] view was not to proselytize people . . . or to evangelize. I had no stomach for that. It seemed almost wrong to even think of that. . . . My focus was the community, the Adventist community. . . . I was becoming more concerned . . . with . . . the pastoral care role of ministry rather than evangelism. . . . I saw high priority in . . . the teacher . . . the ever patient carer-teacher." Only months into his ministry Hansford was convinced that he had made the wrong decision. He explained that the Glacier View trial and subsequent dismissal of Des Ford put paid to his hope that the Adventist Church could change. He concluded that "there was no more openness in the Church" and no future for him in ministry. He commenced "planning" his exit. The actual process of disengagement took almost three years to accomplish, during which time he "marked time . . . [was] intellectually turned off . . . just going through the motions."

Hansford was appointed pastor of a "very conservative little church" where Ford's name was anathema. He experienced difficulties in his preaching. To circumvent the books of Daniel and Revelation, the seedbed of Adventist apocalyptic, Hansford devised an ingenious plan: "to go through the Gospels systematically."

Starting from the beginning and the way I structured it, it would take a long long time to get through the Gospels (laughs). . . . I basically had adopted a harmonic approach, you know, where we sort of look . . . at each passage across the Gospels and sort of move through the set like that and whatever theme there was take it across the Gospels. . . . It was a very rewarding time, spiritually it was very rewarding. . . . I thoroughly enjoyed it. . . . First weeks it was fine, you know, a couple of months was fine, but then [church members] began saying this is going to take a long time to get us through the Gospels, how about something else. I'd say, look there's nothing better than the Gospels . . . we can't better the Gospels surely. Oh dear me, you know . . . come two years I was still chundering slowly, working my way through the Gospels.

He felt guilty at keeping up a front with parishioners. Hansford explained that he "was struggling to survive" in the ministry. Church administrators either did not sense the extent of Hansford's drift or were insensitive to his needs. The Conference president forced him into running an evangelistic outreach campaign. "This is just terrible," recalls Hansford. "[The program] barely ran four nights. They stopped coming after the second night. There was no one there. The third night we sort of had one or two people and then the fourth night there was no one, so it was a good excuse to close it. . . . I purposely didn't . . . want people to come back." He had few conflicts either with parishioners or administrators over theology, but his antipathy toward traditional Adventist beliefs was apparent. One pastor actually sought his advice concerning leaving ministry. Hansford told him that he too was "waiting for the right opportunity . . . to step out."

There was no catalyst to Hansford's resignation. Neither the Conference president nor the Conference evangelist with whom he discussed his intentions tried to persuade him to continue. During his final year Hansford agonized more over his future career than about leaving ministry. He returned to university to study while working part time cleaning the local Seventh-day Adventist Church. He attended church occasionally, and only to protect his "little nest," his business interest as church cleaner. Immediately following his resignation Hansford experienced an "unbelievable" sense of freedom—"the sense was totally elating. . . . I was actually surprised . . . just how wonderful it felt to have this thing just lift off me." But the elation was short-lived. His career was "in shambles." Even worse, the Hansfords were totally isolated by the Adventist community and without friends. The Conference president visited them once at their request, but "nothing came of it." For a time they kept in contact with two former Adventist pastors, but these relationships were short-lived. The incumbent Adventist pastor visited them once or twice, but they found little to talk about because they had little in common. "We found ourselves isolated socially. . . . We had no friends. . . . Adventism was our total social world, our total structure, and we had nothing outside of that." They experienced problems making new friends. "That was a very painful part because we had to start from scratch, and of course . . . who do you make friends with? Who wants to make friends [with you]? . . . Where do you find people to make friends? . . . It's taken [us] years." The most painful aspect of leaving the ministry was telling family members. They anticipated criticism from his father, who was still an Adventist pastor, but were surprised how "mature" he was about it. Telling his parents-in-law, however, was traumatic:

It was really awful. At two o'clock in the morning . . . this wreck of a man crawls into your room and begs, actually woke us out of sleep and begged us not to do what we're doing. . . . (whispers) "Don't desert the truth. Don't desert the truth. You're doing the wrong thing." It was just so traumatic. This guy just could not accept [it]. . . . To him, basically, we were lost. His thinking is just very clear that we are lost people. We argued for hours. . . . "You are the one who has misled my daughter. . . . You've misled my daughter, you've made my daughter a lost soul" (whispers). I just can't forget it. It got very personal. It got very bitter. It was terrible.

Hansford no longer professes to be an Adventist and is unsure whether to even claim the title "Christian." He has no dogmatic views about God and no longer accepts the Judaeo-Christian Scriptures as "God's specifically expressed word to the human family." Depending on his mood at the time he is either philosophical about his Adventist past or, particularly when confronting career choices, angry at having "wasted ten years of my life."

Jonathan Morton

Jonathan Morton served the Seventh-day Adventist Church for more than twenty years as pastor and administrator. He is angry at the circumstances that culminated in his coerced resignation and the fact that Adventist expastors are totally cut off by the church after they leave ministry. Morton converted to Adventism from the Church of Christ as a young man. While working as an apprentice carpenter he was befriended by a workmate who impressed him with his Adventist lifestyle. He attended an evangelistic series, and after eighteen months of regular contact and Bible study with church members he was baptized a Seventh-day Adventist. It was not so much the Adventist theology as the sectarian lifestyle and emphasis on healthy living which, according to Morton, "added a new dimension to [his] Christianity." However, as with all converts, his passage to Adventism involved major discontinuities. Morton had been a keen sportsman, and acceptance of Saturday as Sabbath radically altered his social life; he had to make new friends who didn't work on Saturday. Morton became totally encapsulated in the Adventist social world—the church became his life.

The idea of becoming a minister grew slowly in tandem with his gradual socialization into Adventism. He was encouraged by the pastor who was instrumental in his conversion to consider youth ministry as a career, an idea reinforced by events that he interpreted as signalling God's leading. Morton lacked the necessary academic prerequisites for ministry training, and "made one of those pledges to God that if He meant me to go to Avondale College and did so without my returning to school to complete [secondary school] then I would be a minister. A letter came back telling me that I was accepted. Well, I had committed myself. I had this pledge with God, so now there was no turning back." Morton recalls there were no theological highs during his training for the ministry even though major issues were being debated at the college during those years. Controversy on the subject of perfection generated division among the faculty and students. However, Morton confesses that he didn't understand the theological issues which made more sense to second or third generation Adventists than to recent converts like himself. At the completion of his training for ministry Morton's outlook remained very simplistic but recognizably Adventist. He explains, "I was just a very straight down the line Christian who happened to believe in the Sabbath and the idea of a healthy mind—healthy body and the idea that Adventism was a vigorous church which was taking a message to the world. Theologically speaking I probably was very much a babe in the wood and very naive." He was elected president of the graduating class and sees this as proof that his peers looked upon him as an exemplary up-and-coming Adventist pastor.

Morton advanced quickly up the Adventist ranks. Following an initial three-year appointment to a remote parish, he was promoted to assistant youth leader and for a number of years held administrative portfolios at Conference level, often while pastoring churches. Morton explained: "I enjoyed my life as a minister because I was doing the thing that I liked most. I really loved ministry. . . . I enjoyed my years as an Adventist minister. I feel I was contributing to the Adventist Church in an administrative and creative way." Like many of his contemporaries, Morton met his wife at Avondale College and married immediately following graduation. She was a second generation Adventist with an uncle in ministry and a father who for many years worked for the church selling Adventist books. She "hated" ministry and did not "take a very active role in Church life." Morton explains that "she believed her responsibility was to the children first and not to the church." When she first heard of my proposed research on Adventist expastors and the fact that I was hoping to interview her husband, she told me sarcastically that I should interview wives also and proceeded to recount incidents in her Adventist past of spending hours on end in the car with bored or crying children while her minister husband was "on the Lord's business." Morton conceded that on average he devoted less than one weekend in three to his family, but explains that "the church and church work were my life." So committed was he to the Adventist cause that he became known to non-Adventist contacts as "Mr Adventism" for his sectarian zeal. "If I was in anything for the church. I was up to my ears in it. There was no half-heartedness in what I did. It was a total commitment. My time and energies were primarily for the church; my family came second."

Morton believed that "Christianity was a way of life" and not a set of abstract doctrines, and took little interest in exploring theological matters in depth. All the same, he did not accept blindly the Adventist claims. Early in his Adventist career he questioned the matter of Ellen White's inspiration and had his own views on the doctrine of the Trinity. Nevertheless, he associates the genesis of his problems in ministry not with these private beliefs but with the theological battles being waged in the church during the mid-1970s, a period in Adventism which he interpreted as signalling "a new spirit of evangelical Christianity within the Church." He adds, "I sensed the excitement among young people. . . . I saw older people suddenly become Bible students. It was great." However, Morton was aware that this emphasis was at odds with traditional Adventism; he was excited more over those beliefs Adventists had in common with other evangelical Christians than with doctrines that were unique to Adventists.

As he tells his story now, he explains that his changed theological focus altered his attitude to religion and people. He became, he reports, much more aware of the world beyond the narrow confines of Adventism. He began studying in secular institutions, believing this would better equip him for ministry:

Doing this brought me in contact with people outside of the church. I began to see that my world had been very small and that there were alternative ways of looking at the world and of reading the Bible to the concepts that Adventists had. . . . It was not so much the subjects but the people I met that affected me. They knew I was an SDA [Seventh-day Adventist] minister and in a friendly way sometimes challenged me to look for other ways of seeing things. Adventists generally had things cut and dry. But as I began to read a little more widely I began to sense that there was a part of history missing from Adventism. So my world was expanding. . . . If you look at any Adventist person who has done some study, once they start looking at the bigger world outside Ellen White and the Bible their minds begin to broaden.

With time he identified more with the academics and "innovators" who, like himself, challenged prescribed sect boundaries. Each of the friends he named during the interview had the reputation of being "intellectual" and nonconformist. Morton states that as a convert with "shallow Adventist roots" he was more receptive of revisionist ideas and less troubled by the issues affecting those with Adventist backgrounds. Des Ford's heresy trial and subsequent dismissal affected him differently because he "had no personal history of Adventism, no father and grandfather in the work, so it did not matter to me. I changed once from being Church of Christ to become an Adventist so I could change again." Increasingly he became disillusioned with Adventist doctrine. He recalled a conversation with a pastor friend (who later also resigned), who said to him, "Jon, the coat hanger stuff is blown.[1] He did a diagram on the steps [of the Conference office] of how the 2,300 days investigative judgement was blown." Morton referred to the doctrine of the investigative judgement as "the center of Adventism" and "the big bubble that burst." The inspiration of Ellen White and accusations of her plagiarism compounded his growing disenchantment with the Adventist system. A change of administration at Conference level commenced the final chapter of Morton's ministry career.

The incoming president saw his role as "defender of the faith" and upon taking office immediately set out to cleanse the ministry of "liberal apostates." Pastors were polarized into liberals and conservatives. Morton sided with the "young" renegades and was signatory to a letter addressed by pastors to the world leader of the Adventist movement protesting Ford's sacking and condemning the administration's "cultish, sectarian and narrow" approach to theology. Ford's sacking unleashed a witch hunt aimed at identifying and expelling Ford-minded persons in the Adventist churches. Lay members who did not accept *The 27 Fundamentals* of the church were dismissed from church membership; eight were disfellowshipped in one of Morton's churches and two in another. Along with other minister friends he was harangued by laity and leadership over his preaching. Morton recalls: "I preached very boldly but not theologically, but I tended to echo in my preaching the issues that were being aired. My preaching possibly echoed my thoughts on the issues being debated therefore I was seen as being not one of the dyed in the wool Adventist preachers. I was labelled a Fordite." Acting on information conveyed to him by lay members the president confronted him over his theology. "[He] called me in the office and tackled me on points that I reportedly made in my sermons. We were having to record all our sermons to protect ourselves." Morton is adamant that there was a deliberate campaign on the part of administration "to destroy ministers who were a threat to Adventism." Four pastors in his Conference were dismissed for not adhering to the church's traditional emphasis. "[It] tore my guts out. I knew these men to be honest, straightforward men. I don't think I ever had the privilege of working with a more spiritual and dedicated group of fellows. The church lost something when it lost that group." The dismissals were the turning point in his career. He recalled, "We would go down to the airport to farewell one of these poor souls and we'd have a bit of a laugh but then wonder who was going to be next." Morton says that he "could see the writing on the wall."

A confrontation with the Conference president who questioned him over a statement he had made to a recent convert, was the final episode that led to his resignation. Morton was accused of telling a new member that the Seventh-day Adventist Church "had to do some serious thinking over theology otherwise [it] was going to get itself into a real mess." The Conference president demanded his resignation and informed him that he would not be reelected in the forthcoming triennial elections. The final steps to Morton's disengagement were routine and mechanical. He was asked to sign a short statement to the effect that he was resigning from the ministry "for personal reasons." "[The president then] asked me to kneel with him in prayer. He prayed for me, that God would forgive me. And that was it." Morton continued to work for twelve more weeks following his resignation to wind down his busy departmental program. He claims that this unusual move of keeping him on for a time instead of the usual instant termination possibly was because "someone up top felt kindly toward Jonathan Morton" but thinks it more likely because he was "a political hot potato best handled carefully."

Morton left Adventism a shattered man. His resignation meant that he had to relocate his family to a new social environment. He found it difficult to find work and was unemployed for at least four months. As a middle-aged male, Morton found himself "at the back end" of the labour market. What odd jobs he did get over the next two years were arranged for him by former Adventist friends and involved "cleaning toilets, windows, chook pens, panel beaters' workshops and [some] gardening." He returned to night school to study, and this helped to "re-establish my confidence in myself as a person who could achieve something." "There's no love lost in the Adventist Church," explains Morton. "When you're finished, you're finished, and wiped off like a dirty old rag." He adds:

Seeing something that you have loved for twenty years as a minister, four years training at Avondale plus [two] years as a new Adventist—and totally involved—getting over the hurt is not easy. . . . I felt I was an outcast who was worth nothing. The church did not want me. The commercial world did not want me. Twenty years as Adventist minister was worth nothing, in fact it was a handicap to getting employment. My self-image was zilch.

The dismantling of his career, loss of status and friends, and the collapse of his individual self-image also led to the deconstruction of his entire belief system. "For me as a result of this, I think Adventism was destroyed as was Christianity. What I saw happen . . . among so-called Christian people and how the shocking way they treated each other, shattered my idealism of the Adventist Church. I now see this movement as a sham, just a facade. It is just politics. When you take the veneer off, they were just animals, a cult." Morton now calls himself agnostic. He no longer accepts Christ as the Son of God and questions whether there is even a God. He adds, "If there is a God he's got a hell of a lot to answer for." He sees the Christian faith as "merely an attempt to explain man and his environment" but dismisses Seventh-day Adventism as "a lot of bullshit." On one occasion he met up and tried to converse with the pastor who first convinced him to become an Adventist and who had since become a leading figure in the Adventist Church, but the pastor "simply walked away." Morton explains, "I stood there in utter disbelief, disgusted and shattered. I thought you're just like the bloody rest."

John Dunmore

Dunmore points to his father as the single most important person to influence his career choice. Dunmore's father was a Seventh-day Adventist pastor of some rank, having served the church for more than two decades as evangelist and administrator at Conference and Union levels. Dunmore was raised in a home environment dedicated to ministry, and he too came to view the role of the minister as a supreme calling and the fullest expression of dedication to God. Dunmore loved his father and as a child identified fully with his father's work. But the experience that confirmed in his young mind a sense of calling was his "miraculous" recovery after being hit by a car as a child. The experience, which was interpreted by him and his parents as "a sign that God had a special work" for him, generated in his life a sense of purposefulness that led inexorably in the direction of ministry. His destiny had been decided, like Samuel in the Old Testament, from early childhood, and the possibility of doing work other than ministry never entered his mind. However, it was his training program at Avondale College that gave direction to his sense of calling and deepened his yearning for ministry.

Throughout the four year training program Dunmore endeavored to remain distant and emotionally detached from the theology issues being debated at the college, but the theological mood of the place did affect him notwithstanding. He recalls, "Enthusiasm was in the air. . . . You could sense it all around you. . . . This new enthusiasm for studying [the Bible and the writings of Ellen White] . . . and trying to find some new sense . . . of what our roots were all about was exciting. . . . It made . . . studying exciting. . . . It gave me a new sense of fulfillment." The excitement helped deepen his devotion to the church and reinforced his desire to be a minister. Dunmore explains that the mood of the college had a different effect on him than on college peers who were converts. He was less preoccupied with learning what Seventh-day Adventists believed and more with discovering "newer and fuller answers to our raison d'etre" beyond the "pat answers." Exposure to the revisionist ideas among students raised many questions in his mind concerning traditional Adventist beliefs particularly in the areas of prophetic interpretation and Adventist apocalyptic. At the same time it renewed his zeal for the church. He believed that if this new emphasis could do this to him, then the church as a whole could be revitalized: "I felt that your average Adventist would be interested in growing [spiritually] and discovering a fresh awareness of their Adventist Christian experience." Dunmore explains that from the outset his ministry focused on the Adventist Church; the Adventist membership was his "mission field." His four years of training transformed his thinking "at the roots level." He was unsure of what to do with his new outlook. All the same, he graduated from college and entered ministry feeling ill equipped and unprepared for the work he was expected to perform in the local church.

His first year of ministry as assistant to a leading Adventist evangelist was "a real turn-off." He explains, "If I had a sense of evangelism I lost it with that." The evangelist's material was dated, his presentation stale, and his message altogether irrelevant to contemporary audiences. Dunmore was further disappointed at the "very low level thinking person" attracted to Adventist outreach programs. He became cynical of traditional forms of evangelism. But what changed him most was sharing house with another new entrant to ministry who was "not backward" in his criticism of the Adventist establishment. Dunmore explains that "this added a radical touch to my thinking which possibly wasn't there before." Daily exposure to the unrestrained questioning and criticism of Adventist theology and bureaucracy forced him to focus on and review the theological issues that he avoided while at college. During the Ford heresy trial at Glacier View, Dunmore's house had become the "gossip-line" between Australia and the United States, receiving and distributing up-to-the-minute accounts of the latest developments. His flatmate introduced him to underground Adventist literature and in almost no time their home was transformed into a distribution outlet for literature critical of the organization and traditional Adventist theology. He recalls, "There was almost a sense of clandestineness about [these activities] . . . which . . . added a little excitement as well. [It was] as if we were treading on the edges of forbidden things." Although from the commencement of his ministry Dunmore thought much about the type of ministry he would like to focus on and the direction his career was heading, exit did not enter his thought. He was aware, however, that the highly charged emotional and theological context in which he was operating had changed him. He developed an acute distrust of church administrators, including his own father. He became suspicious of church members and kept his views to himself. He catalogued other ministers in the Conference according to their perceived theological leanings and was careful with whom he discussed theology.

Dunmore traces the beginnings of his questioning of ministry to the Glacier View meetings and Ford's sacking, although he is careful to explain that it was not so much his sympathy for Ford as the administration's response to it that caused him to review all that he took for granted about the Adventist Church, particularly the claim that the Adventist minority had a special role to perform in God's plan of salvation. For him, the dismissal of Ford signalled an absence of Christian virtue; he wondered whether Adventism deserved to be called "Christian." The events leading up to and following Ford's removal he now interprets in political terms, as a struggle over power and control, not theology. When the following year his flatmate was charged with heresy and dismissed, Dunmore lost all sense of respect for church leadership. He also became disillusioned with debating issues of theology. He now had doubts about his calling to ministry and began thinking of exit.

As a pastor, Dunmore identified with the marginal members and with the disaffected—church members who were disfellowshipped for their doctrinal views, or young couple who were refused membership because they were Ford sympathizers. He felt alienated by the actions of his church members, who on one occasion "actually put a sign on the front door [of the church] saying . . . these are the fundamentals of the Seventh-day Adventist Church. If you don't agree with the fundamentals . . . we'd ask you to keep quiet . . . or go somewhere else to worship." He felt antipathy toward the Adventist sectarian mind-set, which marginalized Christian people who thought for themselves. Although Dunmore was careful about what he preached and deliberately avoided entering into theological debates, church members still found fault with his message. A number wrote to the Conference president complaining not so much about what Dunmore said in his sermons, as about what he did not say. At the Church Board members formally demanded in writing his views on the sanctuary, Ellen White's inspiration, and the Adventist interpretation of the prophecies. Dunmore refused to answer these questions because, as he explains, he had not made up his mind where he stood on issues that were still being studied by Adventist scholars. The church requested that he be transferred to a different parish. Support from Conference administrators was not forthcoming. On each of the two occasions the Conference president visited his parish, he sided with the lay majority and refused to consider Dunmore's point of view. The fact that the Conference Executive Committee extended his probationary period in ministry to a third year he interpreted as censure.

The reaction of church members to his wife was "the icing on the cake" in his decision to exit. Although his wife also was born a Seventh-day Adventist, she was not from a "strong Adventist background." She was both "fairly innocent" and "naive" and had no idea of "what was in store for her in the ministry," and did not have the "grin and bear it attitude" to the church that he believes is necessary for wives to survive in ministry. Conflicts in the church and criticisms of her husband's performance she took personally. The dismissal of their best minister friend had a devastating impact on both of them but "ruined her Christian experience." She rebelled. She refused to conform to member expectations of the minister's wife by maintaining close friendship ties with individual members. She flouted the stereotype by training in tae kwon do, which local church elders condemned not only as unacceptable behavior for a minister's wife but also as unbecoming for Adventist women. They complained to the Conference president, who shared their concerns. For the sake of his Christianity as well as his marriage, Dunmore began planning his exit.

No dramatic event as such prompted him to write his letter of resignation. Dunmore made up his mind to quit at the ordination of a fellow minister:

[Seeing a pastor being ordained] I realized that I didn't want to be there. . . . I didn't want to be a pastor . . . (whispers) because to me that would mean . . . that I was fully owned by the church . . . and . . . I didn't want to be owned by the church because the church hadn't shown me that it can be trusted. I lost confidence in it. . . . I couldn't trust their ownership of me, and so it was there that I decided that I was going to do something else.

To make it easier for his parents to accept his decision and to minimize possible negative impact on supporting church members, Dunmore applied for leave to study counselling with the intention of returning to ministry. As it turned out, however, he did neither. With his changed occupational status Dunmore entered a state of "bewilderment" and "confusion." He began to drink alcohol. He grew a beard as a visible expression of his release from ministry—now he could look and dress as he liked and eat what he liked without feeling constrained by church or ministry. His parents reacted angrily to his exit. For more than four years his mother refused to accept his changed identity and insisted that "once God has called you he doesn't go back on the call." It has taken him "years" to get over the guilt of leaving ministry. Dunmore attributes the collapse of his marriage to his experiences in ministry and to the fact that he continued to identify with the Seventh-day Adventist Church even after leaving ministry. He explains that he could not turn his back on Adventism: "There's too much of Adventism in my background to be destroyed, and to do that [would be] to destroy a part of myself and . . . I'd be a lesser person if I did." Dunmore continues to attend church regularly while keeping "a low profile." It has taken him more than four years to "forgive" administrators and stop thinking of them as "devils" and "demons" for the part they played in the collapse of his ministry career. Dunmore states that a return to ministry is now out of the question: "To me there's a freedom [in being out of the ministry] . . . of being my own boss, not having my wage held over me and controlling how I should think . . . and that's quite a relief."

STRUCTURE OF EXIT NARRATIVES

Expastors tell quite different stories that defy classification and reduction into simple linear chronologies of sequenced events. Emotions, descriptions of events, and introspective musings about what happened, and why, are intertwined in the retelling; one memory sparks off another chain of memories. The chronological structure evident in the above case studies is an artificial one, superimposed on the data by the author to communicate to the reader a sequence of developments on the way to exit that is not always clear in the raw accounts. Notwithstanding the individual differences, there are some identifiable patterns in the ways expastors report their exits. First, expastors do not retell an ordered autobiography in which the call to ministry, experiences as pastors, and circumstances of exit are sequenced and linked to form a chronological narrative. They gravitate instead to describing the actual break, the final separation. Morton, for example, launched into a lengthy excursus of events that occurred during the final six months of his twenty-year ministry. With the exception of those who had served as pastors for less than one year, leavers tell a truncated or back-to-front story. They present a highly abbreviated story that focuses on the actual separation *as if* it were detached from earlier experiences; it has only an ending with no beginning. They focus on the "biggest hurts" and most emotionally charged segments of their experiences, and only with prompting from me during interview work outward from there.

The majority of expastors lay bare their very soul in the retelling. The term "confession," defined more generally as self-disclosure or the unburdening of one's private self (Foucault 1978), describes the narratives of at least half of the interviewed expastors. For this reason exit narratives are also intensely personal and charged with "emotionality" (Denzin 1989:29). This is evident in the description of the father-in-law's response to Hansford's decision to leave, in Dunmore's disclosure of how exit affected his relationship with his devoted Adventist mother, and in Morton's sense of alienation when contemplating secular employment.

This emotionality and focus on the social relations story of exit, however, is subordinate to another story. The salient feature of exit stories is their intellectuality. Social and relational factors are pushed to the background while the rational or intellectual issues are given prominence. Leaving the ministry is depicted as an intellectual process and something that occurs almost exclusively "in the head." However, the above three case studies also illustrate that the cerebral process cannot be divorced from, and is more fully understood when examined alongside, the social.

CONSIDERATIONS ON THE ANALYSIS OF ACCOUNTS OF EXIT

C. Wright Mills (1940:904) warns researchers not to treat "an action" as if it were "discrepant from its verbalization." On this point Garfinkel is even more definitive, arguing that descriptions "do things" and should be studied as "action": "The activities whereby members produce and manage settings of organized everyday affairs are identical with members' procedures for making those settings 'account-able' . . . reportable, tell-a-story-aboutable, analyzable—in short, *accountable*" (Garfinkel 1967:1,33; my emphasis). In the present context, the term "account" is used in a technical sense and refers to the procedures people use, in formal and informal speech, to explain and justify action (M. B. Scott and Lyman 1968; Beckford 1978a), excuse it (Austin 1961), attribute causality (Brown 1983:49–52), create an impression of factuality (Wooffitt 1992), or manufacture a particular impression (J. Atkinson and Drew 1979). The truth or falsity of accounts is less relevant, according to Potter and Wetherell (1987:92–93), than arriving at an understanding of how participants make sense of their experiences and attribute meaning to them. But, in turn, that understanding may inform sociological reconstructions of complex processes like exit.

In his study of the conversion narratives of Jehovah's Witnesses, B. Wilson (1978) observed that while the stories differ in predictable ways, he could identify a number of recurrent elements, shared assumptions, and common emphases. The most important common feature was that converts validate decisions to join the movement by reference to ideological terms in which the sect as a collectivity seeks legitimation. In other words, the convert's story matched the group's theology. According to Beckford: "Accounts of conversion [and de-conversion] are constructions (or reconstructions) of experiences which draw upon resources available *at the time of construction* to lend them sense. They are not fixed, once-and-for-all descriptions of phenomena as they occurred in the past. Rather, their meaning emerges in the very process of construction, and this takes place at different times in different contexts" (1978b:260). Wilson (1978:506) argues that "individuals are socialised to conversion and subsequently . . . learn how to express, in appropriate language, just what has happened." Recounting of the conversion experience involves learning how to articulate that experience in an appropriate way. Taylor (1978:319) states that converts formulate convertibility by describing the typically convertible person and by complementing personal experience with the expectations and symbolism of the group with which they identify. In these ways conversion narratives confirm to the group the authenticity of the convert's intentions and reinforce group values and beliefs. Beckford (1978a:249), who observed something similar in conversion accounts of Jehovah's Witnesses, states, "Ideology plays a central role in mediating between the movement's external circumstances, its organisational rationale and its members' ways of accounting for their conversion." In a follow-up essay Beckford (1983) applied this view to accounts of apostasy, arguing that accounts of apostasy similarly are "situated constructions" by means of which leavers justify their actions using reference points and language that are understandable to their audiences.

One may thus generalize that expastors' accounts of leaving ministry are constructed according to a common set of expectations about why pastors leave and a common set of norms for assessing the legitimacy of leaving. An examination of the interview data reveals two distinct yet interrelated accounts of exiting in the narratives of expastors: one which focuses on theology as the reason for leaving ministry (as primary in Hansford's), and a second which highlights non-theological or organizational and interpersonal factors (as primary in Morton's). Our understanding as summarised in the above generalisation of how expastors' accounts of exit are constructed will help us tease out the relationship between these two accounts and the weight to be given to each in generalized accounts of exit.

THE THEOLOGICAL ACCOUNT OF EXIT

The version of exit that most stands out in expastors' accounts depicts exit as deconversion. Leavers are depicted as theological renegades and intellectuals who were prepared to question, challenge, and reject the limits of sectarian belief. Some, including Hansford, locate their initial questioning of sectarian belief in a period prior to commencing in ministry. For others, like Dunmore, the change in outlook was gradual and matured into full-blown doubt while they were working as pastors. A majority of expastors fall into this category, but unlike Morton, who reports that his theological convictions changed "suddenly" after more than two decades of ministry, describe a gradual transformation. What is important in the present context, however, is that all three expastors, in common with most of the other expastors, depict their transformed religious outlook as a movement from conservatism to liberalism, from Adventist orthodoxy to evangelical "heresy" and beyond, from a commitment and devotion to sectarianism to a disillusionment with Christianity itself. The accounts of Hansford, Morton, and Dunmore parallel one another not only in the way the past, which is equated with ignorance and immaturity, is contrasted with present enlightenment and coming of age, but also—and more importantly,—in the fact that all three frame their changes as a deconversion.

Beckford (1985:175) argues that "apostasy is essentially dissimilar from conversion," because disengaging is complex and problematic and presupposes failure or error and not just change. However, Beckford appears to have overlooked the possibility that conversion itself is both complex and can be a painful process. The fact that apostasy and conversion are reported as intellectual processes and occur suddenly may be artifacts of narrative construction. The interviews suggest that exit narratives are constructed to be like Adventist conversion experiences in reverse. In the majority of instances, exit as described, did not occur suddenly but was a gradual transformation. Dunmore, for example, claims that he was often not aware of the full implications of the views he was experimenting with or the implications of his actions, just as in accounts of the early stages of conversion. In the same way that conversion to sectarian belief is riveted on pivotal doctrines of the faith, the narratives of expastors preface exit with the unraveling of the belief system. Finally, exiters emerge with a new way of seeing and interpreting the past, just as converts juxtapose present "enlightenment" with previous "darkness" to emphasize their transition and the resulting changes in outlook. The language of "before and after" in accounts facilitates impression management (Ballis and Richardson 1997); the greater the contrast between present and past, the greater the impact of the narrative.

ATROCITY TALES AND THE SOCIAL RELATIONS ACCOUNT OF EXIT

Expastors' accounts are dotted with anecdotes of disillusionment and reports of experiences that stretched expastors' levels of tolerance beyond bearing. In these narratives expastors describe organizational processes, social relationships, and personal factors that were incongruent with their interpretations of some central premise of Christian ethic. The different versions of exiting compete for attention: the doctrinal account is often the dominant voice that drowns out the other focus on social factors. The relationship between the two voices was poignantly illustrated during one interview where the expastor presented two versions of exit—one on tape, which focused on theological factors as the reasons for exiting, and a second when the tape recorder was turned off, which emphasized personal and relational matters. After several unsuccessful attempts to discuss the immediate circumstances that provoked his letter of resignation, that expastor requested that the tape recorder be stopped and proceeded to give an alternative version, which I subsequently discovered approximated the official one. The Union Conference minutes record that the expastor resigned from ministry on grounds of "conduct unbecoming to a minister." The incident illustrates how this expastor sought to "normalize" his situation by generating a version of exit that, emphasizing theological issues, would show his leaving in a more favorable light, or at least one that would be more acceptable to those who shared his Christian orientation.

No expastor had left the Adventist ministry for purely doctrinal reasons, although it is also true that doctrinal reasons are always *part* of the process. While theology assumes a primary role in the majority of accounts, further narration by the expastors always revealed that concerns over theology meshed with social factors. Expastors' reports of clashes with church authorities and members over theology often have an underlay of "atrocity tales." What is the sociologist to make of these? Are the tales of atrocity in social relations to be accepted as secondary in mainly theological accounts of exit? Our previous considerations would suggest not. But are the atrocities themselves to be admitted into generalized accounts of exit as simple truth?

B. Wilson cautions researchers who seek to understand new religious movements to treat with scepticism and "circumspection" the evidence of "the disaffected and apostate" and to avoid an over-dependence on the testimony of former members. According to Wilson, "The apostate is generally in need of self-justification. He seeks to construct his own past, to excuse his former affiliations, and to blame those who were formerly his closest associates. Not uncommonly the apostate learns to rehearse an 'atrocity story' to explain how, by manipulation, trickery, coercion, or deceit, he was induced to join or to remain within an organisation that he now forswears and condemns" (1990:19). The stories of former members abound with tales of disillusionment and stories of negative experiences. Morton, for instance, describes what he believes was an organized program in his Conference to identify and eliminate deviating pastors who questioned the sectarian beliefs; Dunmore tells of church members who were turned away and advised to worship elsewhere because they expressed sympathy with the views of the recently dismissed Des Ford. One expastor describes how a church member befriended him and secretly recorded many of their conversations and sent copies to the Conference president. If one were to follow Wilson's advice literally, one would be deaf to most things former members would have to tell us in their non-theological versions of their exits.

Other researchers are less dismissive of this type of data. From their examination of published accounts of atrocity tales about the Unification Church Bromley, Shupe, and Ventimiglia (1979) illustrate how negative stories "help construct a moral basis for otherwise illegal actions." Lewis (1989) shows how narratives of atrocities can mobilize and legitimate the persecution of marginal religious movements. Hunt and Benford (1994) suggest that such stories carry an "identikit." By focusing on the self-mortification and rejection of a previous identity, atrocity tales serve to frame an actor's new personal and social identity and mobilize commitment.

The tales of atrocity and disillusionment are many and varied. However, in the narratives of expastors they accomplish several practical objectives. First, the stories identify actors and categorize them as victims or villains. Second, they demonstrate expastors' perception of their own personal identities. Third, they impute to the organization and the sectarian community a collective identity to which they attribute "blame" for their exits. Finally, the narratives are a form of "frame realignment" by means of which expastors "locate, perceive, identify, and label" experiences (Goffman 1974:21) to legitimate exit. In the terms of Snow, Rochford et al. (1986) and Walsh (1981), social narratives and atrocity tales facilitated the "micromobilization" of disillusioned former pastors.

Appreciation of the *function* of atrocity stories in the lives of expastors by no means involves their dismissal as *only* fabrications. As in the appreciation of the constructed character of the theological account of exit, appreciation of the constructed functional character of accounts of atrocities in social relations merely alerts the sociologist to the problematic status of these accounts in any generalized sociological analysis of exit. Appreciation of the constructed character of the accounts warns the sociologist always to contextualize any one expastor's account of exit in the array of accounts, and any one repeated narrative in the array of other repeated narratives. In this study, neither atrocity stories nor theological narratives of exit are dismissed; nor is one type of story (for example, the theological account) reduced to another (for example, the social relations account). Rather, the task of analysis is to show how the developing constructions of reality by the expastors themselves figure in the process of exit, and how the *real* theological issues are fought out in *real* social relations.

SUMMARY

Our examination of the "design features" (Wooffitt 1992:303) of expastors' stories revealed that they were "constructed with group specific guidelines" in mind (Snow and Machalek 1983:175–177). The narratives are best "understood by drawing upon contextual knowledge" (Heritage 1984:142) and presuppose familiarity with Adventism and detailed knowledge of issues being debated in the movement. More than this, the stories mirror the sectarian organizational setting and carry the identity tags of the actors. In this chapter the salience of a theological account of exit in expastors' narratives has been demonstrated. This theological account has been shown to be subordinate in the narratives to accounts focusing on social relations, and particularly atrocities in social relations. Consideration of the constructed functional nature of their accounts, it has been argued, points to the necessity of contextualizing the theological accounts in the social relations accounts, and vice versa, if the end of a generalized sociological account of the process of exit is to be achieved. It is to the first of these contextualizations that we now turn. The following chapters explore the less audible sounds in expastors' narratives in the belief that a knowledge of relational and organizational factors will both provide a necessary context for, and facilitate a more complete understanding of, the theological.

NOTE

1.   The expression "coat hanger" is a cryptic reference to Seventh-day Adventist preoccupation with prophetic interpretation, and more specifically, with the use of prophetic charts to illustrate their interpretation. Prophetic charts became standard equipment used by Adventist evangelists in their public campaigns (see page 175). The term refers to the depiction of the prophecies on these evangelistic charts in which an arc is used to connect the starting point and ending of prophetic time, resulting in a coat hanger shape.

Chapter 5 _____

Loss of Idealism and Cynical Knowledge

During an informal conversation I asked an expastor whether he had come to terms with the way he was dismissed from ministry two years earlier. In his reply the expastor recounted feelings of anger and disappointment dating back many years before his exit that appeared to have no direct bearing on the actual circumstances of leaving. He recalled being threatened with physical violence during a Church Board meeting in his first year of ministry, an occasion when the Conference president mocked him for striving to be innovative in ministry, and described feeling disappointed and hurt by church authorities who promised him one thing but did something else. The final point of separation from ministry was looked upon by this expastor not as an appendage to an otherwise happy ministry but as the end-point of a history of painful encounters. This expastor's response suggests that just as the hurt was not confined to the final months but extended throughout ministry, an understanding of why pastors exit requires that a pastor's work history be considered as a whole. The present chapter examines how previously conservative and conforming pastors progressed from their initial realization that "things are not what they seem to be" in ministry to questioning their future in ministry and full-blown doubting of Adventism itself. At what point in the expastors' ministry did the idea of exiting come to mind? What kinds of experiences generated thoughts of exit? What were the circumstances that compelled expastors to carry out their intentions? These are some of the questions to be addressed in this chapter.

THE ROOTS OF DISAFFECTION

My reading of expastor narratives reveals that processes that culminate with exit, whether by dismissal or resignation, have long antecedents and begin gradually and even imperceptibly. In the same way that a river over time undermines its embankment and alters its flow, the accounts of exit suggest that leavers experience a gradual erosion of commitment. The experiences with which expastors associate the commencement of their disillusionment with ministry often are not significant in themselves, but gain significance in the retelling as types of early experiences that expastors connect with exit. The progression from commitment to disillusionment is not a straightforward one, as if one experience automatically leads to the next. For the majority of expastors exit is prefaced by years of ambivalence—sometimes doubting, sometimes affirming commitment to ministry, depending on the situations that provoke the moods. Most of the time the confused thoughts and contradictory emotions are either suppressed or managed by counterbalancing opposite feelings. At some point in their ministry, however, this delicate balance was disrupted by events that prompted them to review their future as well as their past. Peter Ferguson's case is of particular interest as it portrays both what Ebaugh (1988a:41) calls the "first doubts" stage in the exit process, and critical experiences that intrude into the autobiography and divide it into "before" and "after."

Peter Ferguson

Ferguson believes he is a cast-off from the Seventh-day Adventist Church. He points to the way he finally separated from ministry as typifying the way the church system has related to him through his ministry. He received not a single word of appreciation or even acknowledgment for his eleven-year ministry, and adds, "I have not yet lodged an official letter of resignation, but I have already got final settlement." This confirms in Ferguson's mind that church administrators "are not really interested in me as a person, or in my talents and abilities. It has taken eleven years for it to dawn on me that they are not really interested in me or in the abilities which I know I have got. So I have taken my abilities elsewhere. I will now minister the way God directs me to minister, not the way this lot has directed." Looking back over his past Ferguson recalls numerous events and conversations forewarning him of this final outcome, but confesses that he did not see their full implications while in ministry.

Ferguson's mother was first attracted to the movement by the Adventist health message and encouraged Ferguson and his two sisters to explore the Adventist teachings in depth. Ferguson was fifteen years old when he was baptized into the Seventh-day Adventist Church together with his mother and sisters. He completed his secondary education at an Adventist school, where he enjoyed the sheltered Adventist environment. It was while attending the Adventist school that he first began thinking about ministry. Many lay people commented that he would make a good Adventist minister, and similar comments from a minister friend whom he liked and respected finally convinced him to make ministry his lifetime career. Ferguson commenced training for ministry believing that "to be a good Christian, [one] had to become a minister."

Ferguson explains that he is "a very practical person" with "good one-to-one skills" but not at all theoretically minded. He hoped ministry would develop his interpersonal skills to "better equip [him] to assist people" as "a missionary." But training for ministry at Avondale College, as he recalls, was a great disappointment. Being "idealist [by nature], very conservative, and very very straight," he was "shocked" and "disgusted by the apparent lack of standards," particularly among his fellow trainee ministers. He was put off by the overemphasis on theology, which took precedence in the curriculum over the practical aspects of ministry. He neither understood the finer points of theology discussed in class nor saw the relevance to pastoral ministry of debating abstract theology. The theological issues that caused major rifts on campus made little impression on him. Ferguson explains that he was too preoccupied with his own personal crisis following the death of his mother, and he attributes his "confused and muddled" state of mind to this. He left college traditional in outlook, dismissive of the theological points of view espoused by non-conformist peers, and determined to "keep out of theological debates." The one thing that did become crystal clear in his mind by the end of his training was the desire to specialise in youth ministry.

The practice of ministry proved to be as disappointing as the theory; his very first day in ministry was "a letdown." No one welcomed him when he arrived at his employing Conference, no arrangements were made for his accommodation, and in fact no one even expected him. The Fergusons were temporarily housed (for more than two months) in a run-down shack on the Adventist campground while they waited for the administrators to decide on his initial ministerial duties. He spent his first months of ministry on the campground on his own, painting old sheds.

Ferguson was assigned to assist a senior Adventist pastor in caring for two average sized congregations. He experienced difficulty relating to what he regarded as the trivializing of religion by "parishioners [who] were mentally set in their traditional ways," even though at this time he too was traditional in outlook. Members devoted more time and energy to arguing "over the color of the dustbin to be purchased for the church" than over the vital issue of salvation. He disliked having to continually "listen to all the gossip, the back-biting and arguing about trivia on boards and committees." Despite the fact that he left college conservative in outlook, church members labeled him radical and related to him with caution because he was a recent college graduate. Ferguson reports that early in his ministry he "mentally withdrew" even though "it has taken me years and years to actually make the break." His frustration and disappointment were not confined to the parish. Ferguson explains that the questions pressing on his mind were coming from all directions. The fact that many of his college friends were resigning or being dismissed made him reexamine his own commitment to ministry and wonder whether he too would one day exit. The dismissal and resignation of friends, as he recalls, added to his own disillusionment. What made him most angry were the attitudes of the authorities toward leavers. He became critical of the church system and lost respect for church leaders who pontificated on matters of theology even though the majority had no theological training. His disrespect for administration did not exclude his own Conference president, who told him privately that he believed one thing and publicly preached the exact opposite. Even though Ferguson was "no theologian by any stretch of the imagination," he began to identify with the views of nonconformists. He recalls, "I couldn't match these guys in their thinking, but I respected them very much. If they saw problems from their perspective, this also became problematic for me. And as different people whom I respected stepped out . . . I became even more angry." Ferguson explains that in "[my] mind I was experiencing a separation." "I remember thinking, I work for God and not these people."

For a long time Ferguson's wife, who was a fourth generation Adventist, encouraged him to keep going. In the early years she supported him in his work and encouraged him to persevere despite the many difficulties and disappointments he encountered. She helped him run the Vacation Bible School program during school holidays, wrote study pamphlets and baptismal study material, ran programs for parents, and contributed many hours of voluntary labor by "doing this and doing that and doing something else plus holding my own job." She states, "In the first couple of years I gave it my best shot." For a long time her encouragement kept Ferguson from acting on his doubts.

Ferguson recalls that he often contemplated resignation but "then something would go right and that would keep me going." The one thing that did go right for him after seven years of parish work was his appointment to youth ministry. This appointment was at the same time the realization of his dream in ministry and the commencement of his separation from ministry. Ferguson clashed with one of the departmental leaders with whom he worked. He found it difficult working alongside someone he believed was incompetent and lacked commitment to ministry. At first he found his new work enjoyable but soon found himself reduced to performing menial office tasks. Lay members appreciated his work and invited him to conduct programs in the local churches. His Conference president, however, thought otherwise, and after three years in office Ferguson was told he would be relocated to parish work because he did not function well in administration. Ferguson was devastated and believes the president had someone else in mind for the job: "If I had known then what I know now, I would not have accepted the [Conference] appointment. I wish someone warned me of the politics going on there. I walked into a fire keg. I felt I was never accepted there." The experience was a blow to Ferguson, who believes he was the victim of Adventist politics. "All our hurts from over the years returned, and it just became too much."

Ferguson decided to study at a local tertiary college to be a marriage counsellor. He contemplated moving to the United States to study, but the idea of going overseas was too radical an option. He commenced studying marriage counseling while holding a part-time position as an assistant youth pastor in a local Adventist church. Ferguson explained that his heart was no longer in his work despite the fact that the local Conference president "admitted in writing" that "he had underestimated me." Ferguson did not complete his study because he "found it a waste of time" and also because he made up his mind that he had had enough of ministry. The Conference president tried to persuade him to continue by offering him alternative opportunities in ministry, but Ferguson "wanted out."

He told me that he had churches with vacancies which he needed ministers to fill. . . . He was not interested in me as a person, nor in my talents and my abilities. He only wanted a plug to fill his gaps. I am not just a plug, I am a youth minister. I have got the skills and if they don't want my skills as a youth minister, then they can jump. . . . I wanted another youth position or a church where I could use my creativity. He told me that he does not see that ever happening.

By the end of that year, Ferguson was done with ministry. His two stomach ulcers were a constant reminder of his experiences in the Conference and that he was not happy in ministry.

His wife also had "well and truly turned her back on the system." She made up her mind that it was time for her husband to face up to facts. She became, in her words, "very negative toward the church because of the various things that happened to us along the way." She resented the Conference president's criticism that she was "too ambitious" because she was studying at university and being told that her husband "wouldn't advance in the church because of her." Rumors spread because she was too "trendy" and that "there must be something wrong with my Christian experience." She had "a trendy haircut and wore leather [clothes] and did part-time modelling." Regardless of member gossip, she was adamant she would not conform to church members' expectations of the minister's wife as someone who

is willing to move around, be a sweet little person who spoke to everyone at church, definitely who did some kind of community service like welfare work or whatever, who didn't work or who had very low-key career aspirations, who was always available when they wanted something done and who invited billions of people home for Sabbath lunch . . . played the piano . . . never expressed opinions or ruffled anyone's feathers . . . [and] wore dowdy K-Mart dresses with big floral prints and flat shoes.

She was offended by the way church leaders exploited her labor by having her teach at a church school while paying her below the award wages. But the thing that destroyed her faith and commitment to ministry was the way the authorities treated her husband: "When Peter went into departmental work I started to question things. Here he was working his insides out and doing a professional job but not being treated like one . . . and seeing so many people putting shit on him all the time. . . . When he got kicked out, that was really devastating for me. I questioned the whole system then." Old hurts reared their heads, and, as she explains, "I think all that just built up and built up and built up till I told Peter that we just had to do something about it otherwise our relationship would not survive." She was the one who "forced the issue" in the end: "I started looking for other jobs [for him]. I wrote his resume, got my boss to write references for him, and got him a part-time job while he was still in the ministry."

Ferguson took twelve months' leave on health grounds. He did this "primarily to ease our way out" of ministry. Even if work was offered him in administration in another Conference, Ferguson explains that he would not accept it because the decision to leave ministry was irreversible:

I know there has been a conservative swing [in the church] and possibly one day [it] will swing the other way. But I'm not going to waste six years or whatever of my life [in ministry] waiting for that to happen. I couldn't survive. Really I am going through a mid-life crisis. . . . I have looked at the last eleven years and asked myself, Do I want to spend the next eleven years going through what I have been through? If I don't make a jump now I may not be able to do it again, because I am too old to retrain.

His demotion from administration became the major dividing point in his life, compelling him to recall and reinterpret his past and to reevaluate his future prospects in ministry. Ferguson could now see things in his past which he previously did not take seriously or overlooked that when linked produced one grand narrative of rejection. He could now see this in his impersonal introduction to ministry:

There was no welcome or even a handshake. I saw the president for the first time after being in the Conference for six months, and that was at the steps of the Conference office. There he told me, one, that I was not to leave my [parish] district without his permission and, two, he asked me whether I wanted to be an evangelist. I told him I didn't. He turned and walked off. The next time we talked was two years later, when he called me to his office and tore strips [off me] over gossip that had come to him during those two years—completely unverified gossip.

Ferguson reflected on the way he was pressured to bring more converts to the Adventist Church; his average of six to eight baptisms a year was deemed unacceptable, and in his third year was he appointed assistant to one of his college peers who had specialized in evangelism and who had established a reputation as a "successful soul winner." Ferguson recalled that the president threatened that unless he matched his colleague's number of baptisms for the year his services would be terminated. Ferguson's sense of rejection was compounded by his wife's hurts. She was a trained Adventist teacher who was "tricked" into teaching in an Adventist school for only a portion of the wage agreed on. The promise of backpay did not materialize and the matter was eventually ignored by incoming Conference treasurers. But Helen Ferguson did not forget. She vowed never to teach for the church again. Ferguson sees this decision by her as "significant in the subsequent outcome of events."

The fact that he had to wait six years to be ordained, two years longer than most of his peers, also caused him to be angry now. Ferguson genuinely believed that he was doing good work for the church because "no one ever questioned my theology . . . [and] I kept out of contentious areas and did not stir," yet he was overlooked for ordination. He also recalled how on another occasion during a meeting, "the Division president was next to me sharing a hymn book. He asked me my name. When I told him, he replied, 'That's right, you're a teacher up out west, aren't you?' That told me how far my reputation had travelled." His earlier belief that pastors were to entrust their career to the hands of "the Lord" he now rejected as a myth perpetuated by those in power to keep people like him in a subordinate status. Ferguson now thinks that people who go places in the Adventist system promote themselves and are not content with leaving their career aspirations in the hands of administrators.

Ferguson believes the fact that he was a convert was a handicap in the Adventist system, which promotes and rewards those born and raised Adventists. As his wife explains, "To get anywhere in the Adventist Church, family genetics are essential." Ferguson recalled an offhand remark to this effect during his interview for ordination, during which the Conference president told him that "because you are a new Adventist you were this and this and this when you came into the work, and only now do I think that you have gone from one side of the pendulum into the middle area where you're accepted fully as a minister." What little confidence he had left in the Adventist system was finally dashed by the way he was terminated from youth ministry. According to his wife, "He feels he is nobody, that he is hopeless . . . the Youth Department experience really shook him. He has got really low self-esteem now and feels very insecure. It will take him ages as a person and as a professional to come to terms with that." Moreover, the experience demolished his Adventist doctrinal structure—the central props of his earlier Adventist theology are either missing altogether or radically modified. At the time of the interview Ferguson declared that he was still recognizably an Adventist, but one that adhered to an abridged version of Seventh-day Adventism. He has discarded the salient teachings of Adventist sectarianism—the investigative judgement, the remnant, the sanctuary—and professes to be an evangelical Sabbath-keeping Christian. While he upholds the idea of Sabbath rest, he rejects the Sabbath taboos and now is much more prepared to do things on that day that previously would have been anathema to him. He enjoys vegetarian food, but no longer adheres to a strict vegetarian diet. He occasionally drinks alcohol and enjoys going to dances. His wife made the telling statement that she is now "doing all those things that had been suppressed by my parents. I am having my teenage rebellion at thirty-one years of age." Ferguson claims that his present job as public relations officer in a large organization enables him to "minister" for God, but rejects the traditional Adventist model of the minister as proselytizing agent. He continues to believe in a God but sets aside the "ultraconservative, vindictive and nasty" God of Adventism for the compassionate and accepting God of the New Testament.

LOSS OF IDEALISM IN MINISTRY

The case study highlights two distinct periods in Ferguson's ministry that correspond with two contrasting outlooks toward the Adventist organization and ministry. Ferguson's first six or seven years of ministry are characterized by what I term "loss of idealism." In the final three or four years in ministry Ferguson was more negative and "cynical" toward his work and the Adventist establishment. Loss of idealism and cynicism are complementary processes (Becker and Geer 1973:153), but they are examined separately for the purpose of highlighting why some ministers with doubts continue in ministry, while others leave. What is argued here is that the difference between the two attitudes is not only one of negativity, but also in the types of experiences that generate them. Goldner, Ritti, and Ference (1977:540) differentiate the two responses by contending that the production of cynical knowledge is "a distinctly organizational phenomenon." However, as the Ferguson case study shows, both responses are generated by organizational processes.

Becker and Geer (1973) observed that medical students imbued with idealized images of the medical system undergo a transformation in outlook as they are exposed to the rigors of preclinical training before eventually emerging as fledgling physicians. According to these authors, failure of idealism is the flip-side to acquiring realism in medicine. They contend that loss of idealism is not an attribute of individual students; it is situational in nature and varies not only among students but also according to "the particular activity the worth of which is questioned and the situation in which the attitude is expressed" (Becker and Geer 1973:158). Failure of idealism is functional to the student role and is an important stage in the socialization of medical students into the professional milieu of doctor (Becker, Geer, et al. 1961:439). The interviews with expastors reveal a similar process in ministry.

Loss of idealism is less pronounced among expastors who were born or raised Adventists, although they too report being surprised by what they witnessed and experienced upon taking up ministerial duties. One out of every two expastors who were converts to Adventism states that ministry was not what they anticipated. One was surprised at "how poorly the interpersonal relationships of the church were carried out" and by the fact that members "fought all the time amongst themselves." A second was taken a back "by the ignorance of members and . . . total lack of knowledge [of Adventist] doctrinal beliefs." A third expressed disappointment at the low level of respect given to pastors by church members and administrators:

I was . . . treated so differently from the way that I expected to be treated . . . by Christians. I expected that Christian people would treat their minister with a lot more . . . respect and, ah, you know, treat them fairly rather than the way I was treated. . . . That, that was a real eye-opener. I discovered the essence of the local church; it was not as sweet and innocent as I was led to believe.

Ferguson similarly expressed dismay that church boards devoted time to arguing about "trivial issues" such as what color dustbins to buy. While loss of idealism is experienced by Adventist newcomers almost immediately upon entering ministry, in time all pastors, including those born and raised Adventist, modify their initial high expectations.

LOSS OF IDEALISM AS AN INSTITUTIONAL PROCESS

Only one of the expastors interviewed attributed his disillusionment with ministry specifically to problems related to ministry as an occupation. The expastor explains that he did not have the necessary skills to run a church and attributes this to the administration's failure to provide him with appropriate training before thrusting on him the responsibility of heading two churches in his second year of ministry. The overwhelming majority of expastors trace their loss of idealism to issues specifically to do with the organization and its administration. Expastors' accounts abound with anecdotes pointing out the follies of church leaders. Ferguson's recollection of his first meeting with the local Conference president is echoed by many of the former pastors interviewed. Shortly after his arrival in the Conference one expastor recalls being warned by his Conference president that the "gospel is something we don't talk about in this Conference." This expastor recalled during the interview:

Expastor: What an idiot. . . . He said . . . we don't talk a lot about the gospel, ah, we talk about the good old Adventist message. He said, that's what we're here for. You're an Adventist minister not just a Christian minister of any kind, but an Adventist minister and that's the message you'll preach, the good old Adventist message.

PHB: What did you make of that?

Expastor: Well, it certainly set me back, made me think what on earth had I got into? I couldn't believe that a person would be so blatant as to say that.

An expastor recalls an experience, again involving his Conference president, that took place during the preparations for the annual camp meeting not long after the arrival of this particular minister in the Conference:

The camp meeting was our first appointment in ministry. [The president] was a man who had been involved in all sorts of trades in his time. He was a Jack-of-all-trades and . . . he was a good Jack-of-all-trades too. He had a sound knowledge basically of how most things worked and how to get jobs done around camp time. . . . There were all sorts of problems. There were plumbing problems, erecting the large tent . . . we repaired the toilets. . . . There was a lot of work to do on the camp site . . . and one of the problems that they had was an electrical one. I can remember thinking, the president is not an electrician, he doesn't have a professional knowledge of electricity and yet I had a background in electrical matters. I had a . . . certificate in electrical engineering . . . and I felt I was in a position to give him some advice and I thought with his reputation [of being able to get on with younger ministers] he would be able to accept that advice . . . and so I told him my opinion of what the problem was and how it could be fixed. . . . His response to that was, I know what I'm doing, don't tell me how to run this show, and we had a run-in right from the beginning of camp which was my first appointment in the ministry. He felt I was just a young upstart know-all and totally out of line. As it turned out I was right. No apologies were ever given. . . . So I virtually had to take a backseat from then on.

These responses highlight the marginal status of ministerial interns. More than this, they suggest that some expastors commenced ministry prepared to confront those in positions of authority, an attitude that in the long run proved a disadvantage to their ministries.

Nearly every pastor during the interview commented on the administration's mechanisms of social control. More than half of the expastors interviewed noted that Conference leaders were not content to limit their powers to administration and sought to instruct ministers on what subjects they should preach in their weekly sermons, the direction of their ministry, how they should dress, their daily and hourly movements in the Conference, and even how they should conduct themselves in their homes. According to expastors, church authorities used a variety of means to keep "a check" on ministers. One claims that church administrators used their visits to the pastor's home to "spy" on his family and nonministry lifestyle. Following one such visit by the Conference president and secretary, an expastor was called upon to account for himself, and explains:

The thing that got to me later on [during] camp [was that] they [administrators] hauled me up . . . [and] attacked me over things that they found out by living in my home. I mean they were spies . . . you know, like they got to the fact that my wife worked, um . . . and I mean, they were ridiculous. They said your wife shouldn't work, you know, you be with your husband. I said well . . . she works as a nurse and that's a fairly Christian way to earn a living, to help suffering people. And they said, yes, but . . . she's a minister's wife, she should be beside you. And then my wife said, what do you expect me to do in this [small town]? They said, oh well, you should stay home and help your husband. And I said, in what way could she help me? They said she could answer the phone for you . . . and she could have a book and make appointments for you. I said, serious? (laughs). I mean, they were serious.

This expastor was also criticized for doing "too much housework," a criticism he now cites as proof of the administration's irrational outlook. Eleven former pastors reported that formal minister gatherings, like the camp meetings and ministers' retreats were occasions used by church leaders to promote "Conference propaganda" and to pressure pastors into conforming to their directives. At these gatherings pastors would be told not only what to believe and what outreach programs to conduct in their churches, but how many "souls" they were expected to "win." They were also informed of the tithe status of their congregations. This pressure to conform to Conference expectations encouraged many to invent ways of circumventing "orders." One expastor recalls:

The Conference president would tell you [that] everybody [else] was running a mission, so everybody had to, so it sometimes brought out the cunning and the wild in me, so I circumvented some of those plans. . . . They said everybody was running a health campaign. Well, I made out a way where I didn't run one. I conveniently worked things to be doing something else because I have never seen myself as a pseudo health educator.

Hansford, in the previous chapter, recalls devising an "ingenious plan" of a weekly verse-by-verse study of the Gospels to circumvent preaching on issues promoted by Conference authorities. A majority of expastors conformed to administrative directives either because they feared the consequences of not complying or because they genuinely held to the idealized belief, particularly in their early years of ministry, that church leaders know best. As Goldner, Ritti, and Ference (1977:539) point out, altruism can serve "the purposes of maintaining the legitimacy of existing authority or preserving institutional structure."

One area of activity cited by all expastors as typifying bureaucratic control of pastors is the practice of transferring ministers with complete disregard for the ministers' wishes, their long-term career aspirations in ministry, and the needs of their families. One former pastor recalls: "I felt that . . . I was being transferred continually, that I shouldn't be transferred [as often]. But I had no say. That, you know, that really bugged me. Somebody up there, or some group of people would get together and do things to your life, with no input from yourself at all, you know . . . they never asked you what you wanted to do." Twenty-three expastors describe being "ordered" to relocate. Four were told to either accept where they were being sent or resign. A young intern was "petrified" of the prospect of pastoring a church on his own. He appealed the decision but was told by his president in a "pretty terrible conversation" that "either I do it or I forget ministry." A "successful and budding evangelist" accepted appointment to an isolated parish in a country town of less than one thousand people where it was impossible for him to test his public evangelism skills. He observes: "In my naivete I thought, oh well, the brethren have sent me there, I'll do it. . . . They tried to get others to go but no one else would go there. But I was the intern. I was the boy to do as the president said." Interns were most vulnerable to administrative directives. This expastor thought that willingness to relocate to an isolated rural town would be noted by the authorities and rewarded with promotion into Conference administrative work. He reasoned that "if you want to win their favor, then you suffer this for two years then you get a better posting thereafter." This expastor admits he was wrong in expecting this, as his two-year "banishment" to "the wilderness" was followed by another four yesrs in a different isolated rural town.

An expastor who ministered in a large city church is in no doubt that his transfer to an isolated country parish was "more than just the leading of the Lord." He explains that he "did things [his] way and . . . [didn't] pander or crawl to people" and worked "independently," but realized that independence was not welcomed or valued by the authorities:

I was not getting on . . . or going up the scale [in ministry]. I was always being sent to boundary churches, you know, [names town]. You couldn't get much further from the Conference office, [names town], that's pushing your way up in the sticks, [names town], that was the most remote church from the Conference office, [names town], that was hell, you know, a stinking hot hole with a tiny little congregation and . . . I just felt that . . . the message was coming through, you've got something to learn yet . . . before we put you in charge of some of the bigger churches and ah, more influential parishes.

Relocation was a means of "punishing" ministers who did not comply with the administration's wishes. The way ministers were moved from "church to church often with no rhyme or reason" highlights two additional factors that, according to expastors, contributed to their loss of idealism: the authoritarian management style of administrators, and their insensitivity to pastors' needs. Church administrators were, for the most part, ministers who were promoted to positions of authority as a reward for mission service, success at winning converts, and loyalty to the denomination. Administrators, almost without exception, were middle-aged men who also had no academic qualifications or experience in management other than the knowledge they acquired in the parish. Administrators generally were "good men who have the best interest of the church at heart," according to expastors, but who at the same time were "yes men" and "puppet men" to those above them, and "hopelessly incompetent at managing people." Expastors argue that their authoritative and confrontational styles of management are indicative of an inability to deal with complex organizational and theological issues.

Expastors highlight gross insensitivity on the part of church leaders as another matter of concern. Conference administrators with whom he had dealings were "totally out of touch with people," according to one expastor. A Conference president who was preoccupied "with his own importance" refused to consider a former pastor's appeal against transfer, even when told that the expastor's wife was undergoing long-term counseling therapy. One incident which, more than any other, epitomizes the level of administrator insensitivity, is related by an expastor who was having marriage problems while in ministry. He was visited by his president and describes their meeting in the following way:

Expastor: At this point of time [my wife] and I were having a few hassles. It wasn't real serious but, probably if we had found the right person, they could have helped us, but [by way of advice, the president's] illustration of a successful marriage was his relationship with the secretary-treasurer of the Conference [who also is a male]. I mean, I'm not implying anything about [the president's] sexual preferences. I'm just saying to you that this was his illustration of a happy marriage.

PHB: He used that as illustration?

Expastor: Yeah. He used that to illustrate about husbands and wives. . . . I mean, the man was totally out of touch with reality.

Failure of idealism is also linked with the lack of support shown to pastors, particularly in conflicts with members. Pastor-member conflict was a factor contributing to the exit of one out of every three former pastors. What was even more disappointing, according to former pastors, is that they could not depend on church leaders for support in conflicts with church members. Presidents would side with lay critics, often without first consulting with the pastor. On occasions when the minister was consulted, his version of the problem would be doubted, and he would not be assured of Conference support. An expastor recalls, that the president "would not say whether or not he believed me." The son of a church pastor states, "The only feed-back I was getting [from the Conference] was what church members were doing to me . . . administration certainly weren't providing me with any backup." In a number of instances church administrators actively encouraged members to report on pastors, and one out of every four expastors recalls being confronted by their Conference presidents to answer accusations from lay detractors. Eighteen expastors believe church leaders used lay informants to "keep tabs" on pastors.

While former pastors report that their early idealism was replaced by a more realistic outlook toward the organization, administrators, and parishioners, they stop short of attributing their exit to loss of idealism. Thirteen of the forty-three expastors interviewed report that initial disappointments in ministry made them more determined to continue. One recalls:

[The longer I was in ministry] the more I got to realize that I was small, insignificant and not permitted to think for myself. That was one of the things that really grated on me all through those early years where I found myself slowly being ground down, my independence, my ability . . . my desire to be myself was slowly being taken away from me. . . . Those are the sorts of freedoms I thought we all had. . . . Many times I'd come home and say to my wife, look, I've had enough of this, I'm quitting. [But] then . . . I sort of dig my toes in a bit saying, boy I'm not running. . . . The easy way [out] was to leave . . . and I thought that's not the way I want to go. I want to be a survivor [and running away] . . . was no benefit to anyone . . . and I know for myself I wouldn't have been happy running away.

Many continued in ministry because they believed their problems to be situational or temporary and would be overcome with a change in administration. Four expastors, including Ferguson and the expastor cited above, were encouraged by their wives to persevere in ministry. Still others compensated for their doubts by focusing on positive experiences and the rewarding aspects of ministry.

The point that has been argued thus far in this chapter is that all Adventist ministers, leavers and stayers, experienced a three-stage sequence in ministry regardless of outlook: (1) experiences that generate disappointment in ministry, followed by (2) rewarding experiences and positive reinforcement from significant others, and (3) the postponement of negative thoughts and persistence with ministry. This cycle, which I equate with *loss of idealism* or the acquiring of realism, is evident in all expastors' accounts but did not by itself materialize into exit. All ministers experienced loss of idealism in ministry, discovered inconsistencies in the organization, and learnt of the personal failings of leading actors. However, as in the case of Ferguson, it was when failure of idealism was coupled with the shock of rejection that the path through cynicism to exit was entered.

CRITICAL EXPERIENCES

Social researchers use a variety of expressions to describe events that result in sudden and radical transformation of the person. Strauss (1959:93–100) uses the term "turning points" to describe situations that compel individuals "to take stock, to re-evaluate, revise, re-see, and rejudge." A turning point thus signals discontinuity with the past. Giddens (1991:112–114,142–143) prefers "fateful moments," that is, occasions when persons "are called on to take decisions that are particularly consequential for their ambitions, or more generally for their future lives." According to Giddens, "At *fateful moments*, individuals may be forced to confront concerns which the smooth working of reflexively ordered abstract systems normally keep well away from consciousness. Fateful moments necessarily disturb routines, often in a radical way. An individual is thereby forced to rethink fundamental aspects of her existence and future projects" (1991:202–203). Giddens stresses the consequential nature of these experiences. Greeley (1982:31) employs the term "limit-experience" to describe events and circumstances that push individuals to the limits of tolerance. A "limit-experience," according to Greeley, "is essentially an experience of old perceptions being shattered and new ones being structured." Denzin (1989:15–18) refers to "epiphanies," which he describes as "moments of problematic experience that illuminates personal character" and as a result of which "the person is never again quite the same." An "epiphany" can be a major event, the climax to an accumulation of past experiences, a moment of insight, or a relived experience. Epiphanies are "interactional moments that leave marks on people's lives," according to Denzin (1989:15). Whatever the terminology employed—turning points, fatal moments, limit-experiences, or epiphanies— researchers agree that critical events serve to "mobilize and focus awareness that old lines of action are complete, have failed, have been disrupted, or are no longer personally satisfying" (Ebaugh 1988a:123). Critical moments are not all of one type, but all are painful (Table 5.1).

Twelve expastors attribute the beginning of their disaffection in ministry to a confrontation with Conference authorities or local church members. Conflicts are a common feature of expastors' accounts, however, what distinguishes this group of expastors from the others is not the prolonged nature or extreme manifestation of the conflicts, but that the conflicts triggered a review of their futures in ministry. With only one exception this was the response of expastors who had been in ministry for less than two years. The following account is from an expastor whose ministry lasted only eighteen months, and is typical of how confrontation pushed some recent appointees to their "limit."

By the middle of my second year, the situation [in the parish] had become intolerable. . . . I ran a mission and someone did not like the film I chose. I refused to promote Walton's book, *Omega*. I was angry about this book and would not promote it and a church member came to talk to me about it and had a cassette recorder recording our conversation but did not tell me. Things like my sermons would be taped by one of the elders in the side room without telling me. I would say things to people which would be misconstrued and people would come accusing that I was trying to undermine the church and set up factions, which I wasn't doing. This mentality of suspicion was all around. . . . The youth also began not to relate to me. This guy . . . had teenage children and was leading the youth and on one occasion deliberately and intentionally planned a discussion . . . to provoke me knowing that I would be there. I constantly felt both [that] my ministry with youth was being undermined and [that] I was being questioned by certain individuals as to whether I was fit to be an Adventist minister. . . . The whole thing had become quite ugly. I felt it. Others felt it.

A second expastor recalled: "I was going through these waves where I was having some problems in my local church. . . . I was getting clear vibes back from the local church that I wasn't preaching the Adventist message or preaching the message the way it should be, from the conservative element." Three expastors were accused of moral indiscretion, and this set them reviewing their futures. These charges were not substantiated and were eventually withdrawn, but the very fact that expastors were accused in this way was enough for them to begin questioning "the whole show." One expastor commented, "I knew then that the whole thing was Mickey Mouse." The twelve expastors whose critical event was generated by conflict left ministry without support from either church members or administrators.

Table 5.1
Limit Experiences in Expastors' Accounts

	Expastors (N = 43)
Major clash with parishioners and/or administrators	12
Symbolic protest over the administration's handling of theology issues	8
Growing awareness but suddenly becomes clear	8
Heresy trial	7
Frustration over blocked career path	4
Unusually painful experience not related to ministry	2
Marriage and family problems	2

In contrast to the experiences of the previous group, whose crises were provoked by interpersonal clashes, eight expastors highlight conflicts over interpretation of doctrine as their critical experiences. Three among this group of expastors explain that while they had become alienated from Adventist leadership, their limit-experiences were the result of prolonged, agonizing controversies over their preaching and teaching. Three studied themselves "into a theological corner," having become convinced that they could no longer promote or defend the fundamental teachings of the movement. Four reviewed their futures in ministry following the Glacier View heresy trial and the subsequent defrocking of Des Ford. One of these expastors recalls that following Des Ford's dismissal, "I did not see a future for me as a minister. . . . I became disillusioned with the administration of the Church and its attitude towards the study of the Scriptures. They obviously were not interested in Scripture study except to the extent that it would reinforce the establishment views. I had lost all missionary desire." Once they concluded that they could no longer function as Adventist pastors on grounds of theology, exit followed quickly.

Eight expastors report that their crises were the culmination of a growing unease in ministry. One former pastor in this category states: "Even though I was enjoying [working in that area] and [having a] boat and all that . . . I knew that I couldn't keep it up. I knew that I wouldn't be doing this for the rest of my life and I'm not quite sure when um but I started to look around at what else I could do." In the following response the limit-experience was the realization that the former pastor was not coping in ministry.

Half way through [my third year of ministry] I started to realize that I was not making the grade as a minister, that I was not a good minister. I felt I was struggling with Bible studies. I felt my sermons were boring. I felt people were bored with me as a minister and I felt that I was not helping people spiritually as I believed a minister should. I felt frustrated with the daily routine of the minister's life. I would come home night after night and not feel achieved. I was used to feeling achieved even at college—putting essays in—that was something concrete . . . but as a minister I came home every day having done nothing. . . . It seemed to me that everything I did had no consequence.

A third came to the realization that he should exit during the ordination service of a minister friend. The experiences by which this third group of expastors came to realize that ministry was not something they would do for the rest of their working lives approximates Denzin's (1989:129) "illuminative" or "minor epiphanies."

A fourth group of expastors describe reaching their tolerance limits as a result of a heresy trial or a formal gathering where they were called to defend their views. More than two-thirds of the interviewed expastors had to defend their theology in one of these settings, but seven look upon those events as their "fatal moment." The heresy trial is an example of Garfinkel's (1956) "successful degradation ceremony." According to Garfinkel, for a denunciation to be effective, it is necessary that the feelings of the group be aroused and that the accused individual be called to appear personally and be publicly condemned as acting against the values of the group. Moreover, the denounced person must be "ritually separated from a place in the legitimate order, i.e., he must be defined as standing at a place opposed to it. He must be placed 'outside,' he must be made 'strange'" (Garfinkel 1956:423).

Heresy rituals usually lasted anywhere between three and five hours, during which time pastors underwent ritual shaming through lengthy interrogation and vilification from church members and administrators. Most often the meetings were held behind closed doors and restricted to the Church Board and representatives from the Conference. On one occasion the Saturday afternoon young people's program was turned into a heresy trial. "It was just disgusting," recalls to the former pastor. The meetings were chaired either by a Conference representative (usually the president) or a local elder. On two occasions the trials were not chaired and the meetings degenerated into shouting matches as representatives of the opposing sides accused each other of heresy and misconduct. At one such gathering an expastor was threatened with physical violence for claiming that some of the central Adventist doctrines had no biblical foundation. At these gatherings accused pastors were criticized for their ministry, condemned for their preaching and verbally abused for their theology. The following account is a typical example and depicts both the dynamics of these meetings and the way they impacted on the accused pastors.

Expastor: My doubts were compounded by the fact that my head elder . . . was also on the Conference Executive. Now he came back from the Division meeting which took away Des Ford's credentials and he was determined to clean up the Conference and he was the one who caused so much strife in the Conference. . . . He came up to me and said, ah, we're having a meeting with you this evening. I said, who's we? and he said, the elders and the head deacon, and I said, oh yes, and I said I'm sorry we're having no meeting, ah, I said there's no need for any meeting. What's it about? He said I'm not telling you (laughs). I said that's the more reason we're having no meeting. I said you expect me to turn up to a meeting and you won't tell me what it's about? and ah, he realized he was up against someone who wasn't going to be pushed around, so he got the strength of the Conference.

PHB: The Conference president?

Expastor: Yes. The final upshot was that the president came and chaired a meeting with the Board. They planned to use it as a forum to help me with my questions. The issue was that they felt they had the right to know where their minister stood on the theological issues that had been generated by Glacier View and Des Ford. I challenged that. I said, you don't have the right to ask a person to divulge their personal thoughts on any issue. I said you have a right to expect me in my ministry to represent the church aright, and I said if you have any evidence to the contrary, fair enough, I'll look at it. . . . It was a meeting that lasted for five hours.

PHB: Who was present?

Expastor: The Church Board, which is dominated by this man and his family. They had about eighteen Board members and fourteen would have been his relatives, who were just weeping openly while they just ruthlessly plied me with questions and I wouldn't answer, and I just fobbed them all off. The president sat there as chairman of the meeting, letting people call me a liar over and over again and did nothing to come to my defense or to call people to order. It was an appalling setup. The man should have been shot for it. If I had my wits, if it happened today, I'd have slammed them all in court, those who called me a liar.

Wife: It was a shocking thing, you have no idea.

Expastor: And I had total confidence in the church and its administration still at this stage in spite of what they've done to Des.

Wife: And very unformed theological views. They were asking you what you thought but you didn't know what you thought.

Expastor: At this stage I didn't know what I thought. I was quite confused. I was still running to Ellen White trying to find answers, still wanting to believe that the church was correct.

Wife: At that time the guys were looking to the scholars to give them some answers . . . but the scholars weren't doing it, they weren't giving them answers. We had to get material from all those other fellows who were selling their stuff on the black market, under the table, just about.

Expastor: After that meeting which the president chaired I went home and my wife took one look at me and she knew it had been a bad meeting and she burst into tears and I followed suit. The tension had really built up in me. The Conference president then came in, he was staying in our place and my wife was just crying and crying and believe it or not, this is what the twit said. He looked across at my wife and said, has anybody ever told you that you're beautiful when you're crying?

Wife: That would have to be . . . one of the most hurtful and stupid comments that anyone has ever said to me.

Expastor: I just got up and said, [president's name], would you leave the room and go, and I said, I don't want to see you any more. Just go. . . . That night my wife and I cried all night long. We didn't sleep at all and we cried the next day.

Wife: It was a really bad day.

Expastor: But that was the catharsis. . . . From then onwards it was finished. . . . My eyes were opened. The scales had fallen off. There was nothing left. I had no more feeling for the church. It was finished. . . . I knew then that somewhere in the future I would pull out.

The expastor in the above account prolonged his time in ministry for another three years in a Conference headed by a sympathetic president but was eventually forced to resign by the collective pressure from administrators at Union and Division levels. The fate of pastors accused of theological deviation and labeled heretics was usually decided at meetings such as the one described above. Stigmatized individuals were unable relocate to another parish in the same Conference or to transfer to another Conference. Dismissal or coerced resignation was the most common outcome for expastors who faced heresy trials.

Ferguson's critical point was the way he was terminated from Conference work. The event reactivated old hurts and previous doubts and more important, took on symbolic meaning in the context of his future ministry. It implied that despite his abilities and regardless of his own interests, his future in ministry lay not in the type of work to which he aspired, but in a return to parish ministry. Relocation was interpreted by Ferguson as censure and demotion. He became embittered and critical of church leaders. Exit was something he now actively sought. Three other expastors attribute the commencement of their exit from ministry to actions by the administration which adversely affected their career aspirations: one expastor had his planned ordination overturned at Union level, even though it was approved by the Conference and his ministry was appreciated by church members. A second, who had planned to specialize in public evangelism, was posted to a remote country town. He interpreted this as a deliberate attempt to block his career aspirations. The third expastor had hoped to work among his ethnic community but was not permitted to do so. All four expastors, including Ferguson, responded by contemplating alternative career options.

Regardless of the circumstances that provoked them, what form they took, and the particular issues on which expastors focused, all critical experiences were painful. According to Giddens, critical experiences, or what he terms "fateful moments," are painful because they threaten the routine order of things. "Fateful moments are threatening for the protective cocoon which defends the individual's ontological security, because the 'business as usual' attitude that is so important to the cocoon is inevitably broken through. They are moments when the individual must launch out into something new, knowing that a decision made, or a specific course of action followed, has an irreversible quality, or at least that it will be difficult thereafter to revert to the old paths" (Giddens 1991:114). They are painful also because they are highly consequential and repercussions are felt in many areas, not least on personal identity. According to Berger and Luckmann (1966:172), critical incidents necessitate radical redefinition of the self. Travisano (1981:600) and Berger (1973:76) equate the discontinuity in biography brought about by critical events to "conversion," which Berger defines as "an act in which the past is dramatically transformed." This linking of critical events with conversion is particularly telling, because, as noted in the last chapter, stories of exiting take the form of deconversion narratives. As in conversion, so in the experience of leaving: critical experiences signal a change in outlook that sets in motion processes of radical self-transformation.

CYNICAL KNOWLEDGE

Social researchers have observed that a cynical outlook and radical redefinition of the job often preface career exit. In an autobiographical essay Sarason (1977:189–207) recalls becoming cynical over "organizational craziness" that had reduced him to a mere cog in the machinery of a hospital bureaucracy prior to his exit. Goldner, Ritti, and Ference (1977) observed that Catholic priests adopt a similar outlook prior to leaving the priesthood. Similar observations have been made with regard to police officers (Lester and Butler 1980), nuns and doctors (Ebaugh 1988a:56), and probation officers (Rush 1990) who changed careers. Cherniss (1980:19) therefore argues that cynicism is a "detachment mechanism" or a form of "role distance" manifested by those who have become disillusioned with their work or frustrated by bureaucratic structures of their employing bodies. In the present context, cynicism describes the negative and critical outlook of Adventist pastors following a crisis experience.

The period between the limit-experience and eventual termination is marked by numerous and often prolonged confrontations with administrators and parishioners. Pastors adopt a more militant attitude, become provocative and confrontational, are less cautious about what they say and do, and become apathetic about ministry. Whereas loss of idealism previously prompted ministers to search for ways of improving their work and reforming the church, following a crisis experience the expastors more or less had given up trying to change the system and in some instances were now out to destroy it. The following responses are typical of the post turning-point outlook of pastors.

We were hoping the system will change. . . . It was so dictatorial. . . . But I don't worry about change now because I don't think it will ever change. I realize you can't change the system. Personally I love all the administrators. . . . I've got nothing against them all, you know. But it almost seems as if our church has developed a Dracula in its organization and we don't know how to control it. It's become too much for us and nobody knows how to control it or tame it.

I lost my trust in the administration. My idealism had given way to skepticism. I saw the claims that ministers were men of God who were true to principle, as Ellen White says, as the needle is to the pole, to be a whole lot of rubbish. I looked upon them as political animals [who are out to] either save their jobs or cower to conservative political pressure from within the lay ranks.

The shift in attitude is particularly evident in the colorful terminology disaffected pastors use when referring to church leaders. Administrators are described as "mindless idiots," "uneducated fools," "snakes in the grass," "crazy bureaucrats," "politicians," and "silly bastards" who are "morally immature" and "out of touch with reality." One church leader is labeled "a little shit," another is dismissed as "a bull of a man," while a third is declared to be a "real sharpie" in his business dealings and compared to a used car dealer. An expastor who had been an administrator himself for more than two decades describes church leaders as "intellectually dishonest . . . punitive and violent people, psychologically abused and psychologically abusive." The contrasting positions outlined in Table 5.2 represent the extreme positions adopted by pastors before and after a crisis event. Not every pastor conformed to this "ideal type," and often the post-crisis outlook was not arrived at immediately but was the culmination of a series of adjustments. Crisis events affected pastors' relationships with their superiors and had a flow-on effect in their ministries that impacted on relationships with parishioners.

Table 5.2
Before and After Outlook of Adventist Expastors

Before Crisis Experience	*After Crisis Experience*
Hansford: "The role I saw myself [in] was one of teacher . . . to try and teach the local congregation . . . to bring in a broadness of mind and [an] oneness."	"There is no more openness in the church."
Rowe: "I shrugged my shoulders . . . I would retreat back into my rural world where I had my little thing to do."	"We are a sect, believe it or not."
Lawrence: "[The Conference president] was a Christian [and] . . . we got on quite well together as people . . . but on doctrine we were diametrically opposed."	"The crazy bureaucrats . . . [of that] stupid little ghetto."
Morton: "I sensed the excitement among young people . . . I saw older people suddenly become Bible students. It was great."	"[Seventh-day Adventism]' has to do some serious thinking over theology."
Ferguson: "I kept out of contentious [theological] areas and did not stir."	"[Dismisses the] ultra conservative, vindictive, nasty [God of Adventism]."
Morton: "I really enjoyed my life as a minister because I was doing the thing I liked most. I really loved ministry."	"I now see this movement as a sham, just a facade . . . When you take the veneer off, they are just animals, a cult."

CYNICISM AND BURNOUT

In this chapter I have deliberately avoided using the term "burnout," which was coined by Freudenberger (1974) to describe what happens when an employee is unable to perform assigned duties. Pines, Aronson, and Kafry (1981:3) define burnout as "a state of mind that frequently afflicts individuals who work with other people . . . and who pour in much more than they get back from their clients, supervisors, and colleagues." Cherniss (1980) and Ebaugh (1988a:52–65) employ the concept to describe the pre-exit built up of emotions. Ebaugh (1988a:52–61) views cynicism as a manifestation of occupational burnout and incorporates the concept as a stage in her model of role exit. I have deliberately avoided using the concept of burnout in the present discussion on what expastors experienced in ministry, first of all, because it locates the focus of attention too much on individual actors—the "problem" of surviving in ministry becomes one of "coping." A more important reason for not using it is that while all expastors at one time or another during interview discussed difficulties of pastoral ministry, including meeting unrealistic expectations of parishioners and church administrators, loss of privacy, the loss of friendships, social instability from relocation, the fact that ministers are on call twenty-four hours of the day and have to deal with recalcitrant members—most accepted these outcomes as part and parcel of ministry. It was not so much the demands of the job that wakened in pastors doubts about their calling and prompted them to question the church system, but experiences that often stretched their levels of tolerance beyond reason, challenged some of their central premises concerning ministry, and called into question their individual integrity (see Figure 5.1). In expastors' narratives, cynicism stems not from the demands of ministry, which three expastors describe as a "cushy job," but in response to out-of-the-ordinary attitudes and behavior from those who expastors believe should have known better. The concept as defined by Freudenberger may account for the departure of one expastor who found the work too difficult and the demands too numerous, but does not adequately account for the exits of the other forty-two expastors.

Figure 5.1
Loss of Idealism Among Adventist Expastors

Loss of Idealism	*+ Crisis Experience*	*= Cynicism*	*→ Exit*
Personal gaining of realism plus repeated run-ins with administration.	Events that mobilize and focus awareness.	Negative and critical outlook.	

SUMMARY

Disappointment and loss of idealism are processes integral to working in organizations and professional careers, including ministry. However, while the de-idealizing of ministry and sect organization are matters of concern, in the majority of instances decisions to abandon ministry were triggered by painful and sometimes shocking experiences that pushed expastors to their limits of tolerance. With the exception of a minority whose ministries were short-lived and whose departures were immediate, most reported an interval of several months to three years before their exit. During this interim period and in the aftermath of a crisis experience, failure of idealism gives way to cynicism and blatant attacks on the organization and its teachings. This chapter has focused on key social process that facilitated erosion of commitment to ministry and Adventism. The following two chapters focus on the microscopic social processes and relationships that mobilized expastors' career choices.

_____

Chapter 6

Propagating Cynicism

Every expastor has a story to tell of frustration, disappointment, and hurt in ministry; yet no former pastor whose exit was generated primarily by nondoctrinal issues fails simultaneously to articulate views on theology. The issue of which comes first—the theological doubts or the social and interpersonal disappointments—resists a simple answer, and ultimately the question itself is of little consequence. The intellectual and social are interdependent and do not exist in isolation. In the previous chapter we noted that expastors' attitudes to ministry and the organization underwent significant and sometimes dramatic reversals following a crisis experience. The present chapter expands on the idea that crises leave permanent psychological scars which affected ministry and bred cynicism. The chapter highlights how personal troubles and theological issues interact and reinforce each other in the exit process. It does this by examining the sources to which disaffected pastors turned for inspiration, support, and insight.

MINISTERIAL TRAINING

A multitude of voices can be heard in the Adventist Church arguing that the exodus of Adventist pastors during the 1980s was partly if not wholly an expression of the way ministers were trained. Kapitzke made the same observation in her ethnographic study of literacy practices in a northern Australian Adventist community:

More than a few claimed that "historic" Adventism [was] no longer preached because many in the church had "gone soft" and found "straight truth" too hard-hitting and divisive. . . . A remark frequently passed by members was that the "young pastors feed us on milk instead of meat." . . . Blame for this perceived watering-down of "the message" was squarely laid at the feet of the church's theological colleges. (1995:169)

Exit, according to this view, commences at training with loss of confidence in the traditional Adventist beliefs and gains momentum in ministry with the demands and pressures of parish work. Adventist academics trained in secular academic settings are accused of advocating points of view to trainee pastors that are both at variance with and antagonistic to traditional Adventist teachings (Standish and Standish 1988). The interviews with former pastors, however, reveal that while college training had introduced prospective ministers to methodologies and points of view that conflicted with the sectarian assumptions, the changes in the outlook of former pastors occurred, for most of them, *in* ministry.

Ministerial training changed radically during the 1960s and 1970s, from an exclusive and sectarian focus in earlier times, to one that was more inclusive and open to alternative views. In the decades following World War II the Seventh-day Adventist movement witnessed a radical shift in emphasis, which some describe as Adventism's "coming of age" (Reynolds 1986:207), signifying that the "sect . . . has moved a long way toward becoming a church" (Land 1986:230). According to Land (1986:208), Adventism stepped out of the relative isolation characteristic of its origins and was "moving toward accommodation with other denominations and society at large." There was a concerted push at all levels of the organization for Adventism to be identified with mainstream conservative Protestantism. This preoccupation with gaining recognition and "respectability" is evidenced in the radical policy changes in Adventist education.

In their endeavor to make Adventist theology credible within the wider Christian community, church leaders sought accreditation for Adventist educational institutions and seminaries. Accreditation required that teachers become qualified in the specific disciplines they taught. The introduction of academically qualified teachers at tertiary levels added an element of "sophistication" to Seventh-day Adventist theology (Land 1986:228), which outside observers interpreted in positive terms as signalling that the minority was becoming more liberal (*Newsweek,* 7 June 1971:65–66). Many insiders, however, including academics now looking back saw in these changes an unleashing of forces that ultimately were to impact on all levels of the organization. Bull and Lockhart (1989:231), for example, refer to accreditation as "a turning point in Adventist education" which "bred a sceptical spirit toward the Adventist traditions." Land (1986:226) argues that "in putting great emphasis on education, [Adventism] had inadvertently produced intellectuals who, on the basis of new experiences and new information, were in many ways reformulating Adventism."

According to A. N. Patrick (Interview, 29 September 1987), a leading Adventist academic in Australia and at the time of the interview curator of the Ellen G.

White Estate and SDA Research Centre, the incorporation and use of critical methodologies and systems of thought, which although not directly antagonistic to the Christian tradition in general, were incongruent with the Adventist worldview, undermined the very foundation of the sectarian dynamic. Patrick explains:

From 1950 onwards the church actually had people with university training in the disciplines they were teaching—biblical studies, systematic theology, church history or whatever, and that was having an inevitable impact on Adventism which as a result could never be the same again. . . . These people had a wider frame of reference in their own worldview, they had the perspectives of academic disciplines new to Adventism; they realized that they needed to approach the Bible exegetically instead of just assembling lists of proof-text. . . . This enabled us to look at the classical questions of biblical studies. It started to move us away from the kind of naive, proof-text approach to Scripture we had . . . often employed up to that point. (Interview, 29 September 1987)

These changes produced a new breed of Adventist pastor capable of operating interdenominationally. Patrick argues that the new approaches simultaneously equipped pastors with skills to reassess and question their taken-for-granted sect assumptions.

Ministers were now being taught to ask questions and reach their own answers. . . . In an institution that insisted it had all the answers, you were bound to get conflict. Church members were seldom equipped with this open-ended theological system or to live with questions. . . . Adventism had trained people basically to think that any question that might be asked could be answered by an evangelist standing on a platform with an open Bible; that all questions could be answered definitively so that no more questions needed to be raised, no grey areas left. . . . It was clear, therefore . . . these new approaches [impacting on graduate study] were in fundamental conflict with traditional Adventism. (Interview, 29 September 1987)

The group most affected by these moves were the pastors responsible for "selling" the "Adventist package" (Steeley 1985) to a hostile non-Adventist audience and to a membership that still clung to its conservative ethos. According to Ludowici (Interview, 23 April 1986), Adventist "pastors were encouraged to critically question everything . . . even the sacred cows of Adventist theology." Many conservative (retired) pastors and lay members saw in these trends the destruction of traditional Adventism and became passionate defenders of the old ways and militant critics of the new. Eager to protect the movement from liberalizing influences, conservative Adventist thinkers took to print. The 1960s and 1970s witnessed a proliferation of tracts and cheaply produced pamphlets protesting what their authors perceived was wholesale destruction of "the faith" and calling for a return to old ways. One expastor collected nineteen such pamphlets between 1976 and 1982 accusing theology lecturers of promoting heresy. The no holds barred approach of the conservatives, which angered many Adventists, contributed to the mood of hysteria in which pastors were declared "apostates" and accused of "false teaching."

Typical of this literature is the pamphlet *Is Avondale College in Jeopardy?*, which was co-signed by seventeen retired Adventist pastors, declaring that "a sinister climate of liberation has pervaded Avondale." A similar tract, *Marks of the Current Apostasy: How You Can Detect Error When It Is Heard in the Pulpit or Elsewhere in the Church*, contained forty-nine pointers on how to identify heresy and heretics in the Adventist community. Item 6 told readers to be wary of ministers who placed "emphasis on further study." Items 10 to 15 condemned pastors who preached "Jesus Christ and the gospel" instead of proclaiming "the third angels' message" that was central to Seventh-day Adventist teaching. The opposition encountered by recently appointed ministers from church members is one expression of this change of mood. Tractarians argued that theology graduates were indoctrinated with the "new" theology and that their corrupting influence had to be resisted before it spread to the churches. Nearly half (twenty-one) of interviewed expastors state that they experienced problems in ministry because they were recent starters. Even those ministers who were considered by their peers traditional and conservative in thinking report being treated with suspicion because they were recent appointees.

Typical of these attitudes is a letter from a concerned church member to a newly appointed minister warning him that his theology was under scrutiny. According to this expastor, the letter typified the parish mood in which Adventist pastors and recent appointees had to operate while simultaneously keeping administrators on their side. Three expastors recall upon arrival at their employing Conference being warned by their Conference presidents to avoid preaching on "controversial" issues being debated in the church. One was explicitly instructed to discard "the theology he was taught at college," even though his president had no idea of the former pastor's theological position. Another was told to focus on preaching "the good old Adventist message." In the light of these comments one would expect to find a significant number of expastors confirming that they had become disillusioned with ministry while at college as a result of doubts that they acquired from their teachers. The interviews reveal that the changed academic environment did affect the thinking of some ministers, although in ways that do not verify the fears of concerned critics. A majority of expastors, for instance, received their ministerial training during the 1950s and early 1960s and thus were products of the "old school" of thought. Moreover, more than half (nineteen) of the expastors with ministerial training report graduating from their studies conservative in outlook and with their traditional beliefs and values not shaken.

Fifteen of the thirty-eight former pastors who had trained in an Adventist seminary reported that they graduated from their studies "liberal" in outlook, and of these, only four attribute the collapse of their Adventist world view to ideas and questions acquired at college. One of these four explains that he discovered at college that "Adventism was not congruent with Christianity":

I went to college in search of answers and to a great extent I think I found the answers . . . [but] they weren't what I was expecting to find though, not at all. . . . I found that the teaching of the Scripture was not the teaching of Adventism . . . the gospel was something that was foreign to Adventism. . . . But I didn't think it had to stay that way. I had some hope that it could change. I was still optimistic.

A second claims that he "had a clear impression by the time I left college I wasn't really going to fit in" because the methodology he had acquired during training eroded his sectarian belief. According to this expastor, the lecturers at college "were doing a reformist work. They weren't standing up and saying 'that's wrong,' they were just saying 'this is how you do it.' And by teaching you the method they were giving you the . . . tools to peel the stuff away. . . . I was lucky to be employed. . . . I was lucky to get a job." A third recalls, "By the time I graduated I had gone from a very conservative Adventist to um, someone who . . . could no longer swallow the basic fundamental theology that Adventism stood for. But because I was so convicted to go into the ministry I was prepared to keep my own convictions to myself and go . . . in the ministry without disrupting the local church with my views." It is important to note, however, that all four expastors who traced their changed theological outlook to their training were from non-Adventist backgrounds. Clearly the new critical approach to theology in Adventist colleges was affecting trainees, but the full force of the new emphasis was felt particularly by Adventist newcomers unable to balance the open ended and critical approach to the study of the scriptures they were taught at college with the rigid sect frameworks they acquired when they converted.

It is also worth noting that these expastors, who were to all intents and purposes, in the words of one of them, "unemployable as Adventist pastors," still chose to enter ministry. They did so believing that as long as they upheld the beliefs central to the Christian faith, denominational concerns were of secondary importance to the Adventist ministry. One expastor believed Adventism was sufficiently mature to accommodate conflicting interpretations. A second assumed that there was greater scope in the Adventist Church in the 1970s and 1980s for liberal-minded ministers to make a contribution. All four wrongly assumed that Adventism had embraced evangelicalism and that with their support the remaining vestiges of sectarianism would be banished. As it turned out they underestimated lay and administrative commitment to traditional sectarian beliefs and overestimated the numerical and political strength of the revisionists. Three of them lasted only two years in ministry; the fourth was dismissed after only ten months.

The additional eleven expastors who adopted a liberal outlook at college were all *born Adventists*. The following comments are representative of the views of this group of expastors.

Avondale certainly changed my Adventist thinking at the roots level. . . . I now felt that the pat answers were no longer . . . full answers. . . . I felt that we were going to grow into some newer and more fuller answers as to our raison d'etre.

I learnt that the church was in a worse situation than I initially anticipated. . . . Avondale forced me to look more closely at the church . . . and that inward look led to where I am at the moment. I was not able to reconcile all the things, because the more I looked at the church the more I discovered inconsistencies.

I began studying at Avondale believing it was dangerous to believe in the doctrine of assurance. . . . The final year I concluded it was absolutely essential to have assurance if one wanted to be a Christian. . . . As well Avondale knocked the fanaticism out of me. It was a long and painful process.

What is apparent in the above comments is that despite their more critical outlooks, expastors born Adventists were less extreme and fell short of rejecting the basic structure of Adventist belief. No expastor from an Adventist background who reported graduating from college with a liberal outlook disputed the legitimacy of Adventism's place in the denominational landscape. Indeed, while these expastors were critical of specific points of Adventist teaching and had reservations over the movement's legalistic focus, they nevertheless believed that the problems in Adventism were "just a matter of emphasis" and could be redressed with the growing number of revisionist pastors entering ministry. Expastors who were born Adventists and embraced a revisionist outlook entered ministry believing their "gospel" would revitalize Adventism and framed their own roles in terms of pastor/ reformer with a double mission to extend the Adventist presence in the community and to enlighten the membership.

What is even more remarkable about expastors' recollections of their ministerial training is that six out of every ten graduated from their studies loyal and committed Adventists despite popular claims to the contrary. One former minister and third generation Adventist said, "I was young and . . . I just didn't see issues at all. I was quite convinced that we had the truth. I'd been brought up on that, and ah . . . you know, never questioned it." The response of Ian Peters in the case study that follows is typical of converts who remained loyal Adventists and devoted to ministry at the conclusion of the four-year study program. During the interview Peters explained:

I came out with holy zeal, I guess. You see I never really went there with any questions. The questions arose later. What I learnt there was working quietly in my mind. . . . I didn't go with any preconceived views or judgements, and I thought I don't know Adventism well enough to have formed definite opinions. I hadn't grown up in it and I couldn't understand for the life of me why some people had so many hangups.

Newer Adventists, it would seem, either successfully avoided facing up to issues during training, as Peters had done, or did not comprehend the full implications of what they were studying.

Table 6.1 suggests that the ministerial training program was most "damaging" on trainees from Adventist backgrounds who were thoroughly immersed in the Adventist worldview and able to recognize the implications of classroom-derived knowledge for the movement. The evidence also highlights an important dynamic in the biographical accounts in which *beginnings* and *endings* are juxtaposed and inverted. Leavers who converted to Adventism present themselves as conservatives or as *real* Adventists who were compelled to question their beliefs more by their ministries than by their studies; expastors who were born and bred Adventists present themselves as devotees who dared to question cherished beliefs, and for them the changes in outlook occurred at college. Whether expastors' interpretation of their training is a narrative device used to construct exit in ways I have outlined, or an accurate summation of the impact of the training program, is difficult to judge. What is certain, however, is that only a minority of expastors attribute the impetus for exit to their training. The overwhelming majority account for their decisions by directing attention to lessons learnt and decisions arrived at in the course of their ministries. Expastors' narratives reveal that for the overwhelming majority of leavers, the ministry career was undermined by processes *in* ministry, and not by their training.

Table 6.1
Theological Outlook of Expastors at Time of Graduation

	Born SDA	*Convert*
Conservative Theological Outlook	8	11
Liberal Theological Outlook	11	4

PASTORAL MINISTRY AND ADVENTIST THEOLOGY

With the exception of four converts who jettisoned their Adventist beliefs as a result of college training, a majority of expastors commenced in ministry recognizably Adventist. The belief structure of Adventist pastors, however, is by no means static or fixed once in ministry. Contrary to assumptions in the sociology of religion concerning the relative stability of doctrinal belief among "established sects" (Chalfant, Beckley, and Palmer 1981:123–136; Yinger 1970), the thinking of all Adventist pastors, regardless of theological leanings and subsequent outcomes in their careers, was dynamic and continually modified. If there is any stability in the sectarian world view it is limited to officials with vested interests in guarding the traditions. At all other levels of church life doctrine is debated and fought over. Official church records are replete with narratives of members and ministers who discover "new light," accounts of individuals who promote alternative interpretations of existing doctrines, reports of heresy trials, and stories of ministers who abandon cherished Adventist beliefs. For example, examination of the North New Zealand Conference minutes revealed that between 1920 and 1960 five Adventist pastors were summoned to appear before committees to answer claims of heresy.

The dynamic nature of sectarian belief is well illustrated in the responses of expastors and currently serving ministers to a series of questions in a survey that invited them to record the direction of change in their outlooks while in ministry.

They were asked to select from six pairs of contrasting values those statements which applied to them. Approximately three out of every four continuing pastors (71 percent) state that they were now less preoccupied with debating subtle points of theology than when they began their ministry and more concerned with the practical aspects of faith (Table 6.2). In addition, 51 percent said they were more accommodating of other points of view. The emphasis on practical religion and tolerance is the hallmark of ministry, and it is not surprising that continuing pastors rated highly in these categories. More critical is the fact that 27 percent of stayers report that they are more liberal in outlook now. Although this does not necessarily imply that one out of every four pastors abandoned Adventist theology, it does suggest that for a significant minority of continuing pastors these changes point to a gradual erosion of sectarian values.

Table 6.2

Change in Theological Outlook of Expastors and Currently Serving Adventist Pastors

	% Leavers (N = 50)	*% Stayers (N = 66)*
From theoretical to practical concerns	54	71
From practical to theoretical	10	-
From liberal to conservative theological outlook	-	2
From conservative to liberal theological outlook	74	27
From strictly religious to humanitarian or ethical concerns	70	17
From humanitarian or ethical to strictly religious concerns	-	2
From rather tolerant to stricter religious views	2	-
From rather strict to more tolerant views	82	56
From uncertain in faith to more deeply committed	16	30
From more deeply committed to uncertain in faith	40	2
From caring a lot about theology to caring very little	30	6
From caring very little about theology to caring a lot	20	14

It is to be expected that in all but one of the six categories surveyed expastors' response rate is consistently higher in the direction of radical change. The shift in outlook is more pronounced among leavers and touches a greater number of areas: 74 percent report they were more liberal in their theology prior to leaving ministry, 70 percent replaced previously strictly religious concerns with humanitarian and ethical ones, and 82 percent rejected religious intolerance—the lynchpin of sectarianism. The most glaring contrast between the two groups is that whereas 30 percent of stayers reported being more deeply committed since taking up ministry, 40 percent of leavers reported uncertainty and loss of commitment in matters of religion *while in ministry*. One way to account for these dramatic contrasts is to argue that with appropriate social stimuli, or what I term crisis experiences, expastors' ongoing review of Adventist belief can give way to scepticism and rejection of Adventism. The following case study illustrates these processes.

Ian Peters

Peters went out of Adventism as he had come in—distrustful of religious systems, sceptical of denominational claims, and cautious of being "tricked" into commitment. Ironically, in his account of leaving ministry Peters inverts a popular Adventist metaphor of conversion and compares his years in Adventism to a "dark" interlude, claiming that "it was like entering a dark tunnel with a faint light at the end. . . . I've passed through the tunnel of Adventism out into the bright light of the end." Peters first heard of Adventism through a high school friend who was an Adventist. His association with the movement commenced some years later in his early twenties following an experience that "raised questions in [his] mind about being and direction" for which Adventism had plausible explanations. He was impressed with Adventism's rational approach to religious issues and especially the health emphasis. As Peters became absorbed in the Seventh-day Adventist social world he found himself gradually accepting the doctrines. In time his previously open view of the world gave way to one that was "narrow" and "biased toward other viewpoints." Any doubt he may have had about becoming an Adventist was dispelled by his friendship with a young woman who was an Adventist, and more important for shaping his future career, the daughter of an Adventist pastor. The decision to train for ministry grew from his interest in helping people and the fact that church members encouraged him to find fulfilment in ministry. Although not very impressed with some Adventist ministers whom he considered "arrogant," "worldly," and "dogmatic," overall he had a positive image of the Adventist pastor as someone who was "spiritually oriented and very caring." He observed that in Adventist circles ministers carried status and were "almost revered by some church members." His positive impression of the Adventist ministry was reinforced by his father-in-law, who was a pastor.

Peters commenced his theological training knowing very little about Adventism and even less about the Bible, but willing to learn. The tertiary program, he recalls, was "an enlightening experience," but he found study a challenge. "I wasn't what you might call an excellent student by any means. I had to struggle through . . . but I never really saw academic achievement as a thing of worth." As a married student living off campus he was shielded from daily exposure to on-campus debates, but even so, he puzzled over why doctrine "was causing so much turmoil in the minds of some." He was by nature reserved and "never threw [himself] one hundred percent into anything." He explains that the real reason he was not affected was because he did not have "preconceived views or judgements and didn't know Adventism well enough to have formed definite opinions. I hadn't grown up in it and I couldn't understand for the life of me why some people had so many hangups." At the completion of his training, Peters recalls graduating "with holy zeal" and conforming to the Adventist minister ideal both outwardly and doctrinally, and willing to do "what was expected of me."

He was appointed to care for a small rural church while working alongside a senior pastor/evangelist. Despite four years' training he was surprised by the biblical ignorance of church members and the fact that doctrinal beliefs were accepted without question. He discovered that his parishioners were

still caught up in this idea of righteousness by works. The perfectionist thinking, where I was, was quite noticeable. That amazed me and surprised me. I came into the church thinking that Adventists generally were thinking and evaluating people, but they were not. They accepted what they are taught without questioning. . . . After I gained more confidence I tried to encourage them to think and I used to question everything . . . not only just in doctrinal things but in general attitude. . . . Several objected to it.

He found it difficult to conform to the popular belief that the Adventist minister "should be seen to be apart and separate" from parishioners and rejected the idea as "a whole lot of rubbish." His most painful lesson learnt upon entering ministry was in relation to church leadership. He was shocked at the dishonesty of some Adventist evangelists who were prepared to make outrageous claims from the platform and in advertising brochures to secure audiences and gain converts. He recalls one evangelist who "produced . . . an evangelistic leaflet [in which he] made all these outrageous claims . . . that he was a world traveller and all this kind of rubbish. I raised objection both to him and to the president. . . . He said people will not even worry about it, they won't notice it. Well I wasn't convinced." On another occasion during an evangelistic campaign a leading church administrator presented what Peters now condemns as "an abortion of a program." Peters felt embarrassed by "the way the pastors treated people when they asked questions," the "lies he told," and the fact that people walked out of the meetings "by the hundreds." These experiences and the low success of his own outreach programs shaped his convictions on public evangelism and his impressions of those in authority. But in keeping with his attitude to most things, Peters lacked the "strength of character" to voice the conviction that "evangelism is . . . outdated and doesn't work in this time and age." He recalls telling his wife, "The only man I can really say . . . had a desirable presentation and a very convincing style was Doctor Ford. He had a method of drawing you into what he was saying. It was spiritual. His presentation was rational, it appealed to the reason." However, these experiences convinced him that he was not cut out for evangelism. He also realized that he "was not getting the kind of fulfilment from ministry that he expected."

These feelings and attitudes were compounded by his impressions of church bureaucracy, which he declares "leaves a lot to be desired." "Initially I was given to believe that administrators were very understanding, cooperative, and supportive, but I didn't find them that way at all. In the area where I was, [the president] was not even an able administrator and he just couldn't communicate with people. He had one thing in mind and that was to please the Union Conference president." Peters felt alienated by the administration's preoccupation with evangelism: "That

really got to me—figures, numbers, how I had to amass these numbers of converts."
He came to "detest enormously . . . the controls that the administration placed on
your movements and on your freedom to make decisions." Looking back, he says,
"The whole thing was like a controlling force. Whether this was real or imagined,
at least I considered it to be real." Church members born and bred in the system
possibly felt protected and secure in this closed environment, but as time went by
Peters grew weary of the constraints and of the fact that he was "expected to submit
and surrender my personal freedom to an organization." Outwardly he remained a
"very conservative and typical Adventist minister," but inwardly he was beginning
to rebel. He thought of opting out of ministry but dismissed the idea: "I ought to
give it time, perhaps I haven't got my feet wet." At this time he was still loyal to
the church and clung to the "pig-headed idea that Adventism was right despite all
its faults." These feelings changed with his appointment to work with a team of
pastors on an evangelistic program.

Peters felt utterly frustrated being assigned to work on yet another outreach
program when his heart was not in that type of ministry. The ministers did not get
along with each other, and this made work difficult for him. He began taking a
much greater interest in what was happening in Adventism generally and followed
closely the many theological controversies buffeting the Adventist community. It
unsettled him. The resignations of two close minister friends were a shattering
blow to his confidence in the church system. He was disappointed by "the way the
administration treated its employees." His grievances with the church during the
first three years in ministry stemmed largely from interpersonal and administrative
factors. In his fourth year the focus shifted to theology. During that year feelings
of frustration and disappointment resurfaced regularly and more forcefully than
on previous occasions. That year he was befriended by a sympathetic colleague
with whom he shared his concerns and exchanged ideas. He recalls:

Things really surfaced when I met Pastor J. A. He raised a number of issues with me and
that sort of opened the floodgates. I had heard of other things happening, and the issue with
the Ellen G. White Estate occurred before I went down there. That started me thinking and
asking questions. But when I met J. A. . . . . I started to ply him with questions. He didn't
want to tell me at first because he knew what would happen. But I persisted. We used to
have long conversations, lengthy conversations. . . . J. A. was chewing my ear also, telling
me how helpless he felt and . . . that didn't help either, I might add. I was his ear, I was his
listening piece. But I asked him a lot of questions too. I just wanted to know. Once I had a
doubt about one thing I questioned that and went right through it. I couldn't help myself. I
went through absolutely every other point, about Ellen White, about doctrine. . . . It was
like playing dominoes and I couldn't stop them falling. If I wanted to I couldn't because
everything is so intertwined that once you remove the keystone then the rest collapses, and
Ellen White is that keystone. Adventism is all built around her basically, because she verified
every doctrinal position by a dream. And the dreams were a lot of baloney. They were
dreams and not what she claimed they were. . . . She is no more inspired than you or I.

Pastor J. A. had an elaborate network of contacts who kept him up to date with the latest developments in Adventist politics. J. A. was a key figure in the Adventist underground network receiving and distributing literature on doctrinal and social issues. Through him Peters had on tap the very latest of what was happening elsewhere in the Adventist world. J. A. was instrumental both in focusing attention on doctrinal issues and in raising in Peters's mind the critical questions regarding Adventist theology.

When two officers from the Ellen White Estate held meetings to "sort out doctrinally" ministers in Australia and New Zealand, Peters went to the meetings prepared with questions. "J. A. and I had many sessions before they came and I knew or was aware of a lot of things that they were going to say. . . . We had time to think and formulate questions." As Peters recalls, "Those meetings were really the final straw because I was convinced more than anything from their . . . answers that Ellen White was not a prophet and that she was used by some unscrupulous men in the early years of the movement to discipline and work into shape a sect and to give the movement some cohesion." Distrustful of those in authority and unable to discuss his concerns with lay members, Peters turned to his peers in ministry for support. "In my very last year I had enormous phone bills just to speak to somebody else who was going through a similar sort of thing I was going through, phenomenal phone bills, especially because one got little support from the administration." From this point onward theology became an all-consuming passion fuelled by his ongoing battles with administration.

To get his mind off Adventist troubles J. A. "encouraged" him to study at the local university, but as Peters explains, his study of religious history only made matters worse:

I suddenly realized that what they taught us at Avondale was just touching the surface. When I did all this reading, boy, it was really amazing what I discovered. It just opened my mind so much more. . . . The amazing thing was that the early New Testament church was a movement that was directed by the spirit. There was no need for an ecclesiastical order. The ecclesiastical order actually replaced the spirit. That really hit me. I could see it. I believed it. I appreciated it. Avondale became like a kindergarten by comparison. I guess that happens when you go higher up the tertiary scale. And we did another section on millennial movements of Europe and when they moved across to America. The thing that really got me was all these prophets. There were millions of them, and I clicked in a split second. Ellen White was in that same context, although at the very end of that period. She was in precisely the same context. That's when I came to the conclusion that the way Adventists cottoned on to the Sabbath as the distinguishing feature, because all the other sects that grew up around the prophet all bore some distinguishing characteristic. . . . I went to the professor there and said I really got this problem with Ellen White. He knew about church history. He knew about all the faiths and he said to me, well, every church movement has a skeleton in the cupboard that they prefer to forget. But I said they don't forget this one, it keeps rattling. He really couldn't offer any advice. . . . Gosh, if ever there was an eye-opener that was it. . . . What I learnt that year just destroyed Adventism for me.

The nonthreatening academic environment enabled Peters to explore other areas of Adventist teaching using the points of reference he acquired from J. A. He "came to the conclusion without any reading and without any prior discussion" that the Sabbath, the very heart of Adventist belief, was nothing more than "an identifying doctrine [used] to set apart this movement from other movements in the USA at that time." By the end of his fourth year Peters had become totally disillusioned with ministry and Adventism. He became critical of administrators, the majority of whom, he claims, were "incompetent" and "self-opinionated opportunists." He dismissed public evangelism as "an ego trip" promoted by a group of men whose thinking was still locked into the nineteenth century. He discarded the key Adventist doctrines of the Sabbath and the investigative judgement as unbiblical distortions and labelled Adventism a millennial sect which survived into the twentieth century by capitalizing on the illusions of a self-proclaimed prophetess. The administration's decision to relocate him yet again at the end of his fourth year was "the final straw."

Toward the end of Peters's fourth year in ministry the focus of his conflicts shifted to his wife, who for the first time since they entered ministry insisted that her feelings be taken into consideration. When Peters was told that at year's end he would be relocated, the news precipitated a major emotional crisis for his wife. She was "born and bred and educated in the Adventist womb" and was the daughter of a successful pastor. She had firsthand knowledge of what was expected of the minister's wife and for the first few years conformed to the stereotype by organizing the children's Sabbath School program for the church and conducting cooking demonstrations. According to Peters, "She enjoyed all that. That was her life. She felt comfortable and secure in the church environment and the role that she performed." She was aware of the theological issues causing division in the Adventist Church but did not dwell on them. However, she became unsettled when Peters commenced airing his doubts at home. Peters explains: "She was really having trouble emotionally, coping with the crisis that we were going through at the time, and the church generally was going through over this Ellen White business. She wasn't upset because the church was having trouble with Ellen White, but . . . the emotions and all the in-fighting that was going on and my uncertainty as to where I was going" were troubling her. The counsellor from whom she sought advice regarding her condition noted among other things that "the constant shifting, the uprooting and then having to lay down roots again" were causing her distress and advised that relocation would be detrimental to her health. Peters initially agreed to the transfer, but when his wife protested with tears he resolved to confront the authorities. He requested that the Executive Committee consider his wife's condition and retract the transfer. Unbeknown to him church members signed a petition to keep Peters as their pastor. Church leaders were incensed by this action and launched an "inquiry wanting to know who had put the members up to draw the petition." Peters recalls:

That really made me angry. The dishonesty that went on by the administration behind the scenes to check out on the loyalty of their ministers. To me that was not a Christian thing to do. I don't believe in the devil anyway, but that's a devilish thing. If there's one effective way to destroy the support and the cohesiveness of your ministry, it is to do that kind of thing. From that point on I distrusted decisions that were made by the Executive and by the administrators.

His distrust of church leadership was further confirmed when a member of the Conference Executive told him that the president did not inform committee members about his wife's problems. Peters explains that this information finally "finished me off":

I thought, hell, the guy has lied to me. From that moment on I could never trust a word, or believe a word that man said. I just couldn't trust him. . . . One person that I would never expect to lie almost directly to me, was the president, but then I began to hear of reports of other presidents, the way they were treating some of their men, the lies and the way ministers were preached upon, that, I think, finished me off more than anything. . . . I could tolerate [theological problems] to a fair degree, but what I couldn't tolerate were the moral dishonesty and the lies. . . . That I cannot accept. I guess I'm a very straight person as far as moral issues are concerned, about honesty, integrity, trust. I can't tolerate deviance from those things. That's just the way I am, and [my wife] is much the same. I thought, well, if that's the way the church is going to operate, I really don't want anything to do with it. So from that point on, more than anything, I was looking for an exit. I just wanted to leave.

Peters continued in ministry a few more months but recalls that his heart was not in his work. "Morale was rock bottom. I couldn't go out doing visits. I avoided preaching whenever I could. . . . I was just as flat as flat could be. There were some mornings where I just didn't want to get out of bed. I just didn't want to get up, get dressed or do anything. I could see no purpose in it. All motivation had gone absolutely." For a time he continued to meet with some of the non-Adventists with whom he was studying the Bible but "did not teach Adventism." He spent much of the time "looking around for something else to do," only to discover that his qualifications and experience as pastor of a sectarian community were of little value in the labor market.

Ironically, about this time the Conference president informed him that he was to be ordained at the end of that year, but Peters dismissed this as another of the president's many lies. Peters's apathy by now was visibly apparent, and the president advised him to take six months' leave without pay "to try and sort out [his] doctrinal positions." Peters dismissed the proposal as ridiculous because he was economically dependent on his weekly wages. In his letter of resignation Peters stated that he wished to quit ministry "for family reasons." He did not mention doctrine for fear this may affect severance pay and terms of settlement. Peters left the ministry feeling shattered emotionally and economically. Despite his ten-year "detour" in ministry training he had no career to speak of, no regular work or economic security. He was "virtually penniless" and relied on family members for financial help. He discovered that outside Adventism his academic qualifications in religion and his experience as minister of a sectarian community were not valued and were a handicap to his obtaining alternative employment. He lost one job when his boss discovered that Peters had been a minister of a sectarian community. For two years he changed jobs every two or three months. He worked as a builders' laborer, did fundraising, hospital cleaning, and landscape gardening, and sold insurance, chocolates, and computers before being appointed to his present job as a welfare officer. The unstable nature of short-term employment and the continual task of applying for jobs and being turned down affected his sense of self-worth: "I went through a period of loss of self-esteem. It was really getting quite bad. . . . I was beginning to feel that I was worthless, that I would never be employed again. The bottom dropped out of everything."

His resignation and subsequent relocation put an end to Adventist friendships largely forged while in ministry. His wife, according to Peters, "is in no-man's land." She sends the children to Sabbath School but "objects to the kids being taught stories about angels . . . or about Ellen White." She keeps in contact with "a whole host" of Adventists, fearing she would be "lost and without roots" if she separated completely. For a time he attended the local Adventist Church (for his wife's sake) but more as spectator than participant. He now prefers to stay away and says he is "happy" and "quite content" being on "the outside." According to Peters, the Adventist system is devoid of "basic Christian principles." "Strict adherence to doctrine is the thing that holds it together. . . . It's a web of fear. If you don't keep this, if you don't believe that, if you don't conform then you're lost." Peters believes that central to Adventist belief is a God "who is cold and unfeeling" that "has to be satisfied by works." He regrets he "ever got involved with it." The remaining vestiges of his Christian belief came adrift with the untimely death of a close friend. At the time of the interview Peters described his outlook as neither atheist nor Christian but "a mixture." He does not "believe that Christ existed as a Son of God." He believes "there is a creator who does not interfere. . . . He set the whole thing in motion and now stands back." He says, "God is as personal as we make him." He now sees all "religious organizations, Christian and non-Christian, as attempts to explain the unknown, the inexplicable, and to give a reason for man's existence." In a letter to Peters a former college lecturer expressed hope that "the time will come when the Church will develop a climate within which [Peters] may desire to resume full-time ministry." Return to ministry is unlikely, and Peters dismisses the idea as unthinkable and absurd.

The experience of becoming a member of a sectarian movement and the painful process of disengaging from both ministry and the church community, Peters claims, have changed him as a person. He is now more critical in outlook, less conservative, not as patient, less compliant, and less tolerant of his previous sectarian point of view. He regrets "all the sweat, the tears, the time, the effort, the money that we invested in it that could have been better invested elsewhere," and describes his decade of Adventist association as "a learning experience, but a very costly one, emotionally costly." The only positive element has been that the pain of leaving ministry and disengaging from the movement enables him to empathize with the "down-and-outs" he comes across in his job:

I can understand more of what they go through, why they feel the way they do. One becomes very perceptive of the grief experiences, because the whole thing was a grief experience, one grief after the other. . . . The feeling that I've been lied to, tricked, treated as being dishonest, untrustworthy, then to come back and not be able to get a job, be unemployed, loss of a family member, all that, there's a whole lot of grief. Every time you lose something it's a grief experience. I can pick it up easily now. I have only got to look at a person and speak to them for a few moments and immediately sense if there's something wrong.

MAJOR THEMES OUTLINED

A number of issues are highlighted by this case study regarding expastors' changes of outlook. First, Peters's passage to exit did not begin with his college indoctrination. He is among the 60 percent of expastors in the present study who were as conservative in theology at the conclusion of their four-year ministerial training program as when they commenced. Second, the case study also reveals that the processes that culminated with exit began gradually and imperceptibly. Peters's eventual abandonment of sectarianism progressed from loss of confidence in administration, to his reluctance to seek guidance from those in authority, to his turning increasingly to sources at the margins of the movement for instruction and inspiration in matters of theology. It also demonstrates the role of friendship networks in theological change. The role friends play in exit will be discussed in the next chapter. Suffice it to say in the present context that Peters's frustration with church officials influenced his choice of friends and legitimated acceptance of alternative views on doctrine. The account graphically depicts the changes that occur in expastors' thought processes following crises. In Peters's case, these became evident in his growing fascination and eventual preoccupation with problems and debates in the church over doctrine. Careful examination of what expastors read and the sources to which they turned for guidance provides additional insight into the propagation of cynical knowledge in ministry.

PROPAGATING DOUBT

The literary sources cited by expastors during interview, with few exceptions, had one thing in common: all were critical of traditional Adventist beliefs. Expastors did not foresee the full implications of their reading interests while in ministry and the fact that they were drawn to sources critical of the church and authors renowned for their critical perspectives. The books that made permanent impressions on their thinking while in ministry and shaped expastors' theological beliefs did not bear the denomination's "seal of approval" and were from denominationally independent sources. Only one expastor attributes the genesis of his theological awakening to a denominationally recognized and accepted Adventist writer; but with tongue-in-cheek he explained that his legalistic convictions were overturned by reading a book by Morris Venden recommended to him by Des Ford.

Then again, not everything former pastors read by non-Adventist authors prompted them to reexamine their beliefs. Most often the questions raised by these authors were confined to specific areas of interest and did not threaten expastors' confidence in Adventist teaching. C. S. Lewis and Francis Schaeffer, for example, prompted two expastors to question the focus of Adventist outreach; a third was challenged to reexamine his views of the inspiration of the Old Testament after reading John Bright's *The Authority of the Old Testament* and Haysen Miller's *Israelite and Judaean History*. James Barr's *Fundamentalism* and *The Use and Abuse of the Bible* prompted another to question the fundamentalist leanings of Adventist belief, while Cunningham's *History of the Reformation* challenged yet another to reassess his attitude to the Reformation. Questions raised by these sources were a stimulus to further study and not a catalyst either to abandon Adventist belief or to exit ministry. It was not so much the fact that a book was authored by an Adventist or non-Adventist, but the state of mind of the expastor at the time that determined its impact. Expastors' narratives suggest that a combination of factors interacted with their reading to effect change, including prior disillusionment with Adventism, an immediate set of circumstances that provoked questioning, and exposure to a specific kind of literature.

So long as they were committed to the organization, the belief structure of expastors remained stable and the range of issues and types of material accessed and explored remained narrow. Commitment was a form of closure and set limits to theological exploration. Two expastors explained that in ministry they consciously avoided reading books and articles by Brinsmead and Numbers because they feared the negative consequences of this material. A third says that by virtue of his commitment to the Adventist Church he was not free to pursue questions to their logical end, and explains that since commencing ministry "I had only read Ellen White. . . . I never really questioned Adventism. . . . I believed that Adventism was right and that any doubts I had were my problem, you know, the influence of the devil and that sort of jazz." At some point in this expastor's experience the issues and sources previously ignored or overlooked gained attraction and threatened his seemingly impregnable assumptions about the sect. "I can still remember," states one former pastor, "many of the things that seemed very basic at that time, later brought about the questioning."

CRISIS AND QUESTIONING

Expastors connect the genesis of their changed outlooks in ministry with experiences that unsettled and were antithetical to their perceived order of things. For example, following a period of intense conflict with local church members and the Conference, an expastor states that he "began to look at other Christians to see what they were doing. I remember deliberately not reading Adventist material. I had come to the stage where I stopped doing that." A second recalls that soon after a meeting at which administrators criticized and ridiculed co-workers who dared to question Adventist teaching, he began "to shop around in other bookshops and found there were libraries . . . religious writers outside of Adventism who wrote what now seemed to me to be a lot of common sense, yet who didn't agree with Adventism." An expastor who felt shaken by Glacier View and the subsequent resignation of a close friend turned his attention to exploring theological views outside Adventism, only "to realize that all these liberal non-Adventist nasties were dedicated Christians who simply had a different perspective and that they had a lot of good reasons for some of their . . . perspectives." In each of the cases the broadening of personal theological horizons coincided with or was triggered by experiences that jolted expastors to question their commitment to the church. Peters similarly became more accommodating of alternative interpretations and more accepting of literature critical of Adventist teaching following his clash with the Conference president.

The sources from which expastors drew inspiration when formulating their theological opinions, with few exceptions, conformed to the literary genre of *anti-sectarian tract*. This material was primarily authored by Adventists or, as in the case of Paxton (1978:7), by "sympathetic critics." What gave this literature an edge was its rejection of sectarianism and its anti-establishment flavor. The authors were critical of the Adventist Church's hierarchical structure, authoritarian style of leadership, anti-intellectualism, and approach to theology which limited discussion and conclusions to what was prescribed by Ellen White. The material that did most damage to expastor thinking while in ministry, almost without exception, was produced by individuals well known in Adventist circles for their radicalism.

Table 6.3
Books Cited Most in Expastors' Accounts

	% Expastors (N = 43)
Geoffrey J. Paxton (1978), *The Shaking of Adventism*	17
Robert D. Brinsmead, *Present Truth* (later *Verdict*) and (1980) *Judged by the Gospel*	44
Walter T. Rea (1982), *The White Lie*	33
Ronald Numbers (1976), *Prophetess of Health: A Study of Ellen G. White*	22
Spectrum, A Quarterly Journal of the Association of Adventist Forums	56

Table 6.3 lists the books identified by expastors as contributing to their questioning of the Adventist doctrines. The quarterly journal *Spectrum*, which commenced publication in 1969 had become the mouthpiece of Adventist academia and during the 1970s was the main vehicle for promoting Adventist intellectual concerns. Condemned by church leaders for its radical and often blatant attacks on

the organization, the journal was one of the most talked-about themes in the Adventist community and certainly among ministers. An examination of the table of contents of *Spectrum* from it's founding in 1969 until 1980, the year of Ford's dismissal, reveals that the majority of articles were preoccupied with debating themes central to Adventist theology (Table 6.4). The unrestrained criticisms by leading Adventist theologians, New and Old Testament scholars, Adventist historians and retired church leaders raised questions as to the credibility of some Adventist doctrines. These reinforced in some expastors the convictions that the bureaucracy was not to be trusted and that the Adventist system as a whole was in crisis. More that half (56 percent) of the expastors interviewed attribute some of their disillusionment with Adventism to reading *Spectrum*.

Table 6.4
Themes Featured in *Spectrum* Articles Between 1969 and 1981

	Occurrences
Crisis in Seventh-day Adventist Theology	62
Issues Concerning Ellen G. White	38
Trends in SDA Evangelism/Missions	37
Trends in Higher Education	37
Social and Ethical Issues	30
Church Structure and Bureaucracy	28
Adventism, Science, and Religion	28
Women in the Adventist Church	16
Religion and Politics	15
Church and Litigation	14

A flood of literature appeared during the 1970s by Adventist authors critical of Adventist theology. Among these was the journal *Present Truth* (later *Verdict*), Brinsmead's main platform for promoting his evangelical views. Robert Brinsmead was marginalized by the Adventist community during the late 1950s for his extreme perfectionist views. Following his evangelical "rebirth" during the early 1970s and his close association with Des Ford, Brinsmead's writings received wide distribution in the Seventh-day Adventist Church. *Present Truth* was directed at Protestants generally and especially at Seventh-day Adventists to remind them of their Reformation heritage and how far they had drifted from it. The monthly editions of the journal were distributed free of charge, and the extent of its Adventist readership is reflected in the fact that almost half (44 percent) of interviewed expastors indicated that they regularly received and enjoyed reading the Brinsmead material. The publication of *The Shaking of Adventism* (1978) by Anglican priest Geoffrey Paxton fuelled the Brinsmead debate within Adventism and reinforced the latter's claim that the Adventist doctrine of salvation conflicted with the Reformation teaching on righteousness by faith. *Prophetess of Health: A Study of*

Ellen G. White (1976) was another source that caused a furor in the Adventist community because its author, Ronald Numbers, did not presuppose Ellen White's inspiration. He showed that her health "visions" were embarrassingly similar in thought and often in word to accounts of some of her contemporaries. No sooner had the dust settled from the Numbers book than Brinsmead's *Judged by the Gospel: A Review of Adventism* (1980) kept the debate concerning Ellen White's inspiration alive by questioning her reliability in the area of doctrine. Two years later, Walter Rea, a demoted church administrator, argued in *The White Lie* (1982) that an alarming portion of Ellen White's work showed extensive "borrowing" from contemporary authors, even incorporating historical errors in the process. The issues that Numbers, Brinsmead, and Rea raised were further amplified in various issues of *Spectrum*. An expastor explained that Walter Rea's *White Lie* (he claims his "was probably the first copy of the book in Australia") helped put the Adventist social and theological issues in perspective for him: "I can remember that was really the turning point. . . . When I sat at home and read this thing everything suddenly fell into place. . . . The scales dropped [from] my eyes and I realized . . . the whole thing was based on fraud and I really couldn't, you know, I couldn't entertain being part of it. At that stage I guess my reformist attitudes were finished. . . . I started going for job interviews." Works by nonconformist Adventist thinkers influenced more than half of the expastors to question Adventist beliefs.

The torrent of unpublished manuscripts and copies of correspondence circulated in the church unofficially during these years also contributed to the erosion of belief. The sheer volume of material, its blatant condemnation of Adventist traditional views, and at its times unrestrained vilification of church leaders impacted on the outlook of pastors already struggling to maintain commitment in ministry. As one expastor explained, "I used to get all the underground Adventist literature. In fact I had reached the point of saturation where, you know, I was beginning to say, so what, what's new? . . . I just couldn't handle that kind of thing any more." A second recalls:

Whenever you went somewhere or had someone come and stay, the topic of conversation was, What have you learnt, what have you discovered? You know, it was a search, there was an eager search for new information, new information to add to this growing picture of things that had gone wrong. If I can draw a parallel, I felt like a German in World War II who really believed in the German cause but halfway through the war realized that it had all gone wrong and . . . [was] now trying to back out, but felt obliged to give assent to the war effort because this was expected of him. We wanted to understand, you know, why the lines had fallen.

Two out of every three expastors (67 percent) trace the demise of their Adventist convictions to these sources.

An examination of the collection of material one expastor received via the "Adventist underground press" is indicative of the resources available to pastors. The box of literature, which the expastor donated to my research at the time of his interview, contained 243 items acquired between 1980 and 1982. The collection consisted of 83 letters, 57 unpublished manuscripts, 64 articles, of which the majority were from *Spectrum*, and 39 pamphlets, all of which addressed the crisis in Adventism. Approximately 40 percent of the material (96 items) discussed the authority of Ellen White and the debate over her literary borrowing provoked by the research of Numbers and Rea, and approximately 30 percent (70 items) was preoccupied with Des Ford, the sanctuary, and the investigative judgement. Among the correspondence were copies of letters discussing past Adventist "heretics," including D. M. Canright, A. F. Ballenger, J. H. Kellogg, E. J. Waggoner, L. R. Conradi, W. W. Fletcher, L. Were, and R. D. Brinsmead, and copies of letters relating to the resignation or dismissal of 16 expastors. Also found amid the papers were handwritten notes on two talks this expastor possibly delivered. The notes disclose his state of mind at the time and the impact this material was having on the thinking of some ministers. On the topic of Ellen White's inspiration, the expastor wrote: "I will be quite frank with you—the evidence that I have examined so far leaves me in no doubt that . . . *there is nothing here that can conclusively demonstrate that Ellen White was a prophet of God.*" It is possible that at the time he penned these words he was still a minister and had not thought of quitting.

SUMMARY

The fact that the expastors were prepared to labor over material critical of the organization and Adventist beliefs provides insight into how their social experiences and theological concerns combined and interacted to facilitate exit. In this chapter I have argued that while in ministry expastors' embrace of sources critical of the movement was a symbolic act by which they bypassed existing official channels of information for formulating their own beliefs and utilized resources from the extensive Adventist underground to reinforce their cynicism. This turning away from denominationally sanctioned avenues and preference for negative sources while in ministry is even more pronounced in expastors' social relationships, which are examined in the next chapter.

Chapter 7

Bureaucrats, Scholars, and Friends

Studies on clergy fallout are surprisingly silent on the contribution of significant others in decisions to exit. Much could be learned, however, from tracing the social relationships of leavers about how individuals arrive at decisions to abandon the security of ministry and risk exit. From her study of forty defectors from new religious movements, Jacobs (1989:42) noted that a majority of respondents arrived at decisions to exit as a result of tension-producing relationships. Wright (1987:31–38) found that a "dyadic relationship" was a precipitating factor in a significant number of leavers he surveyed and concluded that attachment to family critical of the movement facilitated defection. This chapter builds on the assumption that in the relative isolation of the sectarian ministry and in an organization with a tight authoritarian structure, pastors developed particularly close friendship ties with other pastors to whom they turned for guidance in matters of theology and on whom they depended for support in difficulty. These relationships were significant in shaping expastors' convictions and attitudes to ministry. The chapter focuses on both the formal and informal associations of expastors and examines the strength of those relationships in ministry and their influence on decisions to exit.

THE ADVENTIST DIVISION OF LABOR

In the Adventist ministry pastors are expected to consult the authorities in all matters pertaining to their work and in particular with questions on theology and interpretation of doctrine. In the previous chapter I noted that expastors were neither forbidden from exploring theological issues nor compelled to read denominationally produced literature. In fact, Adventist pastors were encouraged to "dig deeper" (White 1962:119) while being warned of the pitfalls of independent thought and admonished to trust the authorities for answers. In a meeting with pastors to discuss the ramifications on ministers of what transpired at Glacier View, the Division president advised them, quoting the *Church Manual*, that no individual has "the right to use the pulpit to advocate new light" and that new ideas "should first be presented to the brethren of experience" before being aired in public. The principle outlined by Ellen White is codified in the Adventist *Church Manual*:

> There are a thousand temptations in disguise prepared for any of us who have the light of truth; and the only safety for any of us is in receiving no new doctrine, no new interpretation of the Scriptures, without first submitting it to *the brethren of experience*. Lay it before them in humble, teachable spirit, with earnest prayer; and if they see no light in it, yield to their judgment; for "in the multitude of counsellors there is safety." (1971: 257, my emphasis)

The "brethren" are church administrators who carry the double burden of administering the organization and guarding the Adventist traditions. A cursory survey of the *Seventh-day Adventist Yearbook* reveals that in most Conferences in the South Pacific Division between 1983 and 1985 there was one administrator for every three or four pastors, excluding Union and Division departmental officers and their assistants. There was no shortage of administrators in the Adventist organization to whom pastors could turn for advice. Administrators are appointed by committees, usually for a minimum term of three years, although it has become customary for appointees to continue in administration, and only on rare occasions do they return to previous pastoral duties. If it was not the case during previous generations, then certainly by the 1960s and 1970s appointment to administration was tantamount to promotion, and many pastors saw this as a way of circumventing the demands of parish work. Not surprisingly, appointment to administration was what many pastors sought. Grant, a lecturer in the Division of Religion at the Southern Missionary College in the United States, argues that by the 1980s this view of administration which was underscored by images of the church as a "big business" run by "an intensified *management mentality*," devalued pastoral ministry:

> Administrators are seen as the top power and influence brokers of our structure. Departmental directors are considered necessary to keep the machinery running, but vestiges of a bygone era, who will soon be phased out. The local pastor is the "foot-soldier" lauded in speech and union papers. He is the necessary ally at constituency meetings, but is rarely taken seriously when it comes to deciding policy or theology. Thus for the budding theology student, the pastoral ministry is viewed with disdain as only a jumping-off point to "greater" service. (Grant 1980:63)

In the world of Adventist managerialism, administrators—the men of "experience" who served the church for many years, worked in the mission field and were successful in the art of public evangelism—played a strategic gatekeeping role. As the senior men who were also loyal to the organization and committed to the sectarian cause, administrators provided stability at the upper echelons of the organization by exercising "considerable influence on all major church decisions" (G. Schwartz 1970:188). Pastors advised to discuss their problems and seek the counsel of "the brethren" were required to navigate a system that was both fixed in outlook and conservative in theology.

Expastors recalled being confronted by their Conference presidents regarding their views on doctrine and being reminded that the standard Adventist procedure in matters of theology was to consult the president, who in turn consulted with his Union Conference counterparts, who contacted the appropriate Division departmental men. If the matter was considered worthy of more discussion and study, they in turn communicated with the appropriate General Conference officers and committees (Schwartz 1970:187). At each stage of the process an issue may be rejected and thus terminated or passed on to the next committee for consideration. In this way all "creative endeavours have to run the gauntlet of extensive decision-making bodies" (Sloper and Hill 1985:14).

In the aftermath of Glacier View and Ford's heresy trial, the Division president assured worried readers of the *Australasian Record* (8 September 1980) that while the Adventist organization "is based on a God-ordained, committee representative system, in which it is not possible for one man to take control of the work," it is nevertheless "possible for every member of the church to participate in the church's decisions and its organisation." In reality, however, lay participation at the upper echelons of the movement is minimal (Linden 1978:120). Major policy decisions are usually arrived at by the top levels of organization where church members have only a token presence. In the Adventist order of things, pastors "play a more general conserving role at the periphery" (Theobald 1979:269). Seventh-day Adventism thus resembles Etzioni's (1961:214–215) utilitarian or T-Structure type of organization, which is highly routinized, hierarchical, and authoritarian. In these structures decisions about *means* are left to lower ranked participants, while decisions about *ends* are concentrated at the top. The vertical authoritarian structure depicted in Adventist expastors' accounts is an assembly line, rather than a telephone relay system, in which operations encounter resistance at every junction: few questions filter through to the other end, and fewer answers find their way back.

In such a system the provisions for managing questions of Adventist teaching and criticisms of the organization serve to safeguard the movement against radical change:

Since all doctrinal innovation must gain the acceptance of a religious bureaucracy whose interests lie in theological continuity, it is doubtful that even in times of great stress would this professional hierarchy allow any cognitive resynthesis of traditional ideology to generate a large schismatic body within the church. . . . All decisions about the proper theological response to changing conditions have been thoroughly institutionalized. (Schwartz 1970:187)

The same mechanisms which were aimed at protecting the movement had the consequence of deterring pastors from trusting the authorities. Former pastors familiar with the routines avoided sharing questions with church leaders because they believed that their concerns would not get past the first checkpoint or would get clogged up and lost in the complex machinery of Adventist bureaucracy. Others were cynical of the possibility that theological change could be initiated from below. Half of the expastors interviewed did not anticipate even the collective protests of the mass exodus of pastors to precipitate change. Still others feared the consequences of self-disclosure, noting that Adventist history is replete with stories of ministers who raised their views in committees and were subsequently branded heretics. Two expastors cited the experiences of Louis Were and Robert Greive as examples of men who were pastors one day but labelled heretics the next (Tarling 1981).

CONFERENCE PRESIDENTS AND ADMINISTRATORS

The expectation that troubled pastors would utilize denominationally approved channels of support and discuss problems with those in authority rested on the assumption that the relationship between pastors and administrators was conducive to dialogue and that there was in place an underlying pattern of pastor-administrator sociability. Relative to the importance placed by the authorities on communicating with those in positions of leadership, the interviews with expastors reveal that the social relationship between former pastors and church leaders hindered rather than facilitated communication. Expastors, for instance, rated church administrators low as friends.

In the questionnaire expastors and currently serving Adventist ministers were asked to indicate if they had *close* friends among Conference presidents, administrators, members, pastors, and expastors and whether they sought their guidance with concerns over theology. The survey findings reveal (Table 7.1) that while in ministry three times as many expastors had friends among other pastors (91 percent) and church laity (81 percent) than among administrators up the line— Conference administrators (27 percent) and presidents (31 percent). A higher number of continuing pastors similarly report pastor colleagues (94 percent) and church members (83 percent) among their friends, but many more pastors that expastors list administrators among their close friends. Significantly, two out of every three expastors do not list Conference presidents or church administrators among their friends, a finding echoed in the interview data. Only one of the interviewed expastors refers to his Conference president as a "personal friend," having worked with him on evangelistic campaigns. Expastors depict Conference leaders in negative terms: they are described as "detached," "aloof," "incompetent," "not very bright," "insensitive," and "devious." One Conference president is labelled "dishonest" and "a liar," while a second is angrily dismissed as "a political animal." The interviews indicate that the social relationships between pastors and the authorities were segregated along hierarchical lines. Expastors report feelings of antipathy and distrust in such relationships instead of the reciprocity and confidence that are vital to communication.

Table 7.1
Friendship Network of Expastors and Currently Serving Adventist Ministers

	% Leavers (N = 48)	% Stayers (N = 62)
President	31	48
Administrators	27	37
Other Pastors	91	94
Lay Members	81	83
Expastors	49	59

The relative absence of friendships with those in positions of leadership may be one reason why some pastors fail to continue in ministry. The general impression one gets from accounts is that expastors were socially and relationally removed from those in authority. When we take into consideration that approximately one out of every three expastors with friends in positions of leadership was a second generation minister, then it is evident that these friendships were family linked. Genealogy is important for establishing friendships in the Adventist community and crucial to ministry. This is confirmed by expastors born Adventists, whose friendships with administrators outnumber those of converts four to three. Similarly, twice as many continuing pastors born Adventist (60 percent) had friends among leaders as did converts (34 percent). The absence of close friendship ties with administrators is indicative of a much deeper division between leaders and subordinates in the Adventist community, and this is borne out by the quality of interaction between pastors and administrators.

Expastors describe their meetings with Conference presidents as formal, didactic, and confrontational. They recall being summoned to meet Conference leaders to receive instruction, defend themselves against accusations from church members, or be censured for what they were accused of having said or done. Even with informal social exchanges, social interaction between church leaders and pastors was work-related. The emotional gulf that pervaded the Adventist division of labor affected interaction, reinforced distance, and helped maintain the differential positioning of subordinates and superiors in the Adventist "pecking order." Only one in three expastors discussed their problems with church authorities. The majority (63 percent) turned to their fellow pastors for support.

Expastors present a number of explanations for this division in the Adventist ministry between Conference authorities and pastors. As a general rule the expastors distrusted church leaders. They recalled stories of administrators abusing their power, and of Conference leaders propagating misinformation, breaking confidentiality, being dishonest, and using visiting dignitaries to "spy" on pastors. Irrespective of the accuracy of the claims, the reality is that expastors avoided church leaders and did not trust them with personal or sensitive information. The social and emotional gulf between Conference leaders and those who were led was most apparent in matters of theology. Over half of the expastors mentioned with sarcasm the fact that in the Adventist movement the people authorized to pass judgement on matters of theology were those least qualified to do so. Many church leaders were skilled orators and clever apologists from decades of confrontations with audiences in evangelistic campaigns, but according to expastors were ill equipped to answer questions that required familiarity with ancient languages, expertise in biblical exegesis, and knowledge of recent developments in theology. Expastors declared that church leaders were "Bible illiterates," "out of touch on theology," and "wouldn't have a clue what the issues were," deriding them as "a stupid-looking lot of clowns." If expastors were sceptical that change could eventuate from pastor-initiated talk, they were utterly cynical about the nondemocratic processes church leaders used to shore up doctrine. Expastors adopted a range of strategies to avoid disclosing their thoughts and convictions to church leaders.

At a meeting called by a Conference president to "help me with my questions," one expastor explained that he became defensive and cautious not to "divulge . . . personal thoughts" and states, "I'd been very careful, very diplomatic, and you know, I hadn't put a foot wrong." A second expastor recalled that he "became more and more shrewd and cagey" with church leaders to avoid disclosing personal thoughts. Four expastors avoided answering critical questions by changing the subject. Two "unashamedly" report fabricating answers to conceal their convictions on key theological issues. The atmosphere of hostility that pervaded minister interaction with administration affected expastors' attitudes to ministry. The expastor-administrator avoidance suggests that there is both a historical and a structural dimension to the relationship between bureaucracy and orthodoxy in Seventh-day Adventism. With routinization, sharing with "the brethren" became bureaucratized and depersonalized: the relationships for sectarian orthodoxy thus were relationships established along bureaucratic lines, and, as in any bureaucracy, the *line hierarchy* tended to be subverted by *informal relationships* (Merton 1968:259).

ADVENTIST SCHOLARS

Relative to its numbers Adventism has produced many scholars worldwide who have attained recognition and academic credibility in their respective fields of study (Vande Vere 1972:264). The actual number of such scholars is small, however. In the South Pacific Division between the mid-1960s and mid-1980s only eight individuals carried the scholar tag, and all were associated with the movement's single ministry training facility. Academics receive special mention in the present study because many in the church attribute blame for the clergy fallout to their negative influence. To a conservative church membership which was cliche and slogan riddled and divided over whether the movement should maintain its links with its sectarian past or welcome the possibility of an evangelical future (Teel 1980), the scholars were ambiguously placed. Church members sensitive to the changing social environment were proud of the achievements of Adventist academics, particularly when scholarship was perceived to add credibility to the Adventist cause. Others, intent on preserving the movement's "nineteenth century doctrinal focus" (Butler 1992), were less accommodating and accused scholars of having crossed "local, parochial and provincial lines," "narrowed the gap between the church and the world," and blurred the boundaries that set the movement apart from other denominations (G. R. Knight 1985:37).

Adventist authorities were similarly ambivalent toward scholars. While administrators reluctantly tolerated scholars' control over the minister training program, they maintained rigorous control over the possible spread of alternative views by controlling the processes of appointing pastors to churches. The Conference president ultimately decides who gets a job and where. As well, Conference administrators were able to regulate pastor-scholar contact. Three presidents did this by warning ministerial interns that the theology they acquired at college was "suspect" and not welcomed in their Conferences and instructing them to limit their theological interests to orthodox Adventist concerns. Control over which scholars were invited to what official gatherings, the level of exposure they were to receive, and the subjects on which they were to speak was another means of limiting the potential influence of the academics. The resulting tensions in the Adventist community between sect bureaucrats and scholars parallel the distinctions researchers on organizations make between line administrators and staff specialists. In the same way that line managers perform "jobs that are directly related to the core activities of the organisation" and staff perform jobs that "support the line function" (Vecchio et al. 1992:457; S. P. Robbins 1974), administrators are responsible for the overall running of the church and call the shots on major issues, while the scholars occupy support positions and function in an advisory capacity.

Like some Mormon scholars who feel torn between loyalty to their traditions and intellectual integrity (O'Dea 1957:236), Adventist scholars devised ways of maintaining integrity with Conference authorities while not alienating pastors. One strategy some used was to offset criticism of one set of values with open admiration and defense of another. Others preferred to dissimulate, telling authorities what they wanted to hear, but siding with critics in private. Still others avoided conflict by suppressing their academic concerns and becoming virtual ambassadors and spokespersons for the administration. This was done with noble intentions, reasoning, as Merton (1968:271) does, that "if the intellectual is to play an effective role in putting his knowledge to work, it is increasingly necessary that he become a part of a bureaucratic power-structure." In the climate of hostility and suspicion the exercise of caution by scholars confirmed in the minds of expastors that scholarship and sectarianism did not mix. Adventist historian Anderson (1969:7) notes that "the scholar is the enemy of all tricks, all humbug, all sham, all pretense, all phoniness." The interviews with expastors reveal, however, that the attitudes

Anderson rejects are situationally determined; in certain circumstances the very best scholar is capable of conjuring "tricks." These inconsistencies are at the center of expastor criticism of Adventist scholars. Expastors avoided academics not so much out of disrespect for academia but because scholars were seen to be acting for the bureaucracy.

Of the forty-three expastors interviewed, twenty-seven indicated that their college lecturers played an important part in shaping their emerging theologies. It is worth noting, however, that six were influenced primarily by the scholars' preaching rather than by their teachings, and three others were influenced by the scholars' spiritual devotion. Former pastors were affected more by the personas of the scholars than by their theologies, as is evident in the following responses:

Ford, Patrick, and Lindsay were the bright spots at college . . . these men were willing to share themselves, and were prepared to just come along and say, how are you doing, and taking a personal interest in you.

Men like Ferch, Young, and Jorgenson stand out, but Des Ford stands out as the key figure, most charismatic, most powerful, but above all the conviction that the man had what it takes as a Christian.

Bernie Brinsmead . . . I saw as a man of integrity and a gentle giant. He never ever tried to force his theology on you.

I was impressed with Currie. I saw him as a person who was very congenial; his aim was to win souls and he had this desire to bring people to a relationship with Christ, have them baptized and safely and happily fellowshipping within the growing body of Seventh-day Adventism.

Expastors had only minimal contact with college academics following the completion of their studies, and once in ministry the occasional contact with scholars was restricted to official gatherings. The interviews indicate that expastors did not hanker after input from the academics and scholars do not loom large in exits. Only twelve expastors indicate that they initiated contact with scholars prior to their exit and did so not for instruction in theology but primarily for moral support. Equally significant, six claim that they came away disappointed. The following response is typical of expastor criticism of Adventist scholars:

I looked to the leadership in the church in the form of both the academics as well as the . . . political leaders to provide answers. . . . What was demonstrated very clearly was that the church was not interested in truth. . . . People like Drs X. and Y. came across and started giving answers in gobbledygook, and such extended language no one could understand what they were saying anyway. Privately they tell you one thing and then stand up and say the opposite [in public]. I approached one of the guys a couple of years later and spoke to him . . . and said to him . . . you have a lot to answer for, mate. I said, you know what the issues are, and you have stood by and watched nearly a hundred men leave this church because you didn't have the guts to stand up and say what was right and what was wrong.

This expastor argued that by their silence the scholars perpetuated existing systems of misinformation. Two believe that the silence of the academics was a powerful weapon used by church leaders to quash revisionists and to give legitimacy to traditional sectarian emphases.

What angered the expastors most, however, were attempts by scholars to defend the Adventist position by belittling the questioner. In the following example, the expastor was directed by the Conference president to meet a scholar before deciding to leave the ministry:

I choofed off to see W. . . . He was going to convince me that Adventism was right. Well, I just presented him with my questions but the cunning fellow wouldn't answer my questions. He said . . . first you must decide whether Adventism is right. If you decide that Adventism is wrong, well, then obviously all my answering questions wouldn't matter at all. You first have to decide Adventism is right, and then we can have a look at the questions. Well, that's just totally ridiculous. I said the very reason why I question Adventism is because of these points, these questions, and these are the ones I want answered. Oh, he made excuses because he hadn't unpacked all his books yet, and um, he told me about some fellow, Fletcher, who years ago had left Adventism under similar circumstances, and he said he was a very upright, wonderful looking man, you know, but he saw him some time after he left the church and he said he was, you know, very downcast, and oh, he said, what a shame, and so on. He was trying to make me feel afraid I suppose that something terrible like that would happen to me. It didn't frighten me at all. And, oh yes, another thing he said was that he had done a tremendous amount of study in the Book of Revelation . . . and there were as many interpretations of Revelation as there were interpreters and the only way you could ever arrive at the truth was to let Mrs White decide. I said, this is really wonderful. God wrote a book and he made such a mess of it so he had to send somebody else along to tell everybody what it's all about, you know, how ridiculous can you be.

This account additionally shows that the concerns of some Adventist academics were concealed by the more urgent need to preserve sect values. More frequently, however, refusal to give outright support to troubled pastors was indicative of powerlessness. As one former pastor observed, "I guess . . . I now know where the power base of the church [lies]. It certainly doesn't lie with the teachers, or the theologians or the reformers in the church."

What emerges from this brief overview of expastor references to Adventist scholars is that they played only a minor role in the development of decisions to exit. The scholars' primary impact on expastor thinking was during the four-year ministry training program and featured only symbolically once the expastors commenced on their journey of critical reflection and questioning. The references to scholars in expastor accounts indicate that in the centralized Adventist society church leaders rather than scholars had absolute authority in matters of theology. Insofar as the scholars had an impact on the development of heterodoxy and feature in the process of exit, it was indirectly, through the mediation of informal rather than formal social structures.

FRIENDSHIP NETWORKS

Every organization has an "informal structure" (Selznick 1952:195) or "informal work groups" (Goodrich 1975:37), and churches are no exception. G. Bouma (1992:151) and Blaikie (1979:204–208) observed a general tendency by clergy to develop a network of social support beyond the parish for dealing with their problems. Although expastors' social support networks were located within the broad perimeters of Adventism, they were tangential to the organization; as was noted earlier, the friendships were predominantly with like-minded pastor colleagues and church members rather than with administrators. Salaman (1979:164) argues that rather than reinforce commitment to group values these "informal work groups are more likely to develop and support anti-organisational sentiments and behaviour than to strengthen members' commitment to the organisation." Admittedly not all friendships impacted equally on expastors' thinking. For instance, while church members are rated highly as friends in expastor accounts, they do not appear to have contributed to the expastors' changed outlook. The friendship clusters that had the greatest impact on expastor thinking in ministry were characterized by "inner-cohesion-and-outer-hostility" (Merton 1968:352).

One way of identifying these relationships is by tracking the flow of information and resources among the former pastors. Careful examination of the interview data reveals that the distribution of literature critical of traditional Adventism was an organized and methodical affair. The pattern of circulation discloses an informal and invisible yet effective network of social relationships among the former pastors. The term "network" has become something of an omnibus, according to Bott (1971:319). In the present context the term is used to refer to social and interaction ties that link expastors into recognizable but loosely organized groups. A network of former Adventist pastors is "a circle of friends" (Macionis 1991:182) who have only occasional contact. The concept of "inner-cohesion-and-outer-hostility," which Merton reluctantly endorses because he believes its implied dichotomy does not apply to all social relationships, is appropriate here because it suggests that the informal friendships of expastors nevertheless had cohesion through *shared beliefs* and *common hostilities*. The nuclei of expastors' networks consisted of friendships formed during college training and reinforced with contacts made in ministry. Expastors frequently used a variety of synonyms for these friendships during interview, including, "the guys," "the fellows," and "younger ministers." From these informal friendship clusters expastors drew inspiration for theologies, and during their crises turned to them for support.

Occasions that brought pastors together, such as annual camp meetings (Dick 1977; Goldstone 1983; 1985) and regular ministers meetings strengthened friendship bonds. While only one expastor made up his mind to exit ministry at a camp meeting, twelve others claimed that occasions which brought ministers together were critical junctions in their decisions to exit. Rather than reinforcing commitment to traditional sect values, Conference sponsored get-togethers facilitated exchange of views between ministers critical of the organization. One expastor recalled, "The circle of friends that I was part of were . . . very critically oriented, and so we'd sort of, you know, analyze things and criticize things very openly, and I enjoyed that spirit . . . and I played along with that very much." A second explained that regular contact with a pastor friend helped familiarize him with the issues being debated and contributed to developing his own convictions. The telephone was an important link with other like-minded pastors, as is evident in the following exchange:

PHB:　You mentioned many phone calls.

Expastor:　Yeah, well, we were keeping in touch with one another. . . . The phones were running hot.

PHB:　You kept in touch.

Expastor:　Oh yeah, and it was . . . challenging my theology even more. And I mean it was, that was the stimulation for me. . . . I guess it added a radical touch which possibly wasn't there before. . . . It gave me an added insight into um . . . into um, the questions.

PHB:　What areas in your thinking did these conversations affect?

Expastor:　It added an awareness as to . . . the direction that things were heading. I mean we used to get together and . . . it was a fairly hot gossip line at the time. This was affecting me.

These informal social relations provided former pastors with opportunities to exchange views on doctrinal issues, report on the latest controversies in their neck of the woods and encourage deviating ministers to persevere with their nonconformist convictions. Friendships connected ministers looking for information from the Adventist underground with others who had material to distribute. One expastor who wanted more detailed information on Rea's revelations on Ellen White's plagiarism recalls how a minister friend directed him to "fellows selling their stuff on the black market." To Adventist pastors disillusioned with their work and not willing to discuss problems with church authorities, friendships overcame feelings of isolation by connecting them with the "invisible church" of others asking the same questions and experiencing similar difficulties in ministry.

The association of like-minded ministers was the nerve-center of doctrinal formulation among revisionist pastors. The following responses illustrate some of the ways friendships contributed to the development of expastor theological deviation:

I kept up with all the latest details that were occurring and I mean that was exciting. It certainly was an exciting time. But I didn't know where it was going. . . . C. M. kept me in touch with all of that literature (laughs) which I possibly wouldn't have been in touch with otherwise.

There were a number of us younger ministers that [were] very much in touch. We'd speak about things [going on in the church], discuss issues and pass on the material, underground material, etc.

By means of friendship networks expastors had access to resources that addressed their immediate concerns and satisfied their quest for answers. Informal discussions between friends not only were opportunities to share resources and communicate their views, but also enabled questioning ministers to become acquainted with alternative points of view on the theological debates, which without appropriate tutoring and assistance were difficult to understand. In these groups former pastors found a ready audience with whom to discuss tentative interpretations and test emerging theologies. Moreover, expastors found among their friends others with struggles similar to their own and persons on whom they could role-model. The Ian Peters case study is a graphic depiction of these processes. It also reveals that the theological views that facilitated his exit from ministry were not arrived at by means of "serious" academic research but were the outcome of conclusions formulated in dialogue with Pastor J. A. According to Peters, Pastor J. A. accelerated processes of change that otherwise would have taken much longer to accomplish on his own.

All expastors distributed "underground literature" critical of the Adventist organization and its theology. Four established and operated highly sophisticated systems of distribution. The son of an Adventist pastor explained that he was the main contact for Brinsmead literature during his last two years at college and for a time continued to perform this function in ministry. He claims to have distributed several thousand copies of *Present Truth* over a three-year period. A second transcribed his own sermons and circulated copies to ministers and church members he thought would benefit from such material, and distributed "heaps and heaps of photocopies of Ellen White stuff." When a minister friend gave him an old Gestetner duplicator his literature distribution sideline became a ministry:

I would sit up running this stuff off and stapling it all together. And, actually what I used to do, come to think of it (laughs), I used to post a lot of it to other ministers, to younger ministers whom I thought well, this guy's a bit edgy, you know, he's a bit shaky, so I'll send him the stuff.... The envelopes used to be an inch thick of Ellen White's stuff ... and I'd post it off to them. ... I spent most of my time [in ministry] doing that sort of thing. I figured that most ministers did absolutely nothing anyway, so if I did two-thirds of the time what I wanted to do and one-third of the time what I was expected to be doing, I'd still be doing twice as much as them anyway.

A third recalled that he used to distribute material to friends by mail because "the astronomical phone bills" prohibited this avenue of communication. Literature distribution was a less expensive alternative, with the added advantage that an even greater number of ministers could be reached for less: "I didn't do as much writing as I did sending and receiving photocopied material. Even so, I spent big dollars on photocopying, large amounts. I could have owned a photocopier then."

For one entrepreneurial-minded expastor, literature distribution grew into a relatively successful small business:

I bought a Gestetner and started printing some of Ford's material and I had a lot of young ministers in Australia and New Zealand contacting me for material and I sort of became their major supplier. Together with A. P., G. D., and A. R. we built a program where we were supplying material to fellows in this Division, West Africa, and in Europe. We printed the book that Des and Gil [Ford], wrote called *The Soteriological Implications of the Nature of Christ*. We raised the money and we printed that on Pastor S. M.'s printing press, and he actually agreed to have it done (laughs). . . . Anyway we printed about two thousand copies. We had a friend with a high speed tape copier and we would distribute copies of sermon tapes as well.

Robert Brinsmead encouraged these initiatives and donated "several thousand copies of *Present Truth* which the expastor posted to every Adventist minister he could think of and to about 350 non-Adventist clergymen whose names and addresses he obtained from telephone directories.

The account that follows reveals how friends provided resources for each other and moral support in their search for knowledge. An expastor recalled how another minister in the Conference requested assistance for literature on Adventist doctrinal issues:

P. R. was interesting because we had a couple of talks together [during a ministers' meeting] and he came down home one day specifically to find out if I had stuff that he could read, Ford stuff, you know, the very basic stuff that were [*sic*] sort of relevant three or fours years ago. . . . I said yeah, sure. So he went through all my files and dug it out . . . and took it home to read. He said, I have really not, up to this point of time, grappled with the issues. I've really tried to avoid it. He said that little things had happened and I just can't ignore it any longer. I've got to come to terms with this stuff and know what's it all about. We had a heart to heart talk [and I told him] what I thought about things. I said to him, take this stuff. . . . Don't listen to what I've got to say, take it and read it for yourself and make up your own mind. But I said, you must make up your own mind, you must have an opinion about this stuff, you can't go through ministry without it. So he took it. In a few weeks' time he gave me a phone call and said, look . . . I've been through it all, and he said, I'm just totally done, its totally wrecked me. You know, he said, I just can't see any place for my role in this church. And with that . . . it was a very quick exit, actually in a matter of months he was gone.

The account demonstrates in graphic terms the role friends played in exits from ministry. Expastors with interpersonal or doctrinal problems sought support from like-minded pastors rather than church administrators. Requests for published material on theological issues were occasions for pastors to discuss problems they were having in ministry. The nonthreatening friendship setting was a powerful stimulant for theological change. Not surprisingly, expastors have positive memories of meetings with minister friends. They describe those occasions as "fun occasions," "enjoyable," "dynamic," and "exciting times" from which they got "a real buzz."

One expastor called these occasions the "high points" of ministry. The level of alienation experienced by former pastors is implied by one who is still bitter at the seven years he wasted in ministry, and states that such get-togethers, attended with his wife, were the "highlight of our married life." This chapter has argued that the social distance from leadership facilitated gravitation to pastor friendships and that dissent sprang up in these relationships.

An examination of friends named during the interviews with whom the expastors discussed theology and exchanged experiences in ministry suggests that their informal associations corresponded with Conferences. Figure 7.1 was arrived at by careful analysis of the names mentioned during the interview and depicts the friendship cluster in which Hansford operated. Rowse, according to Hansford, was the leading spokesperson in this cluster of friends. The lines linking the different individuals indicate that Hansford exchanged information with those friends. For example, Hansford had no direct contact with Pastors A. R. and F. B., but knew about them and exchanged information with them through Rowse, who was a close friend of the others. Pastor G. M. was not part of the group but accessed literature available to the group through Hansford. These networks were not self-contained, tightly bounded cells; individual actors had contact with ministers in other Conferences and with some in the same Conference who were "members" of a different cluster. As well, at least four expastors in the present sample appear to have acted independently, and their exits are exceptions to the rule. However, one can conclude with some degree of confidence that there is a direct connection between expastors' networks and exit from ministry.

Figure 7.1
Hansford's Informal Friendship Network

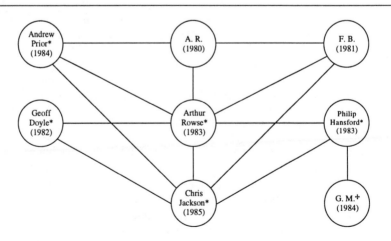

* Interviewed and completed questionnaire
+ Completed questionnaire only

Figure 7.1 additionally shows that attitudes to Adventist theology and ministry ran along friendship lines; the disillusionment and doubts of one former pastor were transmitted to other network members. Each friendship network cluster had at least one person who was central to the group and from whom most members drew inspiration. As the key figure in Peters's network, Pastor Rowse was facilitator to four other exits. These key personalities tended to be senior pastors with greater experience in ministry and elaborate links with other pastors at various levels of the organization. One conclusion we may draw from this analysis is that *exit from the Adventist ministry was a group activity as well as an individual experience.* The cluster effect of the fallout implies that with each subsequent resignation/ dismissal the remaining pastors had even less reason for continuing and experienced an even greater pull to exit.

SUMMARY

Just as in the previous chapter it was observed that expastors underutilized and deliberately circumvented denominationally approved channels for insights on theology, the present chapter showed that expastors turned to like-minded pastor friends for instruction and support in ministry. In this chapter I have argued that the hierarchical organization of the movement both shapes the social world of Adventist ministry and influences the types of social relationships and interactions former pastors experienced with their superiors. The accounts of former pastors indicate that in the Adventist ministry symbolic action and relationships of power stand diametrically opposed to one another and structure socialization, communication and theological interpretation. The theological positions to which former pastors were drawn and which provided the momentum for exit were the manifestation of these structural tensions. The influence of Des Ford on expastors' decisions to exit is examined in the following chapter.

Chapter 8 _____

Charismatic Leadership Versus Bureaucratic Authority

Administrator and lay interpretations of the 1980s attribute the unprecedented fallout from the Adventist ministry in the South Pacific Division to the influence of Desmond Ford, the gifted public speaker and theology lecturer at Avondale College who for more than two decades, until his dismissal in 1980, had dominated theological developments in Australia and New Zealand. Ford concurs with this interpretation. When asked why so many Adventist pastors in this Division left ministry during the 1980s, Ford replied:

Probably because I knew so many of these fellows. You know, the biggest privilege of my life was working with young men at Avondale College [the only institution in Australia for training Adventist pastors]. . . . I think of the years when my wife Gwen was well. We would have whole classes out for a meal. Sometimes we would go to the beach and have a class, you know, all sorts of things like this. I took the boys to the woods for a class, and we would have class as we walked. It was a wonderful time. So I have hundreds of friends among the ministers, hundreds. (Interview, 23 April 1988)

The connection between Ford's activities and pastor fallout, however, is a complicated one, and the simple linear depiction implicit in official and popular accounts ignores the complex processes by means of which the popular teacher-preacher of Avondale became an element in the fallout. Drawing on the interview data and the hundreds of letters and unpublished manuscripts accessed in the course of my research, this chapter examines the nature of Ford's leadership and highlights the politics that developed around his theology. An understanding of the background to Ford's trial and dismissal are essential, and the chapter outlines in some detail the political maneuvers within Adventism leading up to and following Ford's trial at Glacier View. The aim of this chapter is to ascertain in what ways expastors were influenced by Ford and whether their exits can be attributed to his influence.

CONFLICTING OPINIONS

It is difficult to be neutral about Desmond Ford, who is both liked and disliked with equal intensity (Utt 1980a:4). Sympathizers describe him as a "charismatic" and "colourful" personality (Cottrell 1980:21; J. Butler 1980), a "gifted preacher" (Hammill 1992:196), a "brilliant scholar" (Lamp 1980), "a powerful orator . . . and godly Christian" (Chapman 1980). Sympathizing Adventist scholars declare that Ford stands "uniquely among current [Adventist] thinkers" as the man who "championed the cause of the Adventist church over the years" (Thompson 1980). "His years of teaching in Avondale College, his numerous articles and books published by the church, and his participation in the ongoing debate on righteousness by faith, have made him a world figure in Adventist theological circles" (Cottrell 1980:20). These sentiments are echoed by non-Adventist observers. Editorials in *Christianity Today*, for example, described Ford as "a man of great learning and gracious personality" (10 October 1980) and a "brilliant Seventh-day Adventist theologian" (24 October 1980). Even church leaders critical of his theology and ultimately responsible for terminating his ministry describe Ford as "a gifted and charismatic preacher and Bible teacher" (Hammill 1992:183) and "a man of integrity" (Parmenter to Ford, 25 August 1980). Others express puzzlement at his gracious manner and "non-retaliatory nature" (Eastman to Parmenter, 26 September 1980).

At the opposite extreme, Ford's ideological detractors are equally passionate and unreserved in their disapprobation, which abounds in vitriol and apocalyptic. One refers to him as the "Antichrist," "Satan impersonating . . . an angel of light," and "the Omega of apostasy" (Lamp to Lesher, 20 February 1980), thereby equating the popular teacher-preacher with the beastlike forces of evil depicted in the Book of Revelation. The President of the Indiana Conference in the United States denounced Ford as "an enemy of souls" and likened him to "a beast" from within the church, an image derived from the very heart of Adventist apocalyptic (Revelation 13) and calculated to evoke resentment and fear among church members. Others were critical of the fact that a reputable scholar chose to question the biblical foundation of Adventist belief and accused Ford of hypocrisy. Thus in *Victory or Fiasco?*, a pamphlet which received widespread distribution and approval in the Adventist community in Australia and New Zealand, and which at times degenerates into personal attack that borders on defamation, D. Lim (1981) denounced Ford as a "malignant tumour," "a wolf in sheep's clothing," "a first-rate actor," and an "Adventist infidel." One retired evangelist, bitter opponent of Ford, claimed that the thinking of the theology teacher was "bogged down in a sea of theological and so-called scholastic mud." R. Larson (n.d.), the popular Californian pastor, accused Ford of being a producer of "popular fiction," while a group of retired pastors protested Ford's theology, which they dismissed as "verbal gymnastics," "word-trickery," "half-truths," and "ambiguities."

Ford's cheerful courtesy was a further affront to some who believed that his lifestyle was a vehicle to confuse people and promote "heresy." So bewildered were others by what they perceived as being a calculated and deliberate attempt by Ford to destroy the Adventist movement that a rumor was started accusing him of being a Jesuit in disguise. The accusation had a sinister ring to it, echoing Ellen White's (1911:234–235) condemnation of the Catholic order as "the most cruel, unscrupulous, and powerful of all the champions of popery," whose members often "wore a garb of sanctity" to conceal "the most criminal and deadly purposes." These contrasting opinions are indicative of the depth of emotion evoked by Ford and the intensity of debate he generated in the Adventist community. In this climate of extremes, pastors and members, church leaders and non-Adventist observers were obliged to take sides and draw conclusions about Ford.

FORD AS CHARISMATIC LEADER

The personal qualities of the man, his exceptional capacity for recall, clever use of metaphor and analogy, and ability to crystallize complex theological and philosophical issues in simple catch phrases, certainly contributed to his popularity in the Adventist community as a gifted speaker and to his reputation as provocative thinker. According to A. N. Patrick, "Ford was the pillar of Adventist thought in this Division . . . [and] had captured the imagination of Australasian Adventism. He was *the* writer, *the* speaker, *the* scholar par excellence, Mr. Adventism to the nth degree" (Interview, 29 September 1987). Many Adventists viewed Ford's healthy lifestyle, kindly Christian manner, love for Scripture and devotion to the teaching ministry as a personification of Adventist ideals. Pastors were often accused of being Ford clones. Ludowici (Interview, 23 April 1986) mockingly recalls a number of his contemporaries modelling themselves on Ford and mimicking his personal idiosyncrasies:

Des . . . had put a total stamp on the minds of a whole generation of Adventist ministers. . . . I mean we had fellows . . . who even talked like him. . . . He was in fact the father charismatic figure of the trainees. Des was the model pastor-scholar right there on campus. We had fellows who were coming out as interns who wanted to get up at four o'clock in the morning because that's when Des got up, and they've got to have this big meal at breakfast and they've got to be in bed by seven thirty or eight at night because Des did that. . . . Des had stamped his lifestyle on a whole generation of Adventist ministers, there's no doubt about that, his total lifestyle. That's why we had a generation of Adventist [pastors who were] joggers and swimmers. . . . If you wanted to talk with them, they would take you for a walk. That was all Des's influence.

In this sense, Ford is the epitome of Weber's (1948:358–359) charismatic authority—a popular leader with devotees who threaten the security of the established order. However, notwithstanding this limited coincidence with Weber's type, Ford deviates from it in some significant ways. The Ford era was one of prosperity and consolidation for the Adventist community. His activities coincided with a period of institutional development and membership growth. In denominational terms Adventism during the 1960s and 1970s was experiencing a boom (Clapham 1985). Membership worldwide had more than doubled, and sect leaders boasted that the movement was "the most widespread of all Protestant denominations, the largest of all Protestant missionary societies, with the greatest number of missionaries . . . and the most comprehensive single movement to advance the Gospel into all the world" (Oosterwal 1980:1). Australia and New Zealand similarly witnessed a steady membership growth and institutional expansion. The buoyancy of the times was reflected in the unprecedented building program, with upgrading of existing institutional structures, the building of new churches, and the commencement of church schools (Clapham 1985). If the genesis of Ford's activities in the 1960s and 1970s is to be equated with a crisis at all, then it was a crisis "of spiritual identity" (Ford and Ford 1982). The contradiction to which Gaustad (1976) alludes, of a movement which proclaims a millennium in heaven but quietly works at establishing one on earth, highlights the dilemmas of a charismatic sect (B. Wilson 1975:34–43) becoming accommodated to the socioeconomic order of which it is part (Land 1986b; Pearson 1990:277). The delay of the second Advent necessitated a shift of consciousness in the Adventist community, which was now faced with the double task of persuading "the world" that Christ's coming was *still* near and equally important, convincing second and third generation Adventists suffering from apocalyptic burnout of the same. In a sense this was a crisis Ford himself partly generated by questioning the legitimacy of the Adventist interpretation of the prophecies. Ford set out to revitalize a languishing charismatic community that had become bureaucratized. His aim was not to establish a breakaway community or to overthrow the Adventist establishment, but to revive it, although the organization's elite interpreted revitalization as proclaiming its overthrow.

However, it is not so much the intended function but the extent and quality of relationships with followers that distinguish Weber's charismatic leader, and it is on this dimension that Ford as charismatic leader looks a little weaker. Only thirty-one of the forty-three expastors had Ford as a lecturer while training for ministry. The other twelve either predated Ford's years at college, commenced training after Ford moved to the United States, or trained outside of Australia, and thus were not directly influenced by him (Table 8.1). What is noteworthy about these thirty-one expastors, of whom seventeen were raised Adventists and fourteen were converts, is that only a minority (23 percent) report that Ford was a liberalizing influence during ministerial training. Only ten of the thirty-one expastors describe Ford in terms which concur with the claims of critics. One expastor states that Ford "planted the seed" at college that germinated and grew into doubt in ministry. A second explains that "Ford prepared us for the worst" by encouraging students to "go where the evidence leads," even to question the very assumptions on which the Adventist movement was founded. Another reports that Ford made Christianity "exciting and . . . really thrilling" and that his preaching brought "joy" to his faith. A fourth compared the preaching of Ford to "the rebirth of Adventism"; this expastor recalls that the "righteousness by faith emphasis and the whole rediscovery of the Protestant Reformation was like a religious awakening."

Table 8.1
Expastors and the Influence of Ford During Training for Ministry

	Expastors	*Percent*
Ford had minimal or no impact on their thinking	15	35
Ford's teaching helped revitalize Adventism	6	14
Ford provoked questioning of Adventist teaching	7	16
Ford raised initial questions, but Brinsmead's influence led to collapse of Adventist belief	3	7
Did not have Ford as teacher	12	28
Total:	43	100

More important, however, is the fact that only three expastors state that Ford contributed to their rejection of the sectarian world view while at Avondale, but qualify this with the explanation that the Ford issues prompted them to read other critics like Brinsmead, and that it was their reading of Brinsmead that impacted on their Adventist beliefs. According to these expastors, once they read Brinsmead "the Ford stuff was . . . just ho-hum," "a bit watery" and "conservative." One expastor laughed at the accusation that ministers trained by Ford "had idols of Dr. Ford in our living room and bowed to it every day" and explains, "We didn't idolize the man, we just thought that he had a fairly clear message to give." This expastor recalls that toward the end of the four-year training program he was "reading a lot more of what Robert Brinsmead had to say, and, I think some of us had come to the place where we were thinking that perhaps in some areas Dr. Ford didn't go far enough in what he said." The evidence of expastors suggests that the claim that Ford was a radicalizing force is exaggerated. A surprising 49 percent of the expastors taught by Ford reported that the controversial teacher did not disturb their Adventist beliefs but rather revived confidence in the movement. The following responses are typical of the comments of this group of expastors:

Des was there [at Avondale], but all that he was telling us about the gospel didn't mean a thing. . . . I mean, I just didn't see the issues at all. I was quite convinced that we had the truth. I'd been brought up on that, and, you know, never questioned it.

I never really got involved in the Des Ford type of dialectic, you know, it was not something I took up as an enthusiast or as a populist sort of thing. I was more impressed by the scholarly people there, people like Norm Young and Niels-Erik Andreasen, people like that were the people that I thought had the thing sown up. The simplistic sort of, you know, preaching style of Des Ford never really strongly appealed to me.

Being an emotional person, [I was influenced by] the people who vibe emotion and charisma, and Des Ford was certainly there but not primarily from a theological point of view.

In view of the claims of traditionalists, it is quite remarkable that six expastors (14 percent) claim that Ford's teaching actually *reinforced* and *strengthened* their confidence in traditional Adventist teaching. To illustrate his level of conservatism one Ford-trained expastor remarked that the books of Daniel and Revelation in his Bible "fell apart first" because "they were the books . . . used most for giving Bible studies." A similar conservative outlook is evident in the following excerpts from interviews:

I saw myself as an evangelist, and at heart believed that whole religious ferment during those years was God-sent and an evidence of revival. I got involved in street-preaching, and together with the new ideas that were floating around, it affirmed in me strongly that Des Ford was right. I had a personal and emotional conviction about that. . . . I still believed that God was working in Adventism to help it grow up and mature and finally be able to be a missionary church in the way that I understood it. They were exciting days. . . . To me this was the birth of Adventism and I was not about to leave it.

Des Ford, I would have to say, was the one that brought me to a relationship with Jesus Christ, in a way that nobody else had ever done. I hear a lot of people say that Des Ford teaches less on responsibility. . . . In my own experience, I found that the gospel that he presented brought a greater responsibility within me. [Ford] made Christianity exciting, made it into something thrilling, and something that I had never experienced before even though I was brought up an Adventist. I used to sit in his classes and I was like a sponge, just sopping it all up.

The highlight [of my Avondale years] I would have to say was Des Ford, there's no question about that, even though I only had him in my first two years. He was in England during my last two years. I mean, those two classes I had with Des, which were, um, "Life and Teachings" and "Daniel and Revelation" in the first two years were inspirational and ten times more than anything else I had at Avondale as fas as theological training. But that was more on a devotional level than it was on a theological level.

These comments are incongruent with popular claims that attribute the fallout from the Adventist ministry to Ford's influence. Indeed, the above responses also show that while Ford was not traditional in outlook, he was not revolutionary either.

Whereas in Weber's typology charisma is thought of as being volatile but short-lived, Ford's activities extended over two decades, and far from the "irrational" and "emotional" atmosphere typical of *charismania*, his activities were confined to routinized institutional procedures. Ford spoke at meetings to which he was invited, and most often on topics assigned to him by officials. He was an advocate of reform rather than revolution and encouraged ministers and members who shared his convictions wherever possible to persist in the movement and to work to influence change from within. According to one expastor, "Des's idea was to reform the church and to give it new life, and so we all felt, having imbibed his views, we had every reason to call ourselves Adventist, albeit not traditional Adventist. I think we felt a certain solidarity with the Adventist pioneers who had made a break with the traditions of their fathers in order to follow truth as they understood it. So in that regard we were very traditional Adventists." The changes this expastor attributes to Ford's influence amount to a reformation and modification in outlook that approximates *"metanoia"* (Weber 1968:1117). However, the transformations evident in this and some other responses noted above deviate from the ideal type in that the "stripping and welding" functions which Mol (1976:45–49) believes are implicit in the notion of charisma are not evident. Ford did not intend to draw his students down the path of charismatic revolution, nor have them follow him into establishing an alternative "charismatic community" with "definite social structure" and a "charismatic aristocracy" as anticipated by Weber (1968:1111–1119). While in ministry none felt drawn into any *alternative* or parallel charismatic formation. On the contrary, Ford is depicted by six expastors as one who helped deepen religious devotion, reinforced commitment to Adventism, and strengthened resolve to enter ministry. In expastors' accounts Ford is praised for having accomplished well what is expected of all Adventist pastors and teachers.

Only five of the forty-three expastors interviewed linked up with Ford following exit. For a time three met with semi-organized groups of Ford sympathizers, but two became disillusioned with belonging to a community operating on the fringes of Adventism and preoccupied with a belief structure they had rejected. A third continues to maintain contact with Ford but identifies with Baptists with whom he worships regularly. At the time of the interview two expastors were employed by Good News Christian Ministries, the organization set up by Ford and supporters in the United States after his expulsion. Contrary to the claims of Adventist administrators, Ford's organization received only minimal support from expastors.

In many ways, then, Ford is *not* the charismatic leader as typified by Weber: Ford had sympathizers, but no "disciples" in the strict sense of the term; many were moved by Ford's preaching and challenged by his theology, but not to abandon Adventism; some were devoted to him, but for more than two decades devotion did not materialize in the formation of an alternative Adventist community headed by him. In two ways, however, he does seem to have approached the type. First, from the testimonies of expastors, it does appear that Ford developed a charismatic relationship with his students—at least in their perception of him. He was cast as being in special touch with the spiritual font of Adventism; he came to symbolize through his person the Adventist way of life; for some of these expastors at a particular point in their lives to be an Adventist was to be like Ford. Second, based on this charismatic relationship he may be said to have been accorded charismatic *authority*; what Des Ford had to say had special influence because *he* said it. Now, it is in this that there seems to be a germ of insight in the argument that fallout from the ministry is due to a sort of charismatic revolution led and fomented by Des Ford. Only a germ though: the ways in which Ford was not a charismatic leader in the Weberian sense (his working within the organization, his repudiation of secession, etc.) suggest the limitations to the charismatic revolution argument.

NEGATIVE FORCES AND THE LEGITIMATION OF CHARISMA

Theobald contends that in highly institutionalized movements the measure of charismatic success should be gauged not by arguing whether a given leader is or is not charismatic, but by "a detailed analysis of the flow of resources, both material and symbolic, from center to periphery" (Theobald 1978:199). Theobald's claim invites us to focus attention also on the opposition at the centre itself. This perceptive remark suggests that in the process of organizational conflict the center might in effect *construct* a charismatic challenge and set up a charismatic leader in opposition, with or without the presence of a real charismatic leader. The *constructed* charismatic challenge and reactions to it might then become real factors determining organizational outcomes—in this case, pastor exit. This is the possibility that will now be examined. What is argued here is that Ford's opponents at the organizational centers of Adventism effectively constructed him into charismatic leader, and this construction then became an important element in the turmoil of Adventism in the 1980s. The reaction from traditionalist Adventists which grew in tandem and reciprocally with Ford's popularity focused attention on theological issues, forced members and ministers to take sides, and galvanized conservatives into a political force. Ford's notoriety in the Adventist community and the meanings expastors attached to him while in ministry were indicative of and fashioned by these negative reactions to and constructions of him by what might be called an Adventist establishment.

For almost a decade up until his dismissal, Adventist leaders in Australia and New Zealand were preoccupied with fielding questions from conservatives, setting up committees to address issues that Ford raised, and trying to quell conflicts between members and their pastors over the doctrinal issues. In these terms Ford's activity appears charismatic in a sense as suggested by Theobald: a leader at the periphery was setting the agenda for central administrators. In a letter to the Australasian Division secretary (24 August 1981) a group of twenty retired Adventist pastors under the name "Private Action" protested that an "inordinate number of young ministers . . . had either been dismissed or have voluntarily withdrawn from God's work" on account of Ford's preaching. Distressed and angered by this outcome, retired pastors demanded that the administration take definitive action to rid the Division of Ford sympathizers. The retired pastors compared Ford to "a Weet-bix manufacturing machine" that produced a defective product or "seconds." The popular breakfast cereal, which in New Zealand (and to a lesser extent in Australia) outstripped its competitors in popularity and sales, was a major revenue earner for the Adventist-owned Sanitarium Health Food Company. Sanitarium profits subsidize the Adventist work, particularly the church's mission activity in the South Pacific. The analogy of Weet-bix technology is particularly telling. Many an Adventist pastor had worked in the Sanitarium factory situated on the Avondale campus in New South Wales packing Weet-bix to pay college fees and would know firsthand the operation of the Weet-bix oven, how quickly things can go wrong along the production line, and the consequences of malfunctioning machinery. The comparison of training Adventist pastors with the assembly line that produced uniformly shaped and weighted breakfast cereal suggests that diversity and individuality were neither desired nor valued by traditionalists. The accusation that college was manufacturing "reject" pastors and "seconds" was at the same time a criticism that pastors of the 1960s and the 1970s were *qualitatively* different from the traditional pastor type, and Ford was blamed for the difference. To his critics Ford symbolized the changes—theological and social—that threatened sectarian orthodoxy.

There is some justification to the claim that Ford's teaching on a number of themes deviated from the traditional Adventist interpretation, and Ford did not deny this. In his October 27 Forum lecture, which precipitated his heresy trial at Glacier View, Ford claimed that for more than three decades he had held the views on the cleansing of the sanctuary expounded on that occasion. As well, there is evidence that sect leaders knew of Ford's deviation from traditional Adventist interpretation of the sanctuary as early as 1957. In a letter to a New Zealand expastor who was dismissed in 1955 for rejecting Ellen G. White's inspiration, Robert Greive, the former North New Zealand Conference president, who also lost his job over theology, reports being visited by Ford and Pastor Sibley who at the time was the Trans-Tasman Union Conference president. Ford is quoted by Greive to have said that "he did not believe in a two apartment sanctuary in heaven" and that "he did not have to believe it." Greive wrote that Ford tended to "spiritualize E. G. White" and is "so broad in his thinking" that he did not "represent contemporary Adventism." These early references to Ford dating to the 1950s are pertinent because they reinforce Ford's claim of consistency in his theology. Equally as important, they indicate that all along key administrators were familiar with Ford's attitude to Ellen White and the Adventist interpretation of the sanctuary. During the interview Ford reflected on that meeting with Greive and explained that he spoke with Pastor Sibley about his problems with the Adventist interpretation of Daniel 8:14 and the investigative judgement. Ford explains that Sibley advised him to "tell [the students at Avondale] the problems, and just tell them the best that can be done with them." In other words, church authorities tolerated Ford's divergent views as long as he was useful to them as a polemicist to combat critics. The issue, then, is not that in his theology Ford departed from traditional Adventist teaching, but that church leaders who were supportive of Ford in the 1950s and 1960s dismissed him as a heretic in 1980.

THE RECONSTITUTION OF FORD

In a sense it was not so much what Ford said or did, but the way administrators related to him, that helped former pastors see in the destruction of Ford a reflection of their own conflicts with Adventist bureaucracy and frustration in ministry. The administration-traditionalist establishment reaction to what was *constructed by it* as a charismatic challenge had the greatest impact on expastor disillusionment with ministry. Knowledge of the process by which opposition grew from a handful of disgruntled evangelists and retired pastors in the early 1960s to a movement that dominated sect proceedings in the 1970s, gained the support of church leadership, and successfully relabelled Ford a "heretic" in 1980, is useful for an understanding of the role Ford issues played in expastor fallout. Heresy is a social and political construct (Kurtz 1983:1086–1089). Successful application of the "heretic" label entails a contest over authority and power, a process that culminates with public shaming but is prefaced by subtle maneuvers involving redefinition and realignment of relations to institutional power. The stages outlined below are not necessarily mechanical "steps" in the delegitimation of charismatic leaders generally, but descriptive categories of key processes evident in the reconstitution of Ford from hero to heretic.

The identification of Ford with Brinsmead was an important first step in the reconstitution of Ford as deviant. By means of this association with past Adventist heretics, critics were able to harness existing animosities to discredit Ford. Couched in this way, criticism was indirect, subtle, and more effective. Commencing in the early 1960s a minority of vocal but at that time not very influential Adventist personalities began raising questions concerning Ford's theological emphasis and influence over trainee ministers. Protest from traditionalists had been simmering at various levels of the organization for almost a decade (Moore 1980). Clifford and Standish's *Conflicting Concepts of Righteousness by Faith in the Seventh-day Adventist Church* (1976) was an early attempt to voice these concerns in print and is representative of the issues raised by Ford critics. The authors denounced Ford as "dangerous" and "apostate" and condemned his theology as "an aberration of truth." However, at this stage opposition consisted of a minority of retired pastors and some lay extremists, and thus received little support from administration. Their criticisms were often either ignored or dealt with informally. A number of factors, however, helped to galvanize individual protesters into an anti-Ford movement.

According to Bull and Lockhart (1989:74), "the sequence of events that leads from *Questions on Doctrine* to the dismissal of Desmond Ford is a remarkable example of the way in which a web of theological ideas can unravel once a single thread has been cut." Brinsmead's agitation during the 1960s and particularly his theological about-face in 1970 are critical points of intersection in the Ford saga. Robert Brinsmead abandoned theological training in 1958 and was dropped from church membership in 1961 (Wolfgramm 1983; Tarling 1981). Brinsmead reacted to the new-look Adventism which came into being as a result of Adventist dialogue with evangelicals in the United States (Reynolds 1986:185–188; R. W. Schwarz 1979:542–546; Unruh 1977:35–46) and was codified in the 1957 compendium, *Seventh-day Adventists Answer Questions on Doctrine*. The Brinsmead emphasis consisted of a mixture of traditional Adventist teaching which had either been repudiated or played down in *Questions on Doctrine* (for example, that Christ had a sinful nature, and the use of Ellen White's writings) and his own interpretation of the investigative judgement, which highlighted the need for God's people to attain sinlessness prior to the Second Coming. The agitation reached its zenith in the 1960s, during which time Ford was acknowledged as the leading critic of Brinsmead. Ford's emphasis on the Reformation teaching of righteousness by faith was seen as the key teaching for negating perfectionism. However, Ford's critique of Brinsmead was at the same time an indirect criticism of traditional Adventist teachings, which underscored the ideal of perfection (G. Schwartz 1970:102–105). Church authorities tolerated Ford and were prepared to allay criticisms of his teaching as long as he was seen to undermine the legitimacy of Brinsmead (Tarling 1981:186–202). However, Brinsmead's theological turnaround changed all that.

By 1970 Brinsmead "capitulated" to Ford (Paxton 1978:121–145), repudiated perfectionism and embraced the Protestant teaching of justification by faith. These changes, which appeared to bring him closer to mainstream Adventism (Moore 1979:5; Land 1986b:217), had the unintended consequence of simultaneously shifting interest to Ford who was credited with Brinsmead's reversal (R. W. Schwarz, 1979:460). Ford recalls:

When Bob [Brinsmead] recanted of his perfectionism the tempo was increased, perhaps in part it was seen that Bob was following the same heresies that the Bible teacher at Avondale was enunciating in his stress on righteousness by faith. When Brinsmead joined that doubled the threat. Ford had been called Antichrist by respectable evangelist leaders within the Church, men like Pastor Connoly and Pastor Burnside, good old stalwarts of traditionalism who referred to [me] as the Antichrist. So when Brinsmead seemed to be joining the camp which preached the gospel . . . then to many of the concerned brethren the heat was very much increasing. (Interview, 23 April 1988)

Brinsmead's continuing criticism of the Adventist movement for failing to embrace fully the theology of the Protestant reformers now had a Fordian ring to it and raised suspicion in the minds of traditionalists who were charging that "Brinsmead and Ford had linked hands" (Tarling 1981:197). One retired pastor protested that "it [is] impossible to distinguish between the teaching [of Ford] and that of Robert Brinsmead." The "Ford-Brinsmead mateship" (Paxton 1978:128–135; Ford and Ford 1982:22) meant that attacks on Brinsmead now were directed also at Ford (Clifford and Standish 1976:116–117). The same principle of guilt by association was successfully used during Glacier View to discredit Ford by linking him with a host of Adventist "heretics." In a home-printed flier one retired pastor linked Ford with A. F. Ballenger and cited Ellen White's criticism of the latter to legitimize rejection of Ford. In his report on Glacier View, Johnsson (1980), the associate editor of the *Adventist Review*, similarly cast aspersions on Ford by equating him with D. M. Canright, A. F. Ballenger, L. R. Conradi and W. W. Fletcher, onetime pastors who later rejected the "distinctive teaching of the Seventh-day Adventist Church" and were branded heretics, and in this way invoked history and tradition to forecast the fate of Ford.

Ford's close association with Brinsmead fuelled controversy over the credibility of his Adventism and encouraged conservatives to view with suspicion actions and events that otherwise would have been overlooked. Ford's overseas study program is a case in point. His absence from Avondale between 1970 and 1972 to complete a doctoral thesis on apocalyptic under the supervision of Dr F. F. Bruce, professor of biblical criticism and exegesis at the University of Manchester, generated speculation among conservatives who argued that the Avondale College Bible teacher had abandoned Adventism. Ford's decision to seek doctoral supervision from a non-Adventist in order to write a thesis on prophetic interpretation confirmed in the minds of some conservatives that his theology was not Adventist. Moreover, Bruce's remark in the foreword to Ford's commentary on Daniel (1977) that he agreed with and welcomed Ford's "evangelical" focus and interpretation of "the gospel" was taken by many as additional proof of the Avondale lecturer's apostasy. Burnside, the retired Adventist evangelist whom Tarling describes as the "foremost anti-Ford pamphleteer," declared that "Dr Ford has gone to the ranks of our opponents" (Tarling 1981:204). An anonymous mimeographed circular described Ford as a "Doctor of Doubt."

The fact that some college graduates openly questioned Adventist belief and were dividing churches also was cause for concern. By the time Ford returned to Avondale in 1973 the Brinsmead agitation had engulfed the college, and the scene was set for open warfare between traditionalists and revisionists (Tarling 1981:203–221). By mid-1970 Ford critics outnumbered Ford supporters among church authorities, and the anti-Brinsmead/anti-Ford coalition, which had become a lay movement headed by retired pastors, demanded that the college lecturer be called to account for his theology. Convinced that Ford's teaching represented "a radical departure from our fundamental beliefs" (Christensen *Open Letter*, 29 August 1979), conservative pressure groups called on church leaders to weed out the Ford error. *Adventist Observer* (January 1982), issued by a group of conservative Adventists (or "Concerned Brethren") estimated that as many as thirty-five of the forty faculty members at the college were Ford sympathizers. The sentiments expressed in a letter to a theology lecturer at Avondale from a concerned parent echo a widely held belief among conservatives that Ford and Avondale (as a result of Ford's influence) were damaging to the Adventist faith:

I have also seen the harmful effects of [Ford's] new *non*-Adventist theology, particularly with the first two [children], before I woke up. The influence was drastic in undermining their confidence in the Advent message given by God to his people. This cannot be denied and in hundreds of cases young people, once sincere Adventists, have gone home from [Avondale] College with faith in God's message for today undermined, and ready to tell their parents, often ordained pastors, that the old Advent teachings are WRONG.

According to Duncan Eva, a trustee of the Ellen G. White Estate at the General Conference, "Ford tends to present a point of view but not be pastorally sensitive to the results of this." "Ford's views were so divisive that he could not build up the Church" (Hammill 1992:196). Hammill (1992:197) criticized Ford for his lack of pastoral concern and for choosing "uniqueness above the community welfare."

Church authorities thus framed their attacks on Ford as concern for the members. Ford was now the object of double approbium, first because of his links with Brinsmead, and second because he endangered the church. The appointment of conservative administrators and Ford critics to positions of authority during the 1970s helped secure administration-traditionalist control of bureaucratic processes. Ford had freedom to teach and preach as long as he had friends in high places. His downfall, in this sense, was the result of changes in the composition of Adventist bureaucracy.

By the mid-1970s the relabelling of Ford was almost complete; Conference leaders were openly critical of Ford and vocal in expressing concern over his influence in the Division. The anti-Ford lobby had grown into a movement with support at all levels of the administration. One Union Conference president, whom the pastors referred to as "The Ayatollah," is accused of manipulating election processes to appoint like-minded presidents in a number of Conferences in Australia and New Zealand. With the retirement of R. A. Frame and the subsequent appointment of K. S. Parmenter as Division president, Ford critics gained control of key positions in the organization, especially at the very top. Ford explains:

I never would have had this trouble with Brother Frame. Frame was a prince among men. I wrote to Brother Parmenter on one occasion. I said none of your predecessors have been so weak with the opposition as yourself. Don't misunderstand me, I'm not meaning Brother Parmenter was a bad man. But he wasn't a strong man. I said, none of your predecessors had wilted. You're the first one to wilt. I said Naden, Frame, and, who was the one before Naden, the South African man, Clifford, I said none of these men wilted. I said your sons had been in my classes. They know whether I had been pro the best in Adventism or whether I'm out to sabotage. I said, they know the facts. I said, you should know them. Then I gave him a paraphrase of a great English writer, Locke, who said, "The state that circumscribes its men and prevents them thinking, by trying to force them into its own mold, will soon find it has no men of size at all. It will only have diminutive men who can contribute nothing." So I applied this to the church. The church that tries to force its men into a mold of midgets will soon find it has no one who can contribute. But it was this situation in Australia that lent the weight to what happened in Glacier View. (Interview, 23 April 1988)

Ford thus attributes his own downfall to "weak" and unsympathetic leadership.

Intense pressure from conservative groups (Ford 1978:42) forced General Conference and Australian administrators to hold a series of meetings in 1976 to resolve the controversy over whether or not the concept of justification by faith included sanctification. The Palmdale Conference, as it became known, was an early indicator that the theological bias of administration had shifted to the right. Instead of reducing tension, "Palmdale added fuel to the fire of controversy within Adventism" (Paxton 1978:133). While Ford believed that the Palmdale Conference endorsed his view that righteousness by faith includes only justification (Paxton 1978:131), administrator traditionalists argued that it reaffirmed the traditional position. If the Palmdale Conference achieved anything, it was that it took a local Australian conflict and transferred the controversy to the international arena. From this point onwards, General Conference leaders were participants in the debate, openly refuting Ford's teaching. Herbert Douglass's Adult Sabbath School Lesson Pamphlet for the April-June quarter of 1977 was a blatant attack on Ford's teachings on justification by faith. The pamphlet reverberated with perfectionist overtones and argued that Christ had a sinful human nature. Before a Sabbath School audience one pastor tore up the pamphlet in protest, an action that drew immediate condemnation from local Conference authorities.

Ford's relocation to Pacific Union College in California in 1977 was rationalized as an attempt to silence the conservative opposition. Church leaders reasoned that a two-year absence from Australia would appease conservatives and dampen Ford's enthusiasm by exposing him to an Adventist audience more accustomed to the presence of academics in their midst. Ford explains that he accepted the relocation in good faith, with the understanding that he would return to Avondale:

Brother Parmenter, the Division president, had promised me before I left Australia, I was coming back to Avondale. I did not accede to leaving for America until I had that assurance. That was the basis [on which] I left, that I was coming back to Avondale. And I asked Brother Parmenter before I left, now, I understand that if I go I am to return to Avondale. He assured me that was so. But he wrote to me while I was at PUC [Pacific Union College] and said it wouldn't be so. If I was coming back I would not be at Avondale. (Interview, 23 April 1988)

Ford describes his relocation to the United States as his "exile" (Interview, 23 April 1988). The relocation gave him access to an even greater audience (Hammill 1992:184) to promote his views and "to be a nuisance." While in America Ford lectured four days a week and preached for three. He travelled "all over America to ministerial meetings, spoke even to medical men, and [at] College Weeks of Prayer—Loma Linda, La Siera, PUC, Walla Walla, Atlantic Union College—I took Week of Prayer at all of these places." The shift to California extended Ford's influence, but it also weakened his political base. In his absence the Australian administration and conservatives consolidated their domination over all aspects of church life. Retired pastors and other conservatives were greater in number and more vocal in their condemnation of the "new theology," and church pastors were under pressure not to preach on contentious points of theology and to show loyalty to the organization.

Ford's Adventist Forum lecture at Pacific Union College on 27 October 1979 was the catalyst for his heresy trial. The events that followed took Ford by surprise; he did not think his October lecture was so radical as to provoke a heresy trial. "I had been tried before under Frame and under Naden. I had been accused of heresy concerning inspiration and had a court trial under Naden and the thing was wiped because we have enough people within Adventism who are opposed to extreme views on inspiration. And then I had another trial . . . in the days of Brother Frame and we came out of that one OK" (Interview, 23 April 1988). The Palmdale Conference three years earlier may have bolstered his confidence in believing that this too would pass. However, the October lecture differed from previous confrontations in a number of important ways. The Australian churches were in turmoil over Brinsmead's continuing agitation and Walter Rea's revelations of Ellen White's plagiarism. As well, Ford's own indefatigable pursuit of the reformist cause (Cottrell 1980:21) forced the administration, which was already under pressure, to deal with him. The problem "wasn't really so much what was said perhaps, as who said it," according to Ford (Interview, 23 April 1988). The fact that the October lecture came in the wake of Brinsmead's *1844 Re-examined* (1979), in which the author derided 1844 as an "apocalyptic fantasy" and proclaimed that the "gospel is the end of traditional Adventism," strengthened administrator resolve to deal with Ford once and for all. The main difference between this and earlier skirmishes with administration, ultimately, was the issue being debated.

On previous occasions Ford was called to defend his teaching on righteousness by faith, the sinless human nature of Christ, and his position on the subject of perfection, themes which divided a number of Christian denominations over the centuries. Now for the first time Ford attacked in public the central teaching of the sanctuary—the one doctrine that differentiates the Adventist minority from the rest of Protestant Christendom. Church leaders may have tolerated his criticisms of Adventist Christology and soteriology, but his attack of the central pillars of Adventist sectarianism drew prompt response from sect authorities. The "speed and violence" of the reaction of administrators indicates not only that "lines were already drawn" (Utt 1980a:5) but that Ford touched a "raw nerve" in the Adventist psyche (Minnery 1980:76), struck at the movement's "Achilles' heel" (Interview, 23 April 1988), attacked Adventism's "jugular vein." Adams (1993) and Gladson (1992) declare that Ford's message was directed at the Adventist heart: "any hint the investigative judgement harbours theological problems constitutes *a direct attack on the heart of Adventism*" (Gladson 1992:4). Whatever metaphor one employs the message is still the same: Ford tampered with a central "legitimating structure" (Berger 1963:28) which sect members used historically to explain and justify the movement's raison d'etre. In his presentation at the Wahroonga Adventist Church, Parmenter, the Division president, informed church employees that Ford's Forum lecture was "a direct challenge to the fundamental beliefs" of the Adventist Church: "It is not just a peripheral doctrinal matter that is under discussion. . . . We are dealing in this particular issue with fundamental pillars of our church . . . (1) a prophetic message, (2) a prophetic messenger, (3) a prophetic time period" (Parmenter 1980b:3). What transpired at Glacier View was not altogether unexpected. Brinsmead believes that "the administrators had everything cut and dried before they got there" (Wolfgramm 1983:356).

THE DELEGITIMATION OF CHARISMA

Glacier View was the final stage and culmination of Ford's reconstitution. In Weberian terms it signalled "the castration of the charisma" (Weber 1968:1132). Ford was granted six months, leave at the General Conference headquarters to outline his doctrinal position, and a committee was appointed and headed by Richard Hammill, a vice president of the General Conference to assist Ford in presenting a formal statement. The resulting 900-page manuscript, *Daniel 8:14, The Day of Atonement, and the Investigative Judgement* (1980a), was the basis for the Sanctuary Review Committee's deliberations at Glacier View on 10–15 August 1980. From the point of view of traditionalists, the Glacier View meetings could not have been timed better, occurring less than four months after the General Conference Session verified the expanded statement of Adventist beliefs. The ink was barely dry, and Ford's trial at Glacier View was both an early test case and a seal of approval on what some reviewers describe as the Adventist "creed" (R. W. Schwarz 1979:166–167).

Ford was to be tried by a committee of administrators and scholars. The composition of the Sanctuary Review Committee was arrived at with fixed criteria in mind. The occasion provided church leaders with an opportunity to refute Ford's repeated accusation that "the church had never given serious study to the doctrinal problems" concerning the sanctuary (Hammill 1992:192). This was a big committee, signalling that "major doctrinal matters" were being considered. Scholars were present, to answer the charge that Ford was "tried by administrators," an accusation General Conference and Division leaders were keen to dismiss. The committee had to "reflect accurately the thinking of *all* the Church around the world," therefore nine of the ten Division presidents took part in the deliberations and thirty-four participants were from Divisions outside North America. Finally, the committee was to be sufficiently large, because as Hammill (1992:191) explains, church leaders "didn't want it ever to be said that a small group was bottling up major doctrinal issues." According to the General Conference vice president, the "Sanctuary Review Committee represents the most earnest endeavour and the greatest investment in funds and in the time of Adventist workers from all parts of the world field that has ever been given to the discussion of a doctrinal problem in the Adventist Church. The report of the Sanctuary Review Committee deserves more consideration by the Church than it has received" (Hammill 1992:197). Hammill's final sentence is directed at those in positions of authority. In his autobiographical reflections following his retirement, the former General Conference vice president lamented that in the final outcome the deliberations of the Sanctuary Review Committee were overshadowed by the activities of the smaller hand-picked committee of six whose ten-point summary was used to dismiss Ford.

Glacier View certainly had the desired effect on participating authorities (*Ministry,* October 1980:26–27), who spoke approvingly of the "balance of the Committee" (Anderson), the fact that "administrators and theologians" (Smoot) and representatives "from around the world" (Ferch) from "a wide range of backgrounds" (Neall) met to discuss "the Church's historic position on the sanctuary" (Blehm). The American evangelist W. Farag extolled the virtues of the hierarchy, claiming that "freedom of speech" was honored at Glacier View. The expressions participants used to describe the occasion are triumphalist in tone. The meetings were described as "one of the most significant experiences in my life" (Ferch), "a most stimulating experience" (Clark), and a "model for periodic dialogue between church leaders and scholars" (Cassell). One Conference president noted that "the sheer number of Seventh-day Adventist Bible Scholars, New Testament and Old Testament authorities, and worldwide church leaders gathered in one spot was historic, impressive, and thrilling," and doubts "that any subject of Bible truth ever had a more careful or prayerful review" (Blehm).

Seven of the nine participants whose impressions of the Glacier View meetings were published in *Ministry* (October 1980) describe "the remarkable consensus" evident during the deliberations; four highlight the "unprecedented openness" and "freedom of expression." Others make reference to the "love," "mutual trust," and "calm spiritual atmosphere" which five attribute to "the transforming presence of the Holy Spirit." All speak approvingly of church leadership. One participant who came to Glacier View with "anticipation mixed with trepidation" because the issues to be discussed had "the potential to split the Church" went away on a spiritual high after witnessing the "miracle of consensus take place." For Neall, the Glacier View experience was analogous to conversion: "What I experienced this week will affect my teaching methods. I will use authoritarian, lecture-type methods far less, and will involve my students much more in personal and group discovery of truth." All in all, for participants who were granted "immunity" (Ferch) and whose ideas were not on trial and whose careers were not in jeopardy, Glacier View was "a mountain top experience" (J. Butler, 1980) and an occasion of "deep spirituality" during which time "the mind of the church [was turned] to the precious truths that shape the Adventist identity." According to Johnsson (1980), "it was refreshing . . . stimulating . . . [and] reaffirming." The General Conference president saw Glacier View as "an occasion that . . . resulted in great stability for this church" (N. C. Wilson 1980:3).

These acclamations are all the more remarkable in that Glacier View was essentially a *heresy* trial. At the opening meeting the General Conference president informed participants, "A man is not on trial here, only his ideas are" (Ford, Interview, 23 August 1988). Hammill (1992:193), who masterminded the selection of participants, concedes that both were tried at Glacier View. In a letter to the General Conference president, an irate Adventist layman condemned the event as "little more than a thinly veiled heresy trial of Ford." To ensure that the outcome at Glacier View met administrator expectations, the General Conference president, who chaired the meetings, appointed a committee of six to produce an independent critique of Ford's document, which the Sanctuary Review Committee was "explicitly instructed *not* to debate or to vote." Cottrell (1980:21) argues that the ten-point critique of the smaller committee did not reflect a consensus against Ford. In a candid admission Hammill (1992:194) condemned this action as "a serious mistake in tactics" and "an affront" to the members of the Sanctuary Review Committee and dismisses its ten-point summary as an "administration-sponsored report," a "betrayal of Bible scholars," and a reduction of the democratic process to "just window dressing."

For the Australian sect officials the two reports that emanated from Glacier

View were God-sent and were used to serve their double agenda: the ten-point critique to dismiss Ford; the "Consensus Document" of the Sanctuary Review Committee to promote Glacier View to the membership as a breakthrough in the church's teaching on the sanctuary. Glacier View was an attempt to justify an administrative action in theological terms (Butler 1980). In a telephone conversation Duncan Eva explained to A. N. Patrick that the General Conference president's Advisory Committee which produced the ten-point document, "felt Ford should not continue as a minister, not because of doctrine . . . but due to problems of administration." The Ellen G. White Estate Trustee at the General Conference made the remarkable admission that

Des is in some ways a sacrifice as we [the SDA Church] move along. The Colorado statement is quite a modification of the SDA sanctuary doctrine. The consensus statement does move away from some of the stilted and rigid positions we have taken. Ford needs to realize the speed of the convoy is that of the slowest ship. (Patrick, 12 September 1980)

It is an irony, although I would suggest not entirely coincidental given the agenda with which church leaders had been working, that Duncan Eva's depiction of Ford as a sacrifice is derived from the sanctuary typology which lay at the heart of the Glacier View crisis. As sacrificial lamb Ford was offered to atone for the sins of revisionist Adventists who threatened the sectarian foundations.

POST–GLACIER VIEW RITUALS

In the aftermath of Ford's dismissal church leaders went into panic-mode. The post–Glacier View rituals, or what former pastors describe as the "admin-speak," "double talk," "clever footwork," "duck-shoving," together with the "witch hunt" and persecution of Ford sympathizers, confirmed in the minds of expastors not so much the truth of Ford's theology as the fact that the sectarian system had become rigidified in tradition, reactionary to change, and hostile toward reformers. Glacier View participants were eager to attribute blame elsewhere. Hammill, for example, claims that in their haste to dismiss Ford Australian officials acted unwisely, and attributes the controversy provoked by the dismissal to "the ineptitude of the Australasian Division officers" (1992:196). Brinsmead believes that at Glacier View Adventist scholars "proved themselves to be a lot of nincompoops" and "a mob of dead-heads" with "no political acumen": "Adventist academics had proved themselves to be weak-minded, visionless puppets, only fit to be pawns of the all-powerful hierarchy. Hewers of wood and drawers of water" (Wolfgramm 1983:356–357). Cottrell endeavors to absolve scholars of blame with claims that they constituted only a minority of the Review Committee (24 percent) and that a majority of them "acknowledge the same problems in interpreting Daniel and Hebrews to which Ford has called attention." He cites as evidence the results of polls conducted at the beginning and end of the six-day gathering to evaluate the effects of the deliberations on participants (Cottrell 1980:19). On average 23 percent of participants sided with Ford's position, a figure Cottrell believes represents "almost exactly" the proportion of scholars on the Sanctuary Review Committee (Cottrell 1980:26). The General Conference president assured members that church leaders acted "out of a sense of duty to the Lord's work" (N. C. Wilson 1980:66). Brinsmead believes that it was naive of Ford to expect officials to do otherwise: "What Des [Ford] was asking [administrators] to do, was to preside over the disillusionment of Adventism . . . [therefore] they had to make a stand, if they were to preserve the system" (Wolfgramm 1983:356). The dismissal rang like a thunderclap in the Adventist community.

Christianity Today headlined Ford's dismissal as "The Shaking Up of Adventism" (Plowman 1980), thereby echoing Paxton's 1978 prediction. A number of Adventist scholars condemned the outcome as "unjust," "improper," "hostile," and a "misguided reaction of the church apparatus" ("Open Letter," 1980). The maverick former editor of the *Australasian Record* accused church leaders of trying to "out-papacy the papacy in dogma." In a post–Glacier View rage one Adventist scholar claimed, "Takoma Park [the Adventist headquarters in the United States] is the Vatican and administration officials are the Italian Curia" (quoted in Plowman 1980). These references to the Roman Catholic Church highlight a perceived contradiction that Adventism was doing to its reformers what they accuse the Catholics of doing to theirs. In a letter to the Division president, one Adventist layman protested: "In the world of science such administrative action would demand an open inquiry. In our church, administration hope for silence. It will not come! We the laity are also the church and members of the body of Christ and are not satisfied at this time and we will not be until Dr Ford is reinstated. . . . We will not sleep from now on." Another chastises the movement claiming that "the arena of Adventism is strewn with the bones of those who dared to argue." Tarling (1981:234) drew a parallel with Orwell's *Animal Farm*, equating Ford with the condemned Snowball, and asks, "Will we now be subject to endless propaganda telling us that you knew that [Ford] was never really straight? That he did this, and he did that? . . . When will the purge come? [Will] everyone in the work be forced to sign a document? Everybody on the *Verdict* mailing list held suspect?"

Church leaders launched an elaborate campaign to shore up support for their actions. Officials at Union and Division levels and selected academics met with ministers in all Australian and New Zealand conferences to justify Ford's dismissal and to promote the traditional emphasis. The meetings, which were derided as "propaganda sessions," proved counterproductive with some expastors. One expastor made up his mind to exit at one such gathering. What is surprising about administrators' actions following Glacier View is their refusal to allow the Ford controversy to abate. Sabbath School quarterly pamphlets, which members are encouraged to study daily and which form the basis of group discussion on Saturday mornings, deliberately focused on doctrines unique to Adventism and on those books of the Bible and passages central to the Ford controversy. Pastors still recovering from the shock of Ford's dismissal who were uncertain as to where they stood on the theological issues had to reenact the drama each week in Sabbath School. Copies of L. R. Walton's *Omega* (1981), which was in its third printing in its first year of publication and which Johnston (1981:57) describes as a "mischievous little book," were distributed to church employees free of charge. The book, based on Ellen White's cryptic comments regarding the "alpha" and "omega" of heresy, presents an end-time crisis in which persons and ideas critical of traditional sect teaching are portrayed as motivated by demonic forces out to destroy the Adventist movement. The author called for "the unsheathing of the sword against the heretics in our midst." According to Johnston (1981:53), the book's appeal was to "fatigued Adventists" who lost the nerve to fight the bureaucracy. *Omega* targeted Ford and "everyone else not in sympathy with the perfectionist wing of Adventism . . . reflective thinkers and scholars . . . [and] all would-be reformers of the denomination's structure." One expastor who while still in ministry reviewed the book and distributed his critique to parishioners was censured by his Conference president:

The membership of the church up to this time have been informed by the church that *Omega* is a book that they should read. The fact that it was printed in one of our Publishing Houses means that it comes with recommendation. It certainly is confusing to individuals if on one hand the book is recommended in the Sabbath School pamphlet advertisement, but someone such as the pastor of the church states that it is full of inaccuracies and has a false premise as its base. . . . [As] far as your evaluation of *Omega* is concerned, I need to point out that this should have been submitted to the author, the publishing house, or to an administrative committee of the church before it was given to others.

This was one of a series of clashes with authorities which culminated with this pastor's exit. During the 1980 Andrews University summer school held at Avondale College one Adventist scholar commented that Ford's Forum lecture was a "windfall" for the conservative cause and predicted that administrator-traditionalists would use the occasion to return the Seventh-day Adventist Church to its pre-1950 sectarian focus. Neither he nor the pastors present on that occasion, many of whom have since left ministry, anticipated the intensity and ferocity of the backlash or the passion and anger with which church authorities threw themselves into the task of purging the Adventist community of Ford's influence. Glacier View formally endorsed Ford's heretic status and informally sealed his charismatic leadership. For the expastors, the post–Glacier View ritual purge of Ford supporters facilitated the mystification of the man both as victim and villain and stigmatized his supporters.

CLEANSING THE ADVENTIST SANCTUARY

The dismissal of Ford empowered administrator traditionalists to seek out and eliminate revisionist pastors. The General Conference president assured readers of *Spectrum* that the Ford dismissal would not degenerate into a witch hunt:

I have every reason to believe that the administrators of the church will deal patiently and sympathetically with ministers who have questions about some Adventist doctrines and are searching for answers in the Scriptures. We do not believe it is Christian nor morally just to condemn or assign guilt by association. We do not want individuals to be held suspect simply because they are friends of or sympathetic with someone such as Dr Ford, or because an individual might even have similar concerns. . . . The church is not embarking on a hunting expedition to find pastors who teach variant doctrines. (N. C. Wilson 1980:67)

Duncan Eva similarly informed Patrick that he "did not feel Ford's dismissal will precipitate a long series of dismissals." To allay Patrick's fears, Eva informed him that "many hold opinions similar to Ford, [e.g.], not finding the investigative judgment in Daniel" (Patrick, 1980c). In spite of these claims, however, Australian and New Zealand officials launched a coordinated plan to identify and remove deviating pastors. Expastors believe that the purging of nonconformist pastors in Australia and New Zealand was an intentional and planned program orchestrated by Division hierocrats, coordinated by Union extremists, and carried out by local Conference administrator zealots keen to win the approval of their superiors.

This belief is borne out in the correspondence between Conference leaders. At the request of Division and Union officers, local presidents produced biographical sketches of pastors and teachers who resigned or were dismissed, or who they believed were on the verge of exiting. One copy of their compilation was deposited at the Division Office and additional copies were distributed to the respective presidents. One such report, the *Trans-Tasman Union Conference: Ministers and Teachers Who Have Resigned or Been Asked to Stand Down* (1982), listed eighteen pastors and four teachers who resigned or were dismissed. Many currently serving pastors believe that there was an intentional purging of nonconformists. This view is reflected in the following response from one senior church pastor, who requested anonymity:

There has been a purposeful purging of Ford sympathizers. In my opinion Tolhurst is the main instigator, aided by Parmenter and Taylor. . . . Tolhurst was heard to say outside someone's office in the Division recently, "We've cleaned out the ministry, and now we're cleaning out the teachers." This boast, of course, doesn't take into account those who have gone to ground and continue to work in the denomination. I believe many young men who held to Ford's basic ideas were prepared to stay in and could handle the disparity of theological differences but were disgusted with the administrative style. They observed there was no caring concern for the ministers—an obvious lack of basic Christianity, and they had doubts, understandably, whether or not the SDA church was even Christian.

The post–Glacier View purge is analogous to Durkheim's (1976:309–315) "negative rites" in which the infliction of pain is similarly thought to confer positive effects on the group. At official gatherings pastors would often joke among themselves at the way local Conference administrators embraced the harshest Union directives to win the approval of their superiors.

Non-Adventist observers saw the issues primarily in terms of theology, restricting the problem to academics and thus underestimating the true extent of the conflict. A report in *Christianity Today* limited the troubles to "a few [Adventist] theologians" (Minnery 1980:76–77). Those in positions of authority played down the extent of the problem so as not to alarm "the little people of the church." In a letter to one Ford sympathizer the newly appointed conservative editor of the *Record* claimed that the agitation was the work of "a fractionally tiny segment" of the Adventist population in the South Pacific Division. The General Conference president (N. C. Wilson 1980:8) assured readers of *Adventist Review* that "in spite of what some would have you believe, there is no internal upheaval or major crisis in the Seventh-day Adventist Church. This is God's Church, and He has made Himself responsible for its success. There is no reason to become alarmed, unnerved, or panicky." Others argued that the Ford conflict had reached a "crisis" (Ratzlaff 1981) of "calamity" proportions (Suessenbach 1980/1981:37). A report in the *Adventist Observer* (January 1982, no. 2) argued that one out of every four Adventists "espouse Fordian views." Conservatives saw in this figure legitimate grounds for immediate intervention and called on officials to identify and "sack" deviating pastors (Marks [n.d.]). Patrick's calculations were more conservative but equally disheartening. He believed that only 20 percent of the Adventists in the South Pacific Division were affected by the issues—"10 percent on either side of the two extremes" (Patrick 1980b)—but points out that relative to the Adventist population this percentage amounts to "thousands" of Adventists. Whatever the actual figures, the Ford issue was no longer a matter of doctrinal interpretation limited to one particular group of belligerent pastors. Officials had a job on their hands to contain the growing disaffection. In a letter to a friend a pastor states, "The situation has become more than one man disturbing the system. . . . It is a church problem not a Des Ford problem." He further expressed fear that the Ford issue had the potential to "disintegrate . . . the church."

The repercussions of Glacier View affected the church membership and the Adventist economy. Members disillusioned by the issues were leaving in large numbers. Between 1980 and 1985 in one Conference of approximately 7,000 members, 1,158 persons were reported as "apostasies and missing members," a figure equivalent to 16 percent of the Conference's 1985 membership. The loss was particularly visible in major cities, where previously flourishing Adventist communities were emptied and reduced to handfuls of aged members struggling to keep their churches viable. As well, accessions were on the decline. One Union Conference president attributed the low baptismal figures for 1981—"the lowest for the last twenty years"—to rampant theological error, and called on Conference leaders to "encourage our workforce even more energetically" in their responsibility to win converts, but was not optimistic of success: "There are numerous workers who would rather do anything else but visit non-Adventists in their homes, and open up those homes for Bible studies. Such men need earnest counselling by their President, so that they get a few things very clear in mind. Usually these are the men who cry the loudest when we talk about baptismal aims, and it is not difficult to find out which men in our Conference need to be encouraged toward greater soul-winning." A flow-on effect of the high apostasy rate was a corresponding loss of tithe and weekly offering.

One Conference reported "a 22.84 percent decrease in conference tithe" in 1983. When told by officials that their local pastor was under investigation, one local church board threatened the Conference by highlighting the economic consequences of their actions: "If the Administration finds it necessary to crush those who differ, we shall have no alternative but to allocate our tithe for 1982 through other than the regular channels." The commencement of Ford's Good News Unlimited in 1982 was another factor eating away at the economic foundation of the movement. The Trans-Tasman Union Conference president was informed that at least two church members made wills benefiting Ford's organization despite the fact that the Trust Services representative "tried admirably to steer [them] away." The president noted that "these jolly [Ford] rebels are making inroads" and acknowledged that pressure was on administrators to act.

In this climate of suspicion church employees openly critical of the bureaucracy became targets of administrator rage. Academics, for instance, were expected not to air private opinions in public and were instructed to promote the traditional theological interpretations. During a visit to one Conference to meet with pastors, the curator of the Ellen G. White/SDA Research Centre at Avondale College was approached by a number of Adventist pastors troubled with the Ford sacking and uncertain of their future in ministry. Acting on reports of the visit, Union and Conference presidents demanded that Patrick explain rumors of a statement he made to the effect that "if we eliminate Des at this time, we will precipitate a crisis that will progressively rob our administrators of the confidence of thousands of very loyal and committed members." Patrick was "deeply concerned about both the attitudes and the anguish" of pastors and telephoned one minister and former student to encourage him to persevere in ministry. He explained to the Union Conference president that "this was a minimal exercize of one's Christianity if one knows a person is discouraged and might be aided by such an action." The local Conference president reported to the Division secretary that in his meetings Patrick "did not come through as *strongly* supportive of the decision taken at the Colorado meetings and . . . on the related theological issues." The Division authorities demanded that Patrick confirm whether he made the prediction that "within five years all of Doctor Ford's theology will be accepted by this Division." The exchange illustrates how avenues of support were closed to troubled pastors and made it difficult for them to obtain "honest" answers.

With the increased agitation, administrator attention gravitated to the pastors—the footsoldiers of the Conference. Local pastors, as mediators between bureaucracy and the laity, were required to keep the local church operating in the face of massive unrest, continue their evangelistic programs as if the church were problem free, answer questions on doctrine on the very same issues the Sanctuary Review Committee had difficulty reaching consensus, and preach on Sabbath mornings with vigor and conviction on themes hotly debated within the church and guaranteed to generate conflict. Some pastors were still in shock with the outcome at Glacier View and needed time to organize their thoughts on the issues. Most were illequipped to address the technical questions being asked at local church level. Administrators demanded unconditional loyalty from pastors both in word and in deed, especially on the points of doctrine Ford questioned. In his sermon before a large Adventist audience, one Conference official repeated *eleven times* the point that if local pastors "didn't agree entirely with the church on the sanctuary doctrine they should hand in their credentials."

There is a monotonous similarity in the way conflict erupted in Conferences. Confrontation with suspected Ford sympathizers and belligerent pastors often coincided with or was precipitated by visits from Union and Division bureaucrats and occurred during official gatherings at which higher level administrators were present. In each Conference key persons in pastor networks, often newcomers to ministry, were targeted and called to meet with the president or an appointee to discuss their "problems" in confidence. In one Conference three pastors who confided in their president were subsequently declared ineligible for membership on the Executive Committee. In another Conference, ministers who went to their Conference president with their problems were afterwards "asked to seek other forms of employment." In the latter case the President legitimated his action with the claim, "This is not a witch hunt . . . but a sincere and honest attempt to bring unity and loyalty." In a third Conference, a pastor was presented with a "list of questions" to be "answered briefly and concisely." The pastor's colleague protested that "even Dr Ford did not have to go and answer a set of questions like this." This pastor and two friends resigned from ministry soon after the dismissal of the colleague. The impact of the interrogations on the then pastors may be gauged by the comments of one disheartened minister who informed his president that even though he "loved the work," "longed to be a better pastor," and "had given himself to that calling," "ministry has lost its shine for me . . . and I doubt if it can ever be the same again."

The administration's obsession with heresy and heretics issued in new structures of control and vigilance. A Union evangelist acted as informant and warned the Union president of the "very grave situation" concerning sixteen ministers who met with Ford during one of his speaking visits in Australia, adding: "I am concerned that unless we give almost immediate assistance, at the end of the year when this fellow [Ford] comes out [again], it is going to be too late. . . . I think we are going to lose a huge number here in Sydney." He advised his subordinates to be on the lookout for ministers who "met with Doctor Ford in privately-held groups." A file belonging to one Conference president accessed in the course of the present research contained more than two hundred pages of correspondence and transcripts of telephone conversations with ministers, administrators, and lay people reporting on suspected Ford sympathizers.

The "negative rituals" were intended as deterrents to deviating pastors. Among the authorities up the line, the persecution of nonconforming pastors was viewed as devotion to the sectarian cause: to identify and expel the heretic was synonymous with serving God and being committed to the Adventist cause. The rooting out of deviant pastors had become a mission and an integral part of bureaucratic function. In a circular addressed to Conference leaders, one Union Conference president noted that "the work of our Church will never be finished until such times as we are able to restore in the ranks of the ministry a confidence in the distinctive messages of the Seventh-day Adventist Church." The destruction of the bureaucratically constructed charismatic leader thus also provided the legitimacy for the elimination of the bureaucratically constructed charismatic following. What was dismissed by N. C. Wilson as "immoral" and "unchristian" among American Adventists—the elimination of nonconforming pastors—was justified, sanctified, and glorified in Australia by bureaucratic elites.

REPRESENTATIONS OF FORD IN EXPASTORS' ACCOUNTS

It should be clear now that the bureaucracy constructed a charismatic heretic out of the popular preacher-teacher. Administrator elites preoccupied with preserving traditional sect values transposed Ford's competence into the heretic's cunning and his previous devotion into a cloak for deviation. The superlatives noted at the commencement of this chapter are indicative of this process; supporters and detractors saw in the abstracted Ford a representation of their own social and theological biases. Eleven of the forty-three expastors interviewed were adamant that their exit from ministry should not be seen as a protest to Ford's dismissal:

I didn't resign as a protest to Des Ford's dismissal.

[The] Ford thing helped, but it wasn't crucial.

I was not committed to Ford as such, and I sort of couldn't stomach his ideas.

[Ford's dismissal] didn't send me out. That I'm definite on.

I've never had any strong personal affinity with Ford's style or intentions.

I hadn't any great affections for Des Ford. . . . I wasn't a real follower of Des.

I always regarded Des Ford as a gentleman and a scholar . . . [but] it was not his dismissal . . . that affected me.

At the same time, however, they do not overlook the importance of Ford as a factor in their exit. The images of him in accounts highlight the ways in which the Ford issues featured in their experiences of leaving ministry.

All expastors were affected to some extent by the Ford dismissal, and this is evidenced by the "sense of bereavement" in expressions expastors used to describe Glacier View and its aftermath. One expastor found what was happening to Ford at Glacier View "sad to watch." Another states that the news of Ford's dismissal left him "lost for words." Others were "saddened," "shocked," "sickened," "disgusted," "pained," and "devastated" by Ford's sacking. Thirty-five of the forty-three expastors expressed strong feelings on the Ford issue during the interview. When asked whether Ford contributed to his exit, one expastor explained: "What was happening to Ford really was of little interest to me because I was more concerned with what was happening to me. I mean I just saw [Ford's dismissal] as symptomatic of the whole pathetic attitude in a way. It's just all small-mindedness." The difference between Ford's conflict with the administration and the expastors' own conflicts was not one of degree but of public interest. Ford's conflict had a bigger audience. Retaliation against deviating pastors was the same in type, but in its excecution was more emotional, more intense, and more violent than Ford's. Expastors drew strength from this similarity; Ford became the role model for expastors' victimisation.

In expastor accounts the expulsion of Ford is a symbol that carries a multiplicity of meanings. Representations of Ford in accounts are snapshots both of the ways expastors viewed the charismatic leader and what they thought of sect bureaucrats. The references to Ford are grouped into four broad categories: Ford as Bible teacher and reformer; as freedom fighter; as victim of bureaucracy; and as Christian gentleman. Accounts are not hard-edged, so at times expastor descriptions coded under one category incorporate elements of other categories. The images of Ford in expastors' accounts are indicators of the connections expastors draw between their own experience of leaving and Ford's dismissal.

Ford as Bible Scholar and Reformer

Nine expastors attribute their exit to problems arising over their theology which, they state, was influenced by Ford. Four of this group of expastors began ministry conservative in outlook but were challenged by events in their own ministries to study the Ford issues. Eight were born and raised Adventists, while the ninth converted to Adventism as a young adult, married the daughter of an Adventist pastor, and was fully socialized into the Adventist world. This group of expastors are the *true* believers who looked to Ford as their role model in ministry and guide in theology. To them Ford is Adventist reformer *par excellence,* and having identified with his theology they similarly viewed their own ministries in reformist terms. Like Ford, their mission was to enlighten and liberate Adventists trapped inside a nineteenth-century sectarian doctrinal shell. Their preaching was dominated by evangelical concerns and preoccupied with promoting those teachings Adventists hold in common with other Christians. This group of expastors equated evangelical Adventism with the birth of a "new Adventism" or the rebirth of the "old." The tension between reformism and sectarianism is evident in their responses to Ford's dismissal:

[Ford] brought hope where traditional Adventism had only brought condemnation and fear. . . . Des's idea was to reform the church and to give it new life, and so we all felt, having imbibed his views, we had every reason to call ourselves Adventist, albeit not traditional

Adventists. . . . It was sad to watch [what went on at] Glacier View, and yet my feeling was that if the Adventist Church was as intolerant as it was, then he was better off away from it for his own development. . . . I felt [Ford's dismissal] was Adventism's loss, but hopefully the gain of the non-Adventist world.

When I heard about Ford's dismissal I was devastated. . . . I really couldn't believe it. . . . I was bleeding from within. . . . I thought there's no life in the system now.

I never was one of [Ford's] devoted disciples . . . [but his dismissal] turned me from being a most devoted Adventist into um, you know, I started to question the whole thing, starting with 1844, little realizing that once you question that the whole thing will come down.

When the Ford issue exploded . . . I started to have serious questions, and then I looked at the leadership of the church in the form of both the academics as well as ah, the political leaders. And whereas Glacier View should have been an answer, what was demonstrated very clearly there was that the church was not interested in truth, that was all I could say, this church is not honest, it's no different to the JWs [Jehovah's Witnesses].

According to these expastors, Glacier View signalled the sect's rejection of its leading evangelical spokesperson and a repudiation of central Protestant Christian values. As one expastor states, "The church had crucified one of its greatest assets."

Ford as Freedom Fighter

In a *Christianity Today* report Hammill is quoted claiming that Adventism grants all members the right to be heard on all issues and that "the church has a history of being gentle with its creative people" (Plowman 1980). Hammill's remarks sought to portray Glacier View in positive terms, as an expression of Adventist tolerance of religious diversity. The following responses from expastors highlight the opposite:

Ford's dismissal wasn't crucial [to my exit]. In fact I think Ford's just a Seventh-day Adventist, but he's a jolly good Seventh-day Adventist. . . . I admire him not for his belief system but the fact that he would stand up for what he believed in. I didn't like what he believed in. I think he was way out [on some things], but I admired a man who'll stand up for what he believed in, but I saw so many [in the church] who didn't. They were too busy ladder climbing [for promotion].

When they kicked Ford out, it very quickly became apparent to me that there was no more openness really, that [Glacier View] was just a bit of cosmetic stuff. And that was sad, that was very saddening news, and it was a matter of six months basically that um, you know, we both realized that we made the decision that we cannot survive, that we cannot live in the pretense of the Adventist ministry.

Six expastors viewed Ford as the champion of religious freedom. However, it was not so much what Ford said as the fact that he dared to question the establishment that impacted most on the following two respondents:

Des's fairly courageous response at the time resulted in giving many of us permission to maybe name the kind of things that were stirring within. I would say that while it has been a painful road and at times an extremely difficult and painful process to emerge, that has not been negative either. . . . Whatever the dark clouds of Des's activities were, whatever he did to undermine or smash the chains of immature Adventism, for many of us . . . it has become liberty. We have grown up. I would have to say "thanks Des, for nudging some of us to the point where we too were able to make that decision."

I was pained [by the fact] that someone I knew to be a man . . . who should be valued by the church was kicked out. That pained me. But [Ford's dismissal] was significant in the sense that he'd questioned the church but had not been struck down. That gave me some support for my own personal questioning.

More than half of the interviewed expastors reported feeling liberated once they left ministry, but six expastors actually depict Ford as a symbol of liberation. What is more important is that with one exception these expastors were themselves accused of heresy and underwent a process similar to Ford's, including public shaming followed by expulsion. They viewed their own exit from ministry as a continuation of Ford's trials and in this way retrospectively posit Glacier View with feelings stemming from their own experiences of exit.

Ford as Victim of Bureaucracy

In the overwhelming majority of cases the Ford dismissal provided expastors with an opportunity to assess and redress their own hurts in ministry and their attitudes to Adventist bureaucracy. Almost two out of every three expastors (63 percent) interviewed reported that the Ford crisis was an insight into the bureaucratic foundation of Adventist sectarianism.

I was annoyed at [Ford's] dismissal and I saw it as a symptom . . . of a blinkered [and] narrow [Adventist mentality]. We have an institution here [so] don't rock the boat. . . . Dismissing Ford was one of their many mistakes.

What was more a catalyst for me to exit was the [bureaucracy's] approach to the issues that Ford raised.

I could live with the theological issues but I couldn't live with the way the [administrators] had treated Ford and were treating me and others.

Even though I hadn't any great affections for Des Ford. . . . I was angry [at the way issues were] swept under the carpet. . . . [This was a form of] control by the administration . . . and I didn't like that. . . . I'd been brought up [among administrators] and I knew all their stupid lying.

It was not his dismissal but the attitude of the hierarchy . . . that affected me. I still believe that men in the administration are liars.

[Glacier View helped me see] where the power base of the church lay. It certainly didn't lie with the teachers or the theologians or the reformers of the church.

Expastors claim that Glacier View presented them with an X-ray image of sect mechanisms of social control, including the processes of manipulation, exploitation and deception utilized by the authorities to ensure the perpetuity of the sectarian system. One expastor claims that he could cope with theological ignorance, "but I simply couldn't rationalize what I saw them doing with Christianity." Approximately one out of every three cases in which the Ford issues dominate highlight disillusionment with sect bureaucracy as the critical factor leading to exit.

Ford as Christian Gentleman

Whereas for most expastors Glacier View highlighted political processes central to sect bureaucracy, for others, the focus was on the virtues of its central actor. That the "heretic" maintained his integrity, was not bitter, did not cast aspersions on the moral values of his accusers, and remained unashamedly "Christian" throughout his public trial was an indictment of Adventist bureaucracy in the view of nine expastors.

Des had credibility around the Division and around the world. . . . He wasn't bitter [at the outcome of Glacier View], and still isn't. His critics are far more bitter than he is. Des stands head and shoulders above them all, although I disagree with a lot of what Des says.

[The dismissal] was a real shock. I felt that, um, Seventh-day Adventism was for Christians, and um, I didn't consider that Doctor Ford had suddenly changed from being a Christian. . . . [The dismissal] was a terrible shock to me . . . um, and that's when I felt that we were started to go wrong as a church.

Pastor H. actually attacked Ford personally. I mean, he didn't attack him on his theology . . . he not only disagreed with Ford in his theology, but actually implied, um, things about Ford's moral standards . . . without actually saying what he meant. . . . He didn't lower my view of Des Ford but he certainly lowered my view of himself.

Their treatment [of Ford] was to me a total rejection of basic Christian principles. It was a total denial of that.

Eight of the nine expastors who depict Ford as Christian gentleman resigned from ministry voluntarily while the ninth was coerced into resigning. It was not loss of confidence in the Adventist doctrines that led these expastors to exit, but loss of confidence in the Christianity of the Adventist bureaucrats. The attitudes of the "heretic" are thus depicted as more honorable than the "virtues" of sectarian orthodoxy. Two expastors in this category state that they left ministry for the sake of their Christianity.

The representations of Ford in expastor accounts are double-edged and cut both ways. The image of Ford as "Bible scholar" is at the same time a critique of the credibility of the biblical foundation of Adventist theology. The "freedom fighter" contrasts the outlook of Ford and sect preoccupation with protecting the rigid fundamentalist perimeters of sectarianism. The image of Ford as "victim of bureaucracy" contrasts sect bureaucracy with Ford as "hero of evangelical Christianity." Whereas the first three images are critical of the Adventist division of labor and its domination by a minority of powerful elites, the final image calls into question the Christianity of its leading advocates. The post–Glacier View politics and the accompanying witch hunt rituals had the greatest negative impact on expastor outlook. In this case the actions of the parties involved spoke louder than their words.

SUMMARY

The chapter has shown that explanations that attribute the exits from the Adventist ministry during the 1980s to Ford's influence are inadequate and only partially relevant. From the expastors' accounts and other historical records, I have argued that the factor of Des Ford's self-limited charisma thus has a *part* to play in any complete account of the fallout, but only a part. That part may be characterized in the following terms. At the very moment when Adventism was expanding and its administrative structures were stretched to the limit, some of the best and brightest young Adventist pastors came (perhaps despite Des Ford) to accept his charismatic authority. In any case, administrators, an establishment wielding a mixture of what Weber called traditional and rational-legal authority, dreading challenge by expansion, came to perceive a threat to their authority in the rival charismatic leadership of Des Ford. Moreover, insofar as Ford was not by intention or in his following the complete charismatic leader, he was constructed as such by administrators and conservatives like the retired pastors. In their reactions to what was in part their own constructed charismatic challenge, the administration old-guard elite vanquished the charismatic leader, but their pursuit of Ford had become to expastors yet another symbol of administration vindictiveness, distance, and sectarian fervor. The Ford affair, generated by an establishment perceiving itself to be under challenge from charismatic authority, reinforced in some pastors' personal experiences a sense of alienation from, and a sort of betrayal by, the establishment that, as we have seen, is a very central part in the process of exit. The perspectives of wives present additional insight into the social-relational dynamics of fallout from the Adventist ministry and are considered in the next chapter.

Chapter 9 _____

Wives as Facilitators of Exit

She wasn't kicked out
She walked out

—"Eve," K. Llewellyn, 1986.

Wives play a crucial role in the career choices of husbands. What is surprising is that little research has been conducted exploring the contribution of wives to clergy exit. What references there are to wives in the literature are typically negative. This chapter is structured around the testimonies of twelve expastors' wives and draws upon the numerous references to wives in expastors' accounts. The chapter seeks to *bring wives back in* by focusing on some of the ways wives added momentum to their husbands' exit from ministry.

A variety of expressions are used to describe the roles clergy wives play in their husbands' ministries. They are "queens of the parsonage" (Nyberg 1979:151), the ministers' "chief reference persons" (Jud et al. 1970:96), the "strongest" and "most important" support available to ministers (Schoun 1982:161), and the "bulwark of the . . . Protestant minister's support system" (Mills and Koval 1971:56). But wives provide more than emotional support in ministry; they are also traditionally expected to act as co-laborers. Taylor and Hartley (1975:359) picture them as "the gainful unemployed" who represent an "extreme case of the two-person career." There is no other "occupation in which a man's wife is as conspicuous to his clients and in which there is the same degree of opportunity to place demands upon her" (Blaikie 1979:183).

Dempsey (1985:5) found that a majority of the thirty ministers' wives he studied "were heavily involved in their husband's work." "Most wives served as sermon critics, confidantes or co-strategists in their husbands' efforts to accomplish such goals as getting rid of an 'obstructionist' lay leader. It seems most were sources of encouragement and reassurance in situations where organisations were often failing, congregations and financial support declining and lay men and women were often prone to criticise the minister's efforts" (Dempsey 1985:4). The extent of wives' involvement in their husband's work, according to Finch, merits the description "Married to the Job" (1983). Elsewhere Finch (1980:868) uses the term "vicarious contamination" to emphasize that wives are drawn into their husbands' work, often despite their own feelings. However, wives both affect ministry and are affected by it. Built into the role are mechanisms that can have "devastating" social and psychological consequences on wives (Denton 1961:23). According to Pryor (1986:77), "parish ministry is hazardous to clergy marriages."

PASTOR'S WIFE STEREOTYPE

The stereotype of the pastor's wife is nondenominational and interdenominational. Spedding's (1975) description of clergy wives in five denominations in Britain parallels Dempsey's (1985) description of Methodist ministers' wives, and Bottomley's (1977) of Uniting Church ministers' wives in Australia. Adventism stands apart from other denominations in doctrine but shares with them the stereotypical image of the pastor's wife. One reason narratives of wives are included in this study is because wives are considered "helpmeets" in ministry. This fact alone suggests that as co-laborers wives may provide additional light on the processes that lead ministers to exit.

In an Adventist context the role of pastor's wife represents an enlarged and more complete version of the position women in general occupy in the Seventh-day Adventist Church. The attitude to women in the Adventist Church has been shaped by the attitudes and beliefs of Adventist prophetess Ellen White, whose thinking reflects the spirit of nineteenth-century American piety (Bull and Lockhart 1989:185). Ellen White's writings abound with references extolling the virtues of motherhood and describe "in Talmudic detail" (Pearson 1990:137) the domestic ideal as a "sacred" and "holy" duty for women. The mother is "the queen of the household" (*Signs of the Times*, 16 March 1891). Her responsibility for caring for the religious and moral training of children is a ministry that exceeds in importance even that of the minister (1948, vol. 5:594). Ellen White believes mothers are among "the greatest missionaries in the world" (1948, vol. 5:594). Wives are expected to conform to these expectations and in addition to identify with the obligations attached to their social roles as pastors' wives. Among the hundreds of references devoted to describing the roles of wives, the *Comprehensive Index to the Writings of Ellen White* (1962) lists more than 200 occasions in print where Ellen White details how they can contribute to the work of ministry.

Ellen White states that the pastor's wife is a "co-laborer" (1963:140) and a "helper" in ministry (1948, vol. 1:139). She is a "missionary worker" (1946:467–

468) in a true sense, who works alongside her husband and is able to assist in the work of ministry by accompanying him in his travels (1948, vol. 1:452; vol. 2:565), visiting families (1946:437), giving Bible studies, (1963:140) and "holding up the husband's hands by faithful prayers" (1948, vol. 1:137). Ellen White believes that by virtue of being a woman the minister's wife is both able to assist other women and reach out to persons her minister husband cannot (1948, vol. 1:452); she can "smooth" difficulties in the parish with her "womanly tact" and "wise use of . . . Bible truth" (1946:491). For these reasons Ellen White believes the pastor's wife performs a role that is "as great" (1941:203) and "important" as the pastor's (1946:594; 1948, vol. 1:452).

Ministers' wives share the spotlight in the parish and are continuously "watched" by parishioners (1952:355), therefore Ellen White exhorts them to set a "fitting example" and be "exact and careful in influence" (1948, vol. 1:139). Ellen White admonishes wives to be "exemplary, neat and becoming" in outward appearance (1941:450), "plain" in dress (1948, vol. 1:139), and "not extravagant" (1962:180). They are to be "meek, humble and self reliant" (1948, vol. 1:452), "controlled by principle" (1941:206), "careful in conversation" (1948, vol. 1:139) and to "live devoted and prayerful lives" (1948, vol. 1:452). Wives are expected to "come close to people by personal effort" (1962:313) and display "a spirit of self-sacrifice and love for souls" (1948, vol. 1:452). Pastors' wives carry a "double harness" in ministry (Dann 1980:19) with additional responsibilities in the domestic sphere. Ellen White warns wives not to allow "fondness for ministry" to justify neglect of the home and children (1948, vol. 2:620) and calls on them to perform "faithfully their duties in the home" (1941:204–205), be "good wives" to their minister husbands (1948, vol. 2:568), and not "open the door of temptation" to them (1948, vol. 3:325–326). Yet, at the same time, wives are told not to become so preoccupied with domestic and child care chores as to forget parish responsibilities. Ellen White thus admonishes wives where possible to put "housework in the hands of a faithful, prudent helper" and "leave children in good care" in order to engage fully in ministry. To facilitate participation in ministry she recommends that wives who engage in the work of ministry be paid for their efforts (1946:491–493).

The Adventist prophetess argues that the minister's wife can be either a "blessing" or "the greatest curse that ministers can have" (1948, vol. 1:139). Wives have the capacity to "hinder" and even "destroy the influence and usefulness" of the work of their pastor husbands (1948, vol. 1:137). Ellen White's *Testimonies to the Church* (1948) contains numerous references criticizing the negative influence of "unsanctified" wives who frustrate the work of their minister husbands. She mentions some who burden their husbands with "home sick feelings" (1948, vol. 1:450), "indulge in indolence" (1948, vol. 1:627), and harbor a "complaining spirit" (1948, vol. 1:139). She writes particularly harshly of wives who enjoy the status of the role but shirk the responsibilities (1948, vol. 2:542) or who demand "to be served rather than to serve" (1948, vol. 3:229). She advised one minister's wife, for example, to "stay away from [her husband's] place of labor" (1952:356), denounced another as "a medium of Satan" for using ministry as her excuse to ignore her ailing parents (1948, vol. 3:231), and cautioned a third for contradicting in public her husband's preaching (1948, vol. 1:450).

While Ellen White saw marriage to a minister as a privilege and set high ideals for it, she did not overlook the difficulties and called on wives to "take up [their] life's burdens" (1948, vol. 2:446) and be "willing to suffer for Christ's sake" (1948 vol. 1:538), knowing that "suffering" is a mark of the "pioneering spirit" and an integral part of the role (1948, vol. 1:451). She exhorts wives overwhelmed by the demands of their roles to "remember Him who wore the crown of thorns" (1948, vol. 1:138). Ellen White's emphasis on wives' involvement in ministry does not necessarily imply an enlarged role for women in the Adventist community or signal sympathy with and support of the feminist cause. Pearson (1990:143) argues that Ellen White's emphasis arose from a concern with proclaiming the Adventist gospel. Capitalizing on the labor of clergy wives is a logical way of utilizing available labor resources for ministry.

According to Spedding (1975), the stereotype of the clergy wife is neither uniform nor fixed but is something that women acquire and adapt through interaction with relevant others. In Adventism the role of pastor's wife is imposed from above—encoded by Ellen White and promoted by sect bureaucrats. In *The Work of the Pastor*, a pamphlet produced by the Ministerial Association of the General Conference of Seventh-day Adventists and distributed in 1975 to all Adventist ministers as an insert with *Ministry*, pastors' wives are told what is expected of them: "[The pastor's wife] takes a deaconess, an elder's wife, or some other woman in the church with her to call on the shut-ins and the women of the church. A woman's touch of friendship and love will go far in helping bind the members in love and service. . . . The shepherd and the shepherd's wife are one in ministering to the fold" (1975:6W). What Ellen White sketched as an ideal is here presented as something expected of pastors' wives, and, it might be noted, nowhere is it suggested that wives involved in ministry be compensated and rewarded in ways that Ellen White suggested—with provision of household help and payment for services.

The Adventist pastor's wife has role guidelines laid down for her in a way that is not seen in any other denomination. Adventist congregations who are well versed in the writings of Ellen White "know" what to expect from pastors' wives. The problem, of course, lies in the fact that Ellen White sets impossible standards, ones even she herself was incapable of fulfilling. She advised wives not to allow "fondness for ministry" to justify neglect of home and children, yet she did not allow her own children to stand in the way of her duties. It seems that wives can legitimate their personal activities with quotes from Ellen White—as long as this does not involve "secular" employment—while the congregation can criticize them by quoting a different passage from Ellen White. At one level the Adventist pastor's wife is considered "a co-worker in the gospel," but at another level she is very much subordinate to her minister husband. The Adventist pastor's wife has no rights, only responsibilities.

Five of the twelve wives interviewed are harshly critical of the lifestyle and demands of being married to an Adventist minister. Their criticisms, which are very similar, highlight loss of privacy, exploitation of unpaid labor and the fact that family needs come second and are subordinate to the husbands' calling. There are others, however, who describe their time in ministry in positive terms. Seven of the twelve interviewed wives said they enjoyed their "work" as pastor's wife. One recalls thinking while in ministry: "There was nothing I would rather be than a minister's wife. I was so happy, so fulfilled as a minister's wife. It was just using every one of my different skills and talents . . . and I practically felt that was where I wanted to be." Wives who enjoyed the role were also successful in it. Each of the interviewed wives who spoke positively of their time in ministry made a "career" of being married to a minister: one wrote and published devotional short stories in denominational journals; two became "specialist" children's teachers and ran children's holiday programs; another developed her skills as a public speaker and was regularly invited to address women's groups and other church gatherings. These findings recall Dann's (1980:17) observation that "many of the wives of clergy have been outstandingly able women, but held back in their achievements, as most women have been, by the social mores of the time in which they lived." It is likely that in a different social setting these women would have pursued a career, and in a different denomination may have entered ministry themselves.

Expastors' wives who identify with the role and wives who reject it are differentiated by a number of demographics, including "religious background" (Douglas 1961:15). The seven wives who felt fulfilled in ministry were born Adventists, and it should be noted that twenty-nine of the forty expastors in the present study married wives born Adventists (Table 9.1). Expastors' wives in this category had a distinct advantage over converts in ministry. The duration of the average pastoral appointment in the Adventist church is between three and four years. Consequently, wives born Adventist would have known personally between five and ten ministers' wives prior to their own marriages. Douglas (1961:15) argues that "the fulfilled minister's wife . . . usually has had a positive role figure of someone who has done well in the life and enjoyed it." The fact that expastors' wives who were converts expressed the feeling of being "outsiders" to their Adventist communities highlights the importance of "anticipatory socialization."

Table 9.1
Religious Background of Expastors and Wives

	Expastors Born SDA	*Expastors Converts*
Wives Born SDA	18	11
Wives Converts	3	8

The term "anticipatory socialization," first coined by Merton (1968:319–322), has become part of the stock of concepts symbolic interactionists use (Strauss

1959:89–131; Stone 1962:108–109) to identify and explain the process by which individuals learn to adjust to the values of a group or a status to which they aspire. According to Berger and Berger (1972:243), anticipatory socialization is "an intrinsic element of the human condition." McCall and Simmons (1966:211) describe it as "one of the fundamental processes" of life that involves "the gleaning of notions about all aspects of the role: the performances that seem to portray it, the self-expectations and social expectations that it involves, and the self-conceptions and perspectives on social objects germane to it." The "grooming," "training," "rehearsing," and "play-acting" that are associated with anticipatory socialization are necessary and invaluable processes in human conduct without which "we could not stage our lifetime sequence of performances" (McCall and Simmons 1966:212). While anticipatory socialization can be a "mixed blessing" because it can generate "bizarre and unrealistic expectations" in the minds of some, its absence may be even more devastating as individuals feel "estranged" (Berger and Berger 1972:244) and "marginalised" (Berry 1974:73) in their new settings. This may explain why a majority of expastors' wives who as converts had little or no prior exposure to other ministers' wives report feeling disappointment in and antipathy for the role. Conversely, wives born and raised Adventists enjoyed the role and conformed to their role expectations. This interpretation is supported by expastors in their recollections of how their wives felt about ministry (Table 9.2). Indeed, most wives from Adventist backgrounds were reluctant to leave ministry, while most of those critical of their time in ministry and eager to leave were of non-Adventist background.

Table 9.2
Religious Background and Attitudes Toward Exit of Wives as Reported by Surveyed Expastor Husbands

| | Expastor Wives (N = 46) | |
	Born SDA	Converts
Very reluctant to leave	8	1
Willing to leave but preferred to stay	10	1
Neutral	3	1
Preferred to leave but willing to stay	4	5
Very eager to leave	4	7
No response	1	1
	30	16

It is not surprising that age also has a bearing on wives' attitudes to ministry. In society as a whole, younger women have quite different expectations of their roles as wives relative to their mothers. From their 1978 survey of 667 Protestant ministers from seven denominations in the Chicago metropolitan area, Hoge, Dyble, and Polk (1981:142) found that spouses more satisfied with their role as clergy wives were older. In the present study five of the seven wives happy in ministry were between the ages of 45 and 60 at time of exit. Two in their thirties, were born and raised Adventists, had no children while in ministry, and enjoyed the adventure of relocating home each year, meeting new people, and making new friends among church members. By contrast the five wives who were eager to leave ministry were either in their late twenties or early thirties.

A common thread in the narratives of wives is the difficulties they experienced fulfilling role expectations once children arrived. Wives who began ministry with the thought of helping their husbands *in* ministry found themselves confined to doing domestic work and caring for children to free husbands *for* ministry (Sweet 1983:10). This was particularly true of women who enjoyed involvement in their husbands' public ministries but who expected their husbands to share in child care and home duties. Four of the five wives who were eager to leave ministry report that they found it difficult to fulfil role obligations and meet people's expectations once children came along.

Four of the five wives who welcomed their husbands' exits were in their twenties or early thirties, had dependent children, were converts, and were not certain if they were "doing the job properly." One expastor's wife, who described the Adventist ministry as "a game for . . . boys," was a convert, young and a mother with two preschoolers. She is typical of a new generation of pastors' wives who are critical of the patriarchal ethos of the church and reject traditional gender expectations that confine women to the home. For the fifth, who was born and raised Adventist and was the daughter of an Adventist pastor, exit was a symbol of "growing up" and a venturing beyond "the world of mum and dad." Not surprisingly, she provoked the husband's exit by forcing him to choose between her and ministry.

Blanchard (1973:139–140) argues that "the wife's attitude [to ministry] appears . . . crucial in leading men to seek employment outside the pastorate." From his survey of 75 expastors and 176 continuing pastors of the Alabama–West Florida Conference of the United Methodist Church, Blanchard found that the most "consistent" feature differentiating leavers and stayers "is the wife's opinion of the pastorate." What is critical for the present study, however, in contrast to Blanchard's findings, is that the negative attitudes of expastors' wives to ministry did not automatically translate into a preference for exit, nor did a wife's identification with the role automatically signal support for and continuation in ministry. Four expastors' wives who spoke favorably of their work and believed they were successful in it supported their husbands' decisions to leave. The contribution of wives to their husbands' exits, in other words, is complex and not adequately explained by focusing solely on the attitudes of wives to their own roles.

PROBLEM MARRIAGES AND EXIT

A failed marriage can be fatal to the clergy career. Jud et al. (1970:123) believe that the pastor's "family and his occupational system are inextricably intertwined."

Of the 131 expastors Jud et al. interviewed in the late 1960s, 19 percent attributed their exit to marriage and family problems. From this evidence the authors concluded that a "minister's career decisions are heavily influenced by family relationships" (Jud et al. 1970:95). Researchers have not been slow to draw causal links between the quality of clergy marriages and exit from ministry. Schoun (1982:161–162), Blanchard (1973:266–270), Fulcher (1971:58), and Cardwell and Hunt (1979:128–130), to name a few, argue that the quality of the minister's relationship with his wife bears heavily on decisions to exit. MacDonald (1980:18) sees "the number of people leaving pastorates" as being directly related to "the growing incidence of pastor's wives seeking independent careers." M. L. Bouma (1979:43–44) argues that "every year scores of men leave the ministry" on account of marriage breakup and that the true extent of the problem is not known because leavers "are unwilling to implicate their marriages or their marriage partners" in their exits. Researchers thus generalize that ministers who do survive in ministry have happier marriages and supportive wives. Nonsupportive wives and fragile marital relationships are among the main reasons why clergy leave ministry, according to Jud et al. (1970:100), who also highlight the coercive power of the marital relationship as an area needing urgent attention. Jud et al. were surprised, therefore, that not one of the 131 expastors surveyed mentioned family relationships and wives in their list of differences between leavers and stayers. While the authors acknowledged that divorce and separation are not restricted to leavers and that even among continuing pastors it is possible to find relationships on the brink of disintegration, they nevertheless expressed surprise that respondents "scarcely recognize" the impact of family circumstances on career decisions. Jud et al. (1970:98) attributed the omission to "lack of awareness" and an "unwillingness" by leavers to acknowledge the role of wife and family influences in their exit. The authors argued that "this ignorance may well mark the difference between a healthy integration of work and family roles, on the one hand, and unhealthy dependence upon wife and family for the kind of support and encouragement which others gain through their colleagues and constituency relationships" (Jud et al. 1970:100). The argument, however, is circular in reasoning: they interpret the absence of the anticipated response as evidence that family factors do influence decisions to exit. In other words, the researchers know the cause irrespective of what the respondents say. The argument illustrates the difficulties that arise when theoretical premises are not grounded on research findings. An equally plausible explanation, and one that is more in keeping with the evidence they produce, is that expastors do not view the marriages of leavers as qualitatively different from those of stayers. Moreover, Jud et al.'s preoccupation with nonsupportive wives and problem relationships to explain exit overlooks the contribution of wives who are happily married and fulfilled in their roles. Implicit in their preoccupation is the assumption that supportive wives are mere passive recipients of the career choices of their minister husbands and that decisions involving careers are uniquely the husband's to which wives conform.

Although there is some evidence in the interviews with wives suggesting that the critical decisions in ministry were made by husbands and simply announced to wives, expastors' decisions to exit, in most instances, were arrived at jointly. This evidence leads me to question the weighting allotted to problem relationships to explain clergy fallout. The narratives of expastors' wives reveal that a majority of wives contributed in a variety of ways to their husbands' decisions to leave ministry, and that such influence is not limited to poor relationships.

Of course, this is not to deny the importance of marital factors and family circumstances on decisions to exit. Marital issues do feature in the exits. The proliferation of titles on the subject of clergy marriage, including Bouma's *Divorce in the Parsonage: Why It happens, Ways to Prevent It* (1979), Merrill's *Clergy Couples in Crisis: The Impact of Stress on Pastoral Marriages* (1985), and Truman's *Underground Manual for Ministers' Wives* (1974), is one evidence that this is a problem requiring urgent attention. A comparison of the marital status of Adventist leavers with the Jud et al. sample of expastors (Table 9.3) reveals that approximately 7 percent of Adventist expastors and almost the same proportion (6 percent) of expastors in the Jud et al. sample were separated or divorced at the time of exit. As well, 12 percent of Adventist expastors reported that their marriages were in crisis at time of exit—again, about the same proportion as in the Jud et al. survey (11 percent). The similarity of findings between the two groups of expastors indicates that marital factors account for about 20 percent of exits, although this statistic needs to be interpreted with caution. The survey data do not tell us why, if the attitude of the wife and the quality of the marriage are central to exit, no interviewed expastor attributes his exit solely to these factors. The five expastors who said their relationships were in crisis at time of exit and the three who report that their exits coincided with the breakdown of their marriages argue that their failed marriages were the manifestation of pressures in ministry and not the result of either a faulty relationship or poor choice of marital partner. Even if one were to concede that marriage problems account for about 20 percent of the exits, we have not explained in what ways the other 80 percent feature in the process.

Table 9.3
Marital Status of Expastors at Time of Exit and at Time of Interview

	Time of Exit[1]	*Jud[2]*	*Time of Interview*
Married	31	109	24
Married but relationship in crisis	5	14	9
Separated, divorced, and/or remarried	3	8	8
Never married	4	-	2
Total:	43	131	43

[1] Data from interviews with expastors.
[2] Data from Jud, Mills, and Burch (1970:95).

A comparison of how Adventist expastors and continuing pastors rate their relationship with their wives, on first impressions, supports Jud et al.'s conclusions. Table 9.4 reveals that while in ministry proportionately fewer expastors than continuing pastors report that they could talk freely with their wives about their ministries; conversely, more indicate that they received encouragement and support in ministry from their wives. However, the tendency of expastors to report lack of support from their wives during their ministries may be explained by the fact that for 19 percent of expastors the explanations are retrospective and reflect current attitudes (Table 9.3). In other words, it is more than likely that expastors' recollections of how their wives related to their ministries reflect current marital circumstances. A more cautious generalization to draw from surveys of clergy marital relationships would be to argue, as Dudley, Cummings, and Clark (1981) have done, based on their survey of Adventist pastors in the United States, that the marital relationships of leavers are not very different from those of continuing pastors and that the casualty rate for marriages in ministry is constant and high.

Table 9.4
Recollections of Surveyed Expastors and Continuing Pastors of Their Relationship with Their Wives While in Ministry

	% Expastors (N = 46)			*% Continuing Pastors (N = 61)*		
	Disagree	*Neutral*	*Agree*	*Disagree*	*Neutral*	*Agree*
Counselled with wife concerning ministry	15	37	48	12	36	52
Conferred with wife before making decisions	9	15	76	-	7	
Could freely discuss issues with wife	17	31	52	8	12	80
Felt encouraged and supported by wife in ministry	9	31	61	2	20	78
Wife agreed that ministry was where they were meant to be	20	35	46	7	20	73
Took time off to spend with wife	11	59	30	3	47	50

In the present study, approximately two out of every three expastors (61 percent) are clear that their wives *did not* contribute to their exit. Interestingly, a similar percentage of continuing pastors surveyed (63 percent) indicate that if they were to leave ministry, the attitude of their wives would not be a reason. Two conclusions may be drawn from the survey data reviewed so far: first, that the relationships of expastors are not markedly different from those of continuing pastors in terms of marital difficulties; second, the roles expastors' wives played in their husbands' exit appear complex and require that we shift our attention beyond nonsupportive wives and problem marriages. The interviews with expastors' wives help us achieve this shift.

The interview data reveal that it is in problem-free relationships that the importance of wife and family become crucial to exit. In relationships where husband and wife are sensitive to each other's concerns they are also sensitive to the impact ministry is having on family life and family members. A husband is more likely to tolerate the negative impact of ministry on his family if he can see some reward for the deprivation, but if his ministry is problematic, as was the case with the majority of expastors surveyed, and family members were also being affected by the church problems, then the wife also is more likely to contemplate change. One Adventist expastor explained during interview that he and his wife were "happily married" while in ministry, but indicates that his wife nevertheless played a major role in his exit.

The argument thus far has highlighted the inadequacy of two explanations of how clergy wives contribute to exit from ministry—the antipathy of the minister's wife to the role and the problem marriage relationship. The remainder of this chapter seeks to highlight the fact that ministry is a husband-wife partnership or team effort. It seeks to shed light on how wives become incorporated in ministry and figure in the process of exit.

PRACTICAL RELIGION VERSUS THEOLOGY

Whereas husbands received training for ministry, wives were not trained for the tasks they were expected to perform. One expastor's wife recalls that the only instruction she received consisted of two evening lectures at college: "One was on . . . the things that were expected of a minister's wife . . . the fact that you had to be very faithful to your husband . . . and the other one, I think, was something about flower arranging." Most expastors' wives received no instruction at all other than in the form of anecdotes they heard during Sabbath School. Not one of the interviewed wives believed that she was called to be a minister's wife. Sweet (1983:11) observes that women marry ministers "not because of, but neither in spite of or in indifference to, their husband's calling." It is an irony that even though wives receive minimal training in the Bible, and possibly on account of this, they showed little or no interest in matters of theology. Indeed, the one area in which all wives felt alienated in their roles was doctrine, the very thing the husband-wife team was expected to promote in the Adventist ministry.

The following responses are typical of the ways expastors' wives related to theology while in ministry:

I was not really into theology. I know the basics of Adventism and I accepted it as that. I'm not a scholar . . . and I found it hard to understand a lot of the words this long (indicates with hands). I had to study and read a lot about it before I could understand the word, and then if someone used it in a sentence I had a hard time making sense of it. . . . I'm not a scholar;

I'm more a practical person, so scholarly things like theology I listened to and tried to understand and take in what I could. But I trusted the system, um to feed me the right information. . . . I actually looked for practical things to demonstrate to me the difference in the theology.

I don't think I ever had [my own] theology. It is hard to explain. I believed very much that [my husband] was called to ministry. . . . I used to hear the discussions in our home about Ellen White and 1844 and all that sort of thing, but that wasn't really me. . . . I wasn't really into all that sort of thing. I didn't think much about theology.

My outlook [on theology] was always . . . four hundred meters behind [my husband's] (laughs). . . . I guess it's not so much the theology issue for me, as how it affects people.

Another explains that it was not until her husband was accused of heresy that she began to study the issues and questioned her own Adventist beliefs. However, as she explains, the desire to study the issues is one thing; success in understanding is another:

I was forced to do a lot of thinking. . . . I was doing a lot of listening [before] but now I was doing definitely more Bible study. I think we actually had some of Brinsmead's literature what was it called, *Verdict* magazines, yes, [my husband] had a whole stack of them. So I started getting some of them out but I didn't make head or tail of them. . . . I believed that my husband was right, although I couldn't come up with the same theological conclusions. I was willing to stand by him . . . [and had planned] that in the future, yes, I think I' m going to have a look into this. . . . But toward the end of our ministry my mind was more in turmoil more about the future . . . than about the theology of it all.

Only two of the twelve expastors' wives interviewed stated that they were theologically informed and had their own convictions on the issues being debated in the Adventist Church: both were born Adventists and had been in ministry for more than two decades. The other ten explained that they were more interested in the lived experience of people's faith and pleaded ignorance on matters of theology. Younger wives showed less interest in theology than more senior women. One who requested to be present during her husband's interview was surprised at the fact that her husband attributed his exit to rejection of Adventist teachings when he continued to call himself Adventist and identified with the movement. It is worth noting that the husband's questioning of Adventist theology had the opposite effect on the wife.

Rather than undermine commitment to the sectarian belief system, the wife turned her anger on the husband:

Wife: I really can't understand why anyone would want to resign from ministry. . . . But I know that God has been preparing my life for this crisis. What happened with [my husband] was to test my Christianity, and whether I really was with God. It is one thing to believe in God when the going is easy; it is quite another when things get tough. Through it all I have come to trust God and also to believe that there is a real devil [who] . . . has been trying to test my faith to make me turn away from God.

PHB: Has the devil also tested your husband?

Wife: Yes.

PHB: Did the devil succeed?

Wife: Yes, because he became totally consumed with his own theological problems and focused on the people and the church system rather than focus his eyes on God.

PHB: Did you become involved in the theological issues?

Wife: No. I am not a theologian. You and others can run rings around me on theology. I tell you this, though: you may be successful at proving my theology wrong, but you cannot shake my faith in God. . . . I can see God's hand in my life, guiding and protecting me. No one can make me doubt that.

PHB: How has your husband's exit from ministry affected your faith?

Wife: I am a much stronger Christian because of it. I knew all along that God will not abandon me. I believe with all my heart what God declares in the Scriptures, that no temptation will come upon us that we are not able to handle.

This wife remains resolute in her commitment to Adventism. Whereas only ten of the forty-three expastors interviewed remain recognizably Adventist in thinking and lifestyle, nearly twice that number—eighteen of the forty expastors' wives, according to their husbands—continue to identify with the Adventist Church and attend services on a weekly basis. Four are daughters of Adventist pastors; fifteen were born Adventists. An additional point of interest is that eight of the eighteen wives continue to identify with the movement even though their expastor husbands have rejected Adventist belief as unbiblical and irrelevant. What is typical of the overwhelming majority of expastors' wives is that the theological convictions with which they identify are less the result of study and more from commitment to a belief system and lifestyle in which they were socialized.

According to Harstock (1983:295), "men and women . . . grow up with personalities affected by different boundary experiences, differently constructed and experienced inner and outer worlds, and preoccupations with different rational issues." Adventist feminist author Iris Yob promotes the view that women in general "are less involved in the pursuit of doctrinal correctness and the finer points of textual exegesis and more interested in matters of identity and relationship" (Yob 1988:39). Smith (1974) also accepts this duality and argues that the distinction between how men and women conceive of and experience the world produces contrasting outlooks: a *rational-technical* orientation is characteristic of males, and a *relational* focus that begins with the observable and "from where we are" is typical of females (Smith 1988:175). However, it is equally plausible to attribute the general avoidance of theology by the wives to the sectarian ethos in which women are socialized into believing that they are not scholarly. It may be that wives were more concerned with the experiential and relational dimensions of religion because in the Adventist community women are encouraged to "occupy a passive role" (Pearson 1990:151). Even though one expastor's wife acknowledges that women are not altogether excluded from doctrinal debates, she got the impression that in the Adventist Church theology is promoted as a "male activity." The interviews reveal that the wives are just as capable of debating theological issues. One not only was well versed and articulate on the finer points of theology dividing the movement, but also had a depth of understanding that surpassed that of the majority of males interviewed, including her husband.

In the accounts of wives, doctrinal issues are not denied, they are merely devalued in importance. An argument can also be made to the effect that the concerns of wives still involve theology, although one step removed; wives focus at the level of application rather than formulation. Be that as it may, what is argued here is that whereas husbands use the language of theology to articulate their exits from ministry, wives highlight social and interpersonal factors to explain the same experiences. In other words, wives assign to the front stage what their husbands locate back stage. The specific events on which wives focus, and the particular interpretation they assign to them, disclose the ways wives contributed to and even facilitated their husbands' exits from ministry.

MINISTRY AND ALIENATION

The most salient feature of the narratives of expastors' wives, when read alongside those of their husbands, is that wives describe their own exits while recounting the exits of their husbands. His exit from ministry, in other words, was at the same time and in a real sense her exit from the role of minister's wife. Each of the wives interviewed recounts her own disappointments while describing events that culminated with her husband's career crisis. Wives who believed their husbands were "called" by God and who identified with their husbands' ministries tended to internalise and feel personally the problems and conflicts of husbands. This is evident in the following responses.

Whatever affected my husband, affected me. . . . I just felt it was a waste; here was a guy that had a lot to offer and [the organization] wasn't interested, and that hurt me. And it hurt . . . me because it hurt him. I didn't like to see what [church authorities] did to him, and it has taken a long time to come around to feel what he's feeling today.

Church members didn't seem to respect [my husband's] calling. . . . They were more interested in what [he] believed . . . than whether he was called.

The idea that wives tended to view their own roles in terms of their husbands' is not unique to ministry work. Pahl and Pahl (1971) noted a similar pattern among managers and their partners. Wives in some instances support husbands in achieving their career aspirations when they can see benefits in it for them, a phenomenon Gowler and Legge (1975) label "the hidden contract." Marshall and Cooper (1979:76–95) argue that in the work-family interface the wife's attitude is "the key" to the husband's future career prospects. In relation to clergy wives, identification with the work of the husbands extends to include work-related problems. The case studies that follow reveal that support for and familiarity with the husbands' work-related conflicts alienated wives and prompted them to contemplate exit—for their husbands' sake.

A majority of the interviewed wives reported feeling traumatized by church member and administrator attacks on their husbands. However, as the Sue Paynter case study shows, she desired exit not "because of what was happening to my husband, but because of my own experience." Another says that she had her "own reasons for leaving." Five recounted their own conflicts with Conference leaders that led them to question the integrity of some Adventist bureaucrats. One newlywed was taken aback when the Conference president approached her on two occasions to persuade her to abandon paid employment in order to work alongside her husband in ministry. A second is angry that she was paid less than what had been agreed for the teaching she did in an Adventist school and even though she had discussed the problem with the Conference treasurer was unable to seek recompense. A third recalls that she "had Conference presidents call me to their office . . . to advise me that I was too ambitious and that my husband wouldn't advance in the church because of me." An expastor describes the following incident involving the Conference president and the Union ministerial secretary who had called on him and his wife to persuade her to stop working:

I mean, they were ridiculous. They said to her, you shouldn't work, you know, you should be with your husband. I said . . . but she works as a nurse and that's . . . a fairly Christian way to earn a living, to help suffering people. And they said, yes, but . . . she's a minister's wife, she should be beside you. And then my wife said, what do you expect me to do in this [small town]? They said, oh well, you could stay home and help your husband. And I said, in what way could she help me? They said she could answer the phone for you . . . and she could have a book and make appointments for you. I said, serious? (laughs). I mean, they were serious.

Two other wives recalled being criticized by Conference administrators for the fact that they were in paid employment.

The interviews with expastors' wives reveal that eventually some wives lost the capacity to provide emotional support at a time when husbands had no one else to turn to. Approximately two out of three wives had their own personal crises which coincided with and had a compounding effect on their husbands'. It is not unreasonable to conclude on the basis of this evidence that exit from ministry represents the merging and culmination of two quite separate yet interrelated sets of concerns—the expastor's and the wife's.

TYPOLOGY OF EXPASTORS' WIVES

The following case studies depict the variety of ways expastors' wives featured in their husbands' exits from ministry. They have been constructed from interviews with expastors' wives and references to them in interviews with husbands. From the interview data five types of expastors' wives have been identified: embittered outsider, conforming idealist, reluctant feminist, calculating radical, and successful shepherdess.

Embittered Outsider

The "embittered wife" was socially and economically marginal to the Adventist community, and alienated by what appeared to her as the actions of an uncaring organization and an insensitive community. Andy Paddock's wife was at the center of his conflicts with Conference administrators and church members. The case study illustrates how class factors and religious background combined to exaggerate the marginal status of working-class converts in a middle-class and socially elitist Adventist community. The Paddocks left ministry because they could no longer tolerate the "harassment" and criticism of authorities and members.

Andy made up his mind to enter ministry not long after he and Louise were married and joined the Adventist Church. Andy says, "It was what God wanted me to do." Louise agrees: "I always knew he would do ministry; I knew before we went to college that he'd do ministry. I had a feeling he's that sort of person." To the Paddocks, who were from a poor farming background, the image of a well-dressed Adventist pastor who drove a recent model car and lived in a comfortable Conference house was additional incentive to take up ministry.

The Paddocks arrived at college with no savings but planned to pay for the study by working on campus. They both got jobs packing Weet-bix at the Sanitarium Health Food factory on the Avondale campus. Louise worked the night shift and Andy in the afternoons. Their four-year plan had to be revised when not long after their arrival Louise gave birth to their first child. The unplanned arrival turned their world upside down. She suffered from "severe postnatal depression" but kept working because they were dependent on her part-time wage. Louise explains that she was not coping with the demands of looking after a new child, running the home, and working at night. She managed less well when eighteen months later she gave birth to their second child.

Concerned for Louise's health, Andy thought of terminating his studies. As well, study was causing him to question the "conservative Adventist" views he had accepted when he converted. Louise refused to entertain the idea of giving up, insisting, "We haven't gone through all this hardship for you to throw it away now." In his final year of study Andy also fell ill, and the Paddocks were forced to borrow to pay for his college fees and living expenses. The Paddocks were prepared to make this financial commitment and willing to suffer hardship because, Louise says, they had "complete faith and confidence in the church that if we did our best to see our way through college in order to fulfil the requirements to go into ministry, the church would do the right thing by us when we got out." They looked forward to "getting a decent wage" in ministry and to enjoying some of the comforts of life. Sadly, their problems got worse, not better, once in ministry.

According to Louise, their problems began with Andy's initial appointment as an assistant pastor in a large middle-class city church. The Paddocks rented a truck and transported themselves to the new location. Church members found this amusing, and the fact that when Andy was visiting parishioners Louise did the shopping on her bicycle: "We used to cycle down to get all our groceries. I used to have one kid in the seat on the back of the bike and one kid would sit on [the rider's] seat, and I would ride my bike standing up." At first the Conference president was bemused by their lack of sophistication and "complimented" them for their "pioneering spirit." On four separate occasions during their interview Louise remarked that they were "country people" and that she was "a country girl." They were not like the well-to-do city Adventists who "never had it hard," "put on all their airs and graces," were "snobby" and "full of their own importance." They, like country people with whom she identified, were "more friendly," put "people first" in their dealings, and treated life as "fun." One of the college lecturers acknowledged the inappropriateness of Andy's appointment to a middle-class parish but warned them not to be intimidated by class and advised the Padocks "to go up there and be ourselves, scars, flaws, the lot."

Louise and Andy half expected that when they arrived in their new parish they would be accepted and made to feel welcome. Instead, they were "on [their] own." They "didn't know anybody," and no one offered them assistance. With "no friends" and "no one to talk to . . . or confide in," they felt "very isolated." Not once were the Paddocks invited by church members for a meal in their two year ministry. The Conference president told Louise they "won't invite you to their homes and they won't come to yours because . . . [your child] dirtied her pants." Louise believes the real reason for their ostracism is because she and Andy were from a different class.

The Paddocks lived in a Conference home next door to the church, and Louise says this exacerbated what she believes were class-based conflicts. She compares living next door to the church to "living in a glass house"—"we were right under their noses" twenty four hours of the day. "We had no privacy. Every time we walked out our front door we were seen. We couldn't do anything without being seen." The house had no fences or trees for privacy. Members could look "right into our back yard and [see] everything that went on." They complained to the Conference president that the Paddock's "car was never clean," "lawns weren't mown," "the garden wasn't weeded," the "kids weren't tidy," "the house wasn't clean," and they could see "dishes on the kitchen sink." The President adopted the role of courier, conveying member displeasure of the Paddocks.

Louise admits "the house was not spick and span," but adds that her responsibility was to her husband and her children and "not to be a minister's wife." She believes ministry was "Andy's job, not mine"; she was merely "his wife . . . a normal wife" and contends church members had no right to expect her to conform to their expectations of how she should keep house or raise children. She detested the way church members decked themselves with their expensive clothes and jewellery and turned church into a fashion parade.

To make matters worse, Louise had not fully recovered from the illnesses. She arrived at the new location "burnt out" and "about to crack up." Instead of providing her with support, church members added to their woes with criticism: "I feel we were harassed. We were really harassed. . . . I mean how could I look after two children, cope with what I was going through emotionally [and] keep my housework up when I wasn't coping. I wanted help but [church members] all stood back and criticized me. I really needed someone to come and help me. I really needed help, but they couldn't understand that." On one occasion when Andy was away visiting and she was ill and confined to bed, the Conference president called to convey member displeasure. Louise recalls:

[He] came out . . . and told me that some trees that grew in the front yard, some bushes, needed trimming. Andy and I liked the wild and woolly look because we're really natural and I liked them the way they were, so I left them. Anyway, I felt he didn't have any right to come into my yard and tell me what I should do, because it was my house, it was my yard. Anyway, he came back and he said (raises voice), I told you so and so, to cut, fix those trees up. And I was so angry with him I went out and I cut the trees. They were that high (points to shoulder) and when I cut them they were that high (points to ankle and laughs). . . . They went back to their stumps. . . . He really was a horrible man, he really was so horrible.

After two years of continued criticism the Paddocks could stand it no longer and decided to resign. Andy believes that he "was going to be sacked" if he had not resigned. Louise believes that she was the major reason for Andy's exit. "I think I played a big part in [Andy] wanting to leave, I really do. I really think that perhaps I was responsible for a lot of it. I do think that deep down [church members and Conference administrators] felt that [Andy] had theological problems as well, but they never had any proof. I think the children and I played the biggest part in the exit." The Paddocks left ministry emotionally bruised and with massive debts. The loan they took out while at college had not been paid off, and with higher bank interest rates had actually increased. Louise said that it had grown to an amount equivalent to a house mortgage and will take them decades to repay. Andy adds that the debt repayment will be their ongoing reminder of their time in ministry.

Conforming Idealist

Conforming idealists began their sojourn believing that little more was involved in being a pastor's wife than marrying a minister. They had no idea of the complex demands placed on minister couples by Conference and church members and were ignorant of the politics of parish work. The exits of the two husbands in this category were provoked by clashes over theology with Conference authorities and lay members. In each case the wives became disillusioned with the attitudes of some administrators and members and appalled by the hypocrisy of Christians persecuting Christians. Sue Paynter is typical of conforming idealists who did not contest decisions to exit and in retrospect are glad they left the Adventist Church as well.

Sue describes her two years in ministry as "the worst two years of my whole life." She explains that by the end of the second year, "I got to the place where I was just existing. I wasn't really living. That wasn't because of what was happening to Brian [my husband], but because of my own experience." Their brief interlude in ministry left her feeling emotionally bruised and distrustful of people. What enthusiasm she had for ministry "just died."

Sue attributes her decision to join the Adventist movement to the influence of an Adventist aunt and encouragement of Adventist friends. She was raised in a poor family where she and her brothers had to live within the limits of a solo parent's wage. Ministry thus represented a leap in status, although, as she explains, the idea of marrying a minister was not motivated by material and economic concerns. The Paynters had three children when Brian commenced training for ministry. Sue worked part time doing domestic work while caring for her preschoolers, and adds, "We had to go without many things. . . . We literally lived on the smell of an oil rag. We had to go without shoes and clothes and all the rest of it for Brian to get into ministry." Although they lived on the brink of poverty, Sue states that she did not look at the deprivation as sacrifice. "I just believed that [that] was what God called Brian to do. I did not look at it as a sacrifice at all, and I still don't. It was something I believed in very much. I felt that God had called [Brian], so I followed God's calling." On four different occasions during the interview Sue reiterated that Brian was called by God to be a minister and by enabling her husband to pursue his calling she was fulfilling God's will for her life. "Our whole life revolved around Brian and his call [to ministry], not my call," she explained. Sue anticipated that the hardships they endured at college would be short-lived and that life would get better once in ministry. As it turned out, however, "ministry wasn't really what I expected. It was a real disappointment. . . . It wasn't a happy time for me at all . . . from start to finish." She discovered, for example, that a minister's wife lived a marginal existence in the parish. "I felt as though I was not one of the people. I felt that I was not accepted [by them]. . . . I was like a bit of furniture around which church members had to walk." The local church ladies did not invite her to their homes or visit hers. Sue says she "was never really accepted." She did not share church member preoccupation with "what type of car you drove, the sort of clothes you wore and how well or badly behaved your kids were."

She was particularly hurt by church member criticisms of her role as mother. This was a theme to which she returned a number of times during the interview. "I used to find it hard going to church on Saturday morning and everyone would glare at you because your kids were wriggling at church or something. No one ever offered any support or help. I was angry at that." On another occasion Sue explained that church members "expected that because they were [the] minister's children, that they had to sit up [during church] and be perfect, which just didn't work in our case. I used to get real bad vibes from some of the people . . . about how I was bringing up my kids. . . . I never got any good messages from them. They didn't have to say anything, but the vibes were there." Sue thinks that she failed in every sense to live up to church member expectations of the minister's wife: "I couldn't play the piano. I couldn't sing. I couldn't take senior Sabbath School lessons. [Pastor W.'s wife] . . . could do everything I couldn't do. As well I had three young children and everyone at church wouldn't let me even dry a dish at the social evenings because I [was expected] to look after the children. That was my role. I just didn't fit in with their role of the minister's wife." If church members were critical of her performance of the minister's wife role, they were brutal in their condemnation of her husband, whom they labelled a "heretic" and an "apostate."

She was angered by the way church members treated him and by the fact that Conference leaders welcomed misinformation and entertained falsehoods. She explained that theology was "beyond" her and that she "wasn't really into all that sort of thing" and did not fully understand the doctrinal issues dividing the Adventist community. Sue says that she judged theology by the behavior and attitudes of the advocates and thus questioned the Christianity of many in the church. She was "sickened" by the "underhanded and sneaky activities" of some church members in their endeavor to prove that her husband was a heretic. "One of the worst experiences," Sue recalls, was a visit from one of the local church elders who "had a tape recorder [hidden] under his coat and secretly taped conversations with Brian" and sent copies of the tape to the Conference president. Sue puzzled over the sort of religion that motivates people to disrespect personal ethics and human decency. Sue explains that church members were not interested in her or her children and even less in her minister husband. By the end of their second year in ministry her "enthusiasm for ministry just died. . . . We were living such a stressful life."

On one occasion when she was walking home with her children after delivering the car to be serviced, she recalls thinking to herself, "Surely there must be more to ministry than this. It was really boring for me. I really didn't like it very much." The continual negative feedback and rejection and her husband's ongoing conflicts with church members led her to contemplate the possibility of leaving ministry. "I was only there because Brian was there," explained Sue, and she realized that their time in ministry "was limited." All the same, she was surprised when her husband finally announced his resignation. "If he had told me two weeks before leaving that we would be out of the ministry I wouldn't have believed him. . . . I never dreamt that we would leave."

When Brian quit ministry the Paynters severed their links with Adventism. Sue feared the consequences of leaving the church because "Adventism was the only family she had known," according to Brian. She also worried about how they would manage without a regular wage but did not grieve at not being a minister's wife. Sue states that as a minister's wife, she felt devalued and worthless. She describes leaving ministry as her "new birth" experience; "life began" for her when ministry stopped. "I have become my own person now. . . . I have got a lot more confidence. . . . [Now I am] the mother that I naturally was with my kids. . . . [Now] I do things because I want to do them and not because I'm the pastor's wife." Sue still calls herself a Christian but explains that in contrast to her previous existence, she now has her own sense of "calling": "it's no longer Brian's ministry; now it is our ministry."

Reluctant Feminist

The two wives in this category were the only ones critical of Adventist patriarchy and women's subordinate status in ministry. "Reluctant feminists" were wives who were "forced to the limit." Two issues recur in their accounts: the difficulty of fulfilling role expectations, and the conviction that clergy wives are "used" and "exploited" by the organization.

Glenda met her husband-to-be at college; Martin, a convert to Adventism, was in his final year of training for ministry. Glenda went to college not to find a husband but to recover from an earlier failed relationship and because she needed "to make changes" in her life. The idea of marrying an Adventist minister and becoming a minister's wife couldn't have been further from her mind. She believed that she did not have an Adventist pedigree or the right social upbringing for the religious life and high calling with which she equated the minister's wife role.

Glenda was raised in "a divided home." Her mother joined the Adventist Church when she was a toddler, but her father remained "a nonbeliever." She recalls that on one occasion after "some sort of religious crusade in the church" her mother had suddenly "turned fanatical" and became "a very fundamentalist believer," but Glenda was not "turned on by religion." Her mother's change of heart created problems for her and her brother, who found it "difficult . . . adjusting to [doing] things that we had not been used to." Glenda attended church regularly but describes her Adventism as "lukewarm"; she was not troubled by "eating meat [or] drinking tea and coffee." The year prior to going to college she "had virtually left the church." She cites these experiences as proof that she was an unlikely candidate for the minister's wife role. Glenda admits enjoying her time at college, but explains that the company of "all the lovely people" convinced her that she "was not a fundamentalist Adventist like everyone else there."

Glenda loved Martin, but not the prospect of becoming a minister's wife:

The last thing I wanted to be was a minister's wife. I felt I was not a person who was fundamentally and inwardly Adventist. Outwardly I could be an Adventist, but in myself I did not think [that] I was capable of being what an Adventist minister's wife would have to be. . . . I felt my temperament was not quite in keeping [with the] Adventist minister's wife [stereotype]. I like to think what I like to think and do what I want to do without being told you must do this and you mustn't do that.

Once in ministry she discovered that the reality of the minister's wife role was even more austere than she had imagined. She believes Adventism is a "restraint" and compares being a minister's wife to imprisonment. She discovered that church members expected the pastor and his wife to showcase the Adventist message. The wife, for example, is "expected always to be there to be supportive" and "have housework and cooking done by sunset Friday." They were expected to be early birds and some church members actually used to telephone "early in the morning just to see if you were up after being out till midnight the night before."

Glenda resents the fact that by marrying a minister she forfeited her privacy. While she accepts that ministry involves sacrifice, she did not think that this entailed sacrificing her husband. She was angered by "the fact that [she] could never have Martin to [herself]." Glenda says church member expectations were unrealistic and uncompromising. Members expected and sometimes demanded that the minister's wife would invite people home for meals and entertain guests in her home. She recalls, "We used to entertain many people on the weekend. In fact, a week after giving birth we were entertaining. My God, what a time. . . . I hated entertaining. To this day I hate entertaining. You are lucky you got something to eat! I am now letting out all my frustration once more, for the last time probably." According to Glenda, the Adventist minister's wife is "expected to be always smiling, always welcoming, never angry, never turning anyone away, which I had done (laughs). Oh dear, there's a limit isn't there. . . . The minister's wife, I felt, always had to be available. That was what we tried to live up to with no limitations. But of course, you always do have limitations and therefore you feel guilty." She describes the artificial existence wives are forced to live and the fact that "people . . . could not be themselves around the minister's wife . . . they couldn't swear and be themselves." She was expected to be socially detached and to avoid establishing close friendships with church members. Glenda found the isolation difficult to bear.

For the first two of years in ministry Glenda was relatively unaffected by the demands of her role. "We were very romantic and happy and wanted to work together as a minister-wife team." She avoided getting paid employment because she genuinely wanted to "do the right thing" and "work together with Martin." Her husband, who was present during the interview, said, "You actually liked doing some of that jazz." Glenda replied in jest, "Yes, but that was because I felt you wanted me to be pure for the church." The arrangement of accompanying the pastor when visiting parishioners and assisting with programs worked well until they had children. Glenda states that once their first child came along she "resented . . . going out with a small baby." "When the second child came along, I refused to go." The questioning of her role as minister's wife began earlier, but was accelerated by the fact that children forced her to reevaluate her loyalties. "I started feeling I wasn't going to do what everybody else made me feel that I should do, [and] I suppose all this came home to me when the children came on the scene. I now wanted to be with them. I resented having to leave them in someone else's care." In addition to abandoning the arrangement of accompanying her husband in his work, Glenda now found that, as a mother, she had neither time nor energy to devote to housekeeping:

You see, the job was always around. Martin would come home and go upstairs to study and he didn't like to be disturbed no matter what. The building could be falling around, kids screaming, oh dear. I mean, if he had been in another job I still would have had the kids screaming, but I wouldn't have to put up with that type of thing, I could have just let everything drop. But I couldn't let everything drop. There was always something on the go, day in, day out—Friday night, Saturday night, Sunday evenings.

Glenda began feeling house-bound and confined to looking after children from "five in the morning . . . till seven at night." The only time she and Martin had to themselves was eleven at night, when he came home. That was when they "saw each other and had [their] long discussions." The demands from church members did not stop, and Glenda recalls a "blowup" when she turned away a church member who "turned up to have a brief chat" while she was cooking the evening meal and children were screaming. In retrospect, Glenda thinks that "children [have] a lot to do with whether you survive [in ministry]. There's just two static roles of male and female, and then the children come along, and then other things come into it. The wife now has a second role to fulfil, at the same time as keeping up the relationship. But you can't do it. Something eventually breaks." She is of the view that the stereotypical role of minister's wife is more appropriate for newlyweds with no children or couples with grown up-children.

Once she began to question her role as pastor's wife Glenda questioned other aspects of ministry, including the social organization of the church. On two occasions Glenda accompanied her husband and "several other ministers and their wives" on a work-related holiday. During the trip she observed that wives of senior pastors "had to do everything for their husbands." This made her determined that she was not going to be "a servant." "If I went on holiday, I was not going to wash up for any husband; he had to wash his own dirty clothes. No way will I do that. . . . I mean I had enough problems on holidays washing nappies once the kids came along." She now thinks Adventist ministers are "male chauvinist pigs" and ministry is "a game for the Adventist boys."

She also is critical of the fact that in ministry wives are obliged to invest unpaid labor in the husband's work. She recalls that on one occasion [the city evangelist] got me to copy out all these old fluorescent charts of Daniel 2, which took me many hours. Five hundred dollars, I was supposed to be paid. It all went on Martin's trip to Israel and then over to Egypt. . . . I did all the hard work. [The evangelist] was paying me to do [the job], but he took the money out of Martin's expenses for the trip. The money I earned ended up . . . paying for film so that [Martin] could go on the trip to the holy lands, so that he could show pictures in his missions. . . . I had to stay home because I was seven months pregnant. They went just before I was to deliver.

Glenda believes that to be successful, a minister's wife needs to have "a lot of self-esteem." For a time she tried to make excuses for herself, to forget her disappointments and overlook her frustration. "I tended to brush aside those things, but deep down, I suppose, all those things do accumulate." In time, Glenda became "sick of the whole thing," and "toward the end of our sixth year, I felt that was it. I thought, blow God. I don't think I ever felt unjustified [for thinking like that], although I was made to feel that I was not making it [as a minister's wife]." She was "fed up" with having to live up to people's expectations and glad when Martin finally had announced that he had resigned. Martin believes that some of the difficulties his wife experienced in ministry were because of his own insensitivity to gender issues: "I actually felt that was what you were meant to do. . . . I admit some things were pretty excessive . . . but [I saw them] as being purely necessary to do what I perceived was the minister's role. I admit it does sound awful when I think back on it."

Calculating Radical

Only one of the expastors' wives interviewed is in this category. Gail Reid requested to be present during her husband's interview, and although I arranged to interview her separately, at different times during interview she interjected with her own interpretation of events. The following exchange is one such example. The excerpt illustrates poignantly how, in this instance, the actions of the wife were deliberate and calculated to shock. This expastor was forced to reexamine his commitment to ministry because of the actions of his wife. In the final outcome, both husband and wife, who were born Adventists with parents in ministry, reacted less against Adventist theology that against the sectarian culture.

Expastor: I just had a radical wife who didn't want to be a minister's wife.

Wife: (laughs)

Expastor: Who used to swear in church all the time.

Wife: One Saturday I accidentally dropped my bag and I said, "Oh shit."

Expastor: At the top of her voice in front of the Concerned Brethren.

Wife: I once wore red, white and blue colored hair to church. I wore it to work and forgot that I was going to church the next day.

PHB: (to the expastor) How did you handle that?

Expastor: I didn't.

Wife: Things like this nearly broke up our marriage. When we married he loved me for who I was and because I was different. I had promised that I would try to survive being married to a minister. To start with I really tried, um, I was a martyr, something I promised myself I'll never be again.

PHB: You didn't enjoy it?

Wife: Of course not.

Expastor: If I hadn't been a minister I wouldn't have cared less how she dressed or what she did. But . . . in a church where my ideas were not accepted . . . I had to fight for my ideas, and she wasn't helping me. That's why I had a lot of anger at the time.

PHB: Did you expect your wife would assist you in ministry?

Expastor: Actually, I wanted the opposite. I wanted to keep her out of my ministry altogether. I didn't want her involved.

Wife: When I did get involved I didn't like it.

Expastor: She was just an obstruction.

Wife: Even though everybody really liked me.

Expastor: Yeah, that's the funny thing. People did like her. But I saw the colored hair and all that sort of thing as a threat to my ministry.

Wife: My theology wasn't radical. . . . My interest was helping people to love each other.

Expastor: She just reacted all the time, you know, any little thing that didn't suit her . . . she would react; she would go and dress the opposite way to what the people expected.

Wife: Quite deliberately.

Expastor: Yes, she would do the very opposite to make people react. And that just made me angry.

Wife: The first time I went to church with him I cried for three hours when we got home. . . . He couldn't understand, he had no idea, how much pain I was going through each time I attended church.

Expastor: I was feeling her lack of support. I was always getting bad vibes from Conference and some church members about her, and there was no support from her.

Wife: But I wasn't well. I was advised by a psychiatrist who was a Christian that I had to stop going to church. It was after this that [my husband] began to understand my reactions.

Expastor: Yeah, but the fact that people were reacting to me because of her started to eat away at me.

PHB: What did you do?

Expastor: The problems with my wife [were] really starting to affect me.

Wife: I wasn't coping with church.

Expastor: She wasn't coming to church. I was trying to minister [to these people] without a wife there at all. It was a very lonely place to be preaching from the pulpit without your wife there. I didn't have support. I didn't care if she didn't get involved, but I at least wanted her, you know, wanted her to be there. Ah, that hurt in a big way. . . . The tipping point, if you want to call it that, was that, I suddenly, for some reason, started to . . . see why she was reacting so much. I don't know what it was, what exactly it was, but for some reason like a flash of light I suddenly understood why she was reacting. I still didn't agree with her reacting as she did, but I could see her whole background. I suddenly understood where she was coming from. She could have told me a hundred times but it suddenly sunk, something just flashed, you know.

Wife: Every time I went to church I would be sick for days, critically ill.

Expastor: I suddenly understood her at that time, and, you know, I just said, oh well, if that's what church is doing to her, and I can see that it is in a very big way responsible for her being that way, her whole background . . . I decided to pull out of ministry.

PHB: If your wife was not having problems with church would you still be in ministry?

Expastor: That's the funny thing. It's just that, ah, having to fight through things within our relationship made things clearer quicker, that's all, yeah, that's all. . . . The thing that was biggest in my mind, the thing that hurt me most was that Adventism, the culture of Adventism, had sucked me into being angry at my wife, when I loved her so much. . . . I had started to condemn her because I was so enthusiastic for my ministry, and I saw that, ah, here I was a person who had a certain ideal for myself, and here I was becoming part of the system that was condemning. That really gave me a big shock, and that was the thing that really wrenched me out of the ministry.

Successful Shepherdess

Five of the expastors' wives interviewed, including Julie Walker, whose case study follows, were successful shepherdesses, wives who enjoyed their role, were successful in it, yet supported their husbands' decision to exit, albeit reluctantly. A majority of interviewed expastors' wives fit this category; three were middle-aged or older, and all five were born Adventists.

The Walkers came closest to Ellen White's ideal of the Adventist pastor-wife ministry team: both had an impeccable Adventist pedigree with parents and relatives "in the work," were committed to promoting the Adventist cause, and enjoyed and were successful in their "ministries." Robert was a successful pastor, while Julie embraced the role of pastor's wife. Julie did not marry Robert because she aspired to the role of pastor's wife, but says that once in ministry she developed a certain "flair" in her role and that she was "a good minister's wife." She claims that her background was an advantage because she "knew beforehand what the standards were" for minister's wives and was not troubled by them. She describes herself as "goody, goody and a legalist at heart who liked to do the right thing." Unlike other expastors' wives who are critical of the lifestyle, particularly the continual moving of minister families, Julie states that she "enjoyed change and variety" and the "new challenges" of shifting to a new location, although even she was alienated by the administration's "method of decision making" in relation to appointment of ministers. She admits that relocations became less bearable and "much harder with the kids."

As pastor's wife Julie "dressed simply" and "modestly." She was frugal and "didn't go out buying five hundred dollar designer suits and that sort of thing." Money was never something she and Robert complained about while in ministry. Julie describes the ideal minister's wife as "someone who is always there to support her husband . . . who is always at every meeting she was meant to be at, who helped run Vacation Bible schools, who was there to prepare the food when the big boys came down from Conference, and who just did it all without complaining." Julie read the appropriate literature, like the *Youth's Instructor* and *Ministry*, and "tried to fit the model" of the minister's wife. The idea of pursuing a career did not enter her mind while in ministry. She recalls telling a group of ministers' wives on one occasion that "ministers' wives should not have a job because being a minister's wife was enough of a job if it were to be done properly." Julie enjoyed planning and organizing and she "brought that aspect to her husband's ministry"; he tends to "go with the flow" rather than planing things ahead of time. She played a leading role organizing activities for the local church, assisted in Vacation Bible school programs, ran cooking demonstrations, and enjoyed playing music for church, in addition to her regular contributions to Adventist journals as a freelance writer. Julie believes she "was contributing a fair bit" to her husband's ministry. "Publicly, by attending the various programs and by just being there. Privately, I think a wife can often see things from that little bit of distance that's needed, and I think women are a bit more sensitive than men." She used to spend "a lot of time . . . pouring oil on troubled waters."

The one issue that concerned her prior to the circumstances that culminated with their exit was the fact that the contribution of pastors' wives to ministry is "undervalued" and "needs to be acknowledged more." She regarded herself as "a worker" and resents the fact that at ministers' meetings wives were "not part of the team" and confined to the margins. She recalls that on one occasion a Conference president "actually asked wives not to come to ministers' meetings" and that "if they were to come, we were asked to bring our own meals." She states, "I was very angry about that and I was ready to ask the Conference president who was coming to stay at our place to bring a cut lunch."

Julie and Robert were not "blind" to the failings of the Adventist leadership, and even though they had some "minor skirmishes" with Conference bureaucrats, in general, they were not preoccupied with the institutional processes of the organization, at least not until her husband became the focus of a Conference initiated post–Glacier View inquisition aimed at routing Ford sympathizers. Julie explains that her husband was "evangelical" but "not radical" in outlook and thus was "shocked" that Conference administrators and a group of laymen accused him of heresy. She was hurt by the way church leaders "crucified Des Ford at Glacier View" and was baffled by the church's response to "men leaving ministry, good men, men that I respected." She was utterly "disgusted with Adventist leadership" for the way her husband was treated. "I just lost complete respect, you know, for the [Conference] guys concerned. I lost respect for the Conference president, you know, as a man I have virtually no respect for him. He is the pits." Following the "heresy trial" of her husband, Julie began paying closer attention to what "the pastors were saying." As pastor's wife, Julie was

content for my husband to give me the answers [on doctrine]. I've not studied theology . . . and I often used to say that if Robert wanted to know about how something was cooked, well, he'd come and ask me, and if I wanted to know what the Bible was really saying about something, I would ask him that. That's theologically. Experientially I certainly did not believe I was going to get to heaven by the fact that my husband was a minister. I had my own experience but I didn't delve deeply into the Bible.

Ford's dismissal and her husband's experience forced her to take greater interest in matters of theology. She became more critical of the "corruption" and "hypocrisy" of church authorities. For a time she stopped attending church and "came up with all sorts of excuses to try and get out of attending." Robert left ministry after serving the Adventist Church for almost two decades. During his interview, Robert explained that the exit, "was definitely from me. Julie was probably, in her mind, much more wanting to continue being a minister's wife . . . than see me leave. In fact, I probably denied her a role. . . . I took it away from her. From being a minister's wife with a very distinct role and position in life, she was suddenly no one, and she had as much rethinking to do as I did. She did not influence me to leave but she supported me in that decision."

Expastors' Wives and Exit

The categories outlined in this chapter depict the variety of ways wives were involved in their husbands' exit from ministry. In some respects the extreme responses highlight the range of attitudes at the time of exit. The categories are used here to bring out the *different* ways expastors' wives related to their husbands' ministry and contributed to exit. The five categories reveal that the contribution of wives to exit is not uniform. The "embittered outsider's" feelings are pivotal in her husband's decision to exit ministry. The "conforming idealists" lose their idealism and youthfulness as pastors' wives and figure in exit as committed wives. "Reluctant feminists" are not reluctant about leaving, but confused about feeling they were used and exploited in ministry. The "calculating radical" is the reaction of wives who were born and bred in "the Adventist ghetto" (Lawson and Lockwood Carden [n.d.]). In the same ways that Old Testament prophets used "symbolic" or "parabolic actions" (R.B.Y. Scott 1968:99) to confront the values of their contemporaries, "calculating radicals" use radical behavior to shock conservative Adventist members and their own husbands to change. Finally, the "successful shepherdesses" are sad examples of wives who became part of the exit process by their devotion to their husbands and to the minister's wife role. They represent the majority of expastors' wives who enjoyed the pastor's wife role, were successful in it, and preferred to remain in ministry, but who also were committed to their husbands and identified with their hurts. Each of the wives in this last category has no misgivings about her husband's leaving ministry, and none has expressed a longing to return. The overwhelming impression of "successful shepherdesses" is that in losing an expastor the organization lost two workers with the one exit.

Only one of the wives interviewed does not fit comfortably into any of the five types listed above—she continues to be angry that her husband has left ministry. She converted to Adventism together with her husband when in their early thirties. Because of the continual criticism of relatives and friends and the fact that they had accepted the Adventist Saturday as Sabbath, they sold their business and moved to Avondale College, where the husband commenced training for ministry. The severity of their experience of conversion to sectarianism and the radical social and relational changes it necessitated may explain why this particular wife had refused to undergo a second religious transformation and all that it implies.

In the final outcome, twelve of the fifty expastors who completed the questionnaire, including Louise Paddock's husband, rate wife and family concerns high among their reasons for exit. Two of the wives interviewed believe they were "responsible" for their husbands' leaving ministry. One took matters in her own hands: she searched the national papers and found a job that she believed would suit her husband, wrote and typed his curriculum vitae, arranged for her boss to act as referee, and finally drove her husband to the interview, because she believed he deserved to be treated better. She explains, "A few years ago I would have worried how I was affecting [my husband's] career, but I think that both of us had progressed to the point where we didn't care any more."

SUMMARY

Theorizing that equates exit with faltering marital relationships not only views the influence of wives on the careers of husbands in negative terms, but also sees leaving ministry in negative terms, an assumption contested by approximately half of the wives interviewed. What is argued in this chapter is that the versions of exit told by wives highlight social processes which in expastor accounts are overlooked, disguised, or assigned to the "back stage." The narratives of expastors' wives provide additional insights that reinforce what has been argued in earlier chapters regarding exit as a social process. Far from being passive observers of their husbands' career crises, a majority of expastors' wives contributed to the career change of their husbands by reinforcing, facilitating, and in some cases actually precipitating the exit. More than this, the chapter shows that expastors' wives most devoted to their husbands and involved in their ministries also were most supportive of the decision to leave ministry.

Negotiating Exit

The actual separation from ministry most often occurs with a whimper rather than a bang. It involves cutting the remaining threads of a career that had come apart much earlier, the culmination of months, and in most cases years, of agonizing. The final stage is merely a routine event—there are no surprises, no tears, and no dramatic outbursts. The separation is dramatic only insofar as it marks the cessation of ministry and the commencement of a new episode in the life of the expastor and his family. It is dramatic *not* in how it is accomplished but in the radical changes it necessitates. What is argued in this chapter is that the timing of exit, writing the letter of resignation, notifying sect officials, and informing parishioners, family members, and close friends, are mechanical actions regulated by organizational procedures and routines.

TIMING EXIT

Researchers on the process of exiting organizations and social relationships emphasize the importance of catalysts and dramatic events to explain why individuals separate when they do. According to Ebaugh (1988a:123), the catalyst "mobilizes and focuses awareness" and "provides individuals with the opportunity to do something different with their lives." From her interviews with more than 160 individuals representing a variety of exit situations, Ebaugh identified the major types of catalysts, including, "specific events," "the straw that broke the camel's back" experiences, "excuses," and "moments of realization." What is common among the different types of catalysts is the fact that researchers (and some participants) cite them to explain action. In this study about half of the interviewees do not cite an explanatory catalyst. That 49 percent of expastors neither identify a point of time in their experiences of leaving nor focus on specific catalyst events prior to exit required explanation. The following responses are typical of twenty-one of the forty-three expastors interviewed:

> There was no real catalyst in my experience. . . . I was enjoying my ministry in the country, the bush walks and all that [but] I knew that I wouldn't be doing this for the rest of my life. . . . I'm not sure where but . . . it started to dawn on me that I didn't want to do this and I started to look around at what else I could do.

> There was no particular incident in my experience. Just this smoldering buildup. And that was it.

> I really don't know if there was a catalyst. I never sat down to analyze it. . . . I still cannot put my finger on what happened. You might be able to understand it better than I do, as an observer.

Expastors do not fragment exit into a sequence of identifiable stages characterized by specific attitudes. Exit narratives emphasize continuity between initial doubts and final exit; the circumstances that initially led former pastors to contemplate exit and the experiences prior to leaving are looked upon as being connected. Shaffir and Rockaway (1987:99–100) note that ultra-orthodox Jews similarly "without exception" defect after "a long period of doubts and soul-searching." This does not overlook the fact that more than half (51 percent) of expastors refer to what an outsider might regard as catalyst experiences during their interviews. However, expastors point to these experiences more to illustrate the social milieu and culture of the organisation at time of exit than to explain why they acted when they did. The events to which expastors attach special meaning do not fall within the range outlined by Ebaugh. While twenty-two expastors actually use the term "catalyst," sixteen describe events that do not even remotely correspond to Ebaugh's definition. Eight describe experiences that occurred between one and three years prior to leaving—one mentions a "heresy trial" two years before final separation, and a second describes a confrontation with an administrator eighteen months earlier. What is questioned here is not the importance of "limit-experiences" on expastor decisions to exit, but the status passage hypothesis which predicts that exit will be preceded by unusual or shocking events and the assumption that radical change necessarily follows out-of-the-ordinary experiences. Chapter 5 discussed at some length the types of experiences that erode idealism and generate cynicism among Adventist leavers. A consistent feature of expastor accounts is that exit from ministry is not attributed to unexpected or unusual circumstances, but to a proliferation of disappointments experienced over a number of years. It is the cumulative effect of a host of similar experiences that eroded expastor confidence in ministry and led to exit, whether by resignation or dismissal. For a minority of expastors who were in ministry for a short time, the buildup was brief and intense, and events normally separated in time occurred almost concurrently. With the majority of expastors events and changing relationships culminating in exit took place over a number of years. In all instances, however, the experiences that immediately precede exit are neither unusually harsh nor rare but typical of what expastors had come to expect in ministry.

A common denominator in expastor accounts of circumstances that precede exit is *the timing*, not the events themselves. Of the fifty-seven expastors whose exits were noted in official church records, 75 percent communicated their intention to leave between the months of October and February, with the greatest number of exits (40 percent) occurring in November (Figure 10.1). There are a number of possible explanations for this clustering in the timing of exits. One is that the timing coincides with the winding-down of Adventist operations, and thus exit occurs during the "quiet times" in ministers' lives. The evangelistic programs concluded, pastors conduct their planned baptisms of new converts, and the Adventist community seemingly enters a period of nonactivity and pastors take their annual leave. On this basis one might hypothesize that the decision to exit occurs when the minister is freed from the ongoing demands of regular ministry and has time to reflect on his work circumstances and personal needs. But the assumption that the year-end months *are* the quiet months of ministry does not bear scrutiny. In actual fact, the end of year period can be the busiest in the Adventist minister's program.

Figure 10.1
Monthly Pattern of Exits From the Adventist Ministry

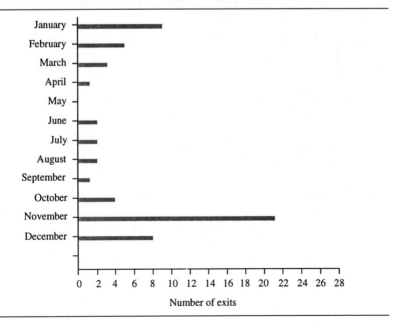

Number of exits

An alternative explanation is that the end of the year period is a high point in the Adventist community calender when Conference employees and lay constituents come together during the annual camp meetings to study and be "recharged" for the coming year. Ministers meet together often for between two and three weeks at a time, to prepare camp, pitch the tents, and plan for the occasion. The camp meeting is a rare opportunity for ministers, who for most of the year work on their own, to share ideas and exchange concerns with other pastors (Dick 1977). Indeed, I have argued in Chapter 6 that informal friendship associations play a critical role in expastors' exiting ministry by providing them with a venue to raise questions and an opportunity to have doubts reinforced, and it is especially at such gatherings that friendship networks were reestablished. However, the explanation that former pastors resigned after meeting other pastors with similar concerns is not supported by exit narratives. Only one expastor indicates that he made up his mind to exit ministry at a camp meeting, and he did not actually resign until the following year end.

The most plausible explanation as to why a majority of exits occur between November and February is that the timing reflects organizational processes and conforms with the Adventist calendar. The average pastoral appointment in the Adventist Church in the South Pacific Division was between two to three years, with many ministers relocated every year during internship and prior to ordination. During the months of September and October administrators finalize pastoral staffing for the Conference, and decide the direction of the future ministry of pastors. They then announce the changes during October and November. Because the pattern of ministerial appointments affects the operations of the local church, individual members and church boards often take advantage of the predictable patterning of pastoral appointments to communicate their preferences to the authorities. The last quarter of each year is thus a stressful time for pastors, whose performances are closely monitored and whose futures in ministry are being decided. Two of the expastors interviewed attribute their exit to clashes with Conference administrators triggered by the ubiquitous arguments over transfer to a different parish. Both contend that they were not consulted regarding their relocation, and one claims that his transfer was insisted upon despite a doctor's advice to the contrary. The timing of exits from the Adventist ministry depicts a common patterning that is generated by the Conference's annual review and transfer of ministers. The following response from one expastor is a case in point:

I was on the Conference Executive Committee at the time and the president rang me because we were dealing with staff changes. He rang me on a Monday and said, I have a difficulty and I need to talk with a committee member about such and such a person who we were going to transfer, and so forth. And I said, well, look, I wasn't going to tell you this now but because it affects the whole planning, I should let you know that I have decided to leave ministry.

This expastor was not "on trial" himself. However, talk of appointments and transfers prompted him to make public his intention to exit. The number of pastors resigning between the months of October and February does not necessarily imply that exit was a reaction to direct provocation by problems of pastoral evaluation. However, the clustering effect does suggest that, whether consciously or unconsciously, tensions surrounding pastoral appointments did come into play. The clustering of exit during these months may be indicative of an atmosphere of pastor evaluation that, as expastors' accounts suggest, degenerated during these months into open hostility against pastors out of favor with authorities or labelled doctrinally suspect. Whatever the actual reasons for the decisions to leave ministry during these months what is clear is that exit was not a spur of the moment action, as is the case with some defectors from new religious movements (Beckford 1985:157), but a decision that was thought about and agonized over. As one expastor explains, "I was under an enormous amount of stress at the time. . . . I just wanted to get out. I just couldn't handle the agony and pain of it all any longer."

RESIGNATION LETTERS

For expastors, the letter of resignation was a formality produced to meet bureaucratic requirements. While the news of the expastor's exit surprised some, there are no surprises in the letters, which signal the inevitability of exit. "I had well and truly finished with ministry and . . . the resignation letter was just a formality. It was just the tidying up of the paperwork," said one expastor. Another explained, "My resignation was the final step . . . and my letter made it clear . . . that I had been dying in ministry over the last two or three years." An expastor states, "We were already mentally packing up and going" even though "physically [I had not] put in my resignation letter." This expastor explains that his letter was merely "an outward expression of an inner state of mind." The terminology this pastor used had an Adventist ring to it: the letter of resignation was analogous to the baptismal certificate which Adventists consider to be an outward expression of a baptismal candidate's inner attitude to the church. The fact that one expastor received final settlement even before he submitted his resignation in writing suggests that the letter of resignation was a symbolic act and a bureaucratic formality.

The sixteen resignation letters collected in the course of the research fall into two categories differentiated by length and content. Nine expastors produced brief statements of between one and two pages, expressing disappointment at leaving ministry. In these letters, which are marked by economy of language, expastors highlight personal and family reasons for exit and only hint at the deeper social and theological problems experienced in ministry. Other expastors produced theological treatises of between six and eleven pages detailing their criticisms of Adventist doctrine, administration's intolerance of diversity, and loss of confidence in the sectarian worldview. We are not to conclude that longer letters imply more painful exits. Three expastors explained that they were instructed to produce "short statements" stressing that they were resigning from the Adventist ministry "for personal reasons," and two arrived at the wording with the assistance of Conference personnel. The following exchange during interview indicates that some expastors deliberately produced letters highlighting family and personal concerns, believing that they could jeopardize their terms settlement if they mentioned doctrine:

Expastor: Finally I wrote a letter, and I signed it and sent it off.

PHB: What did you say in this letter?

Expastor: You really are testing my memory now. I couched it in words that didn't specify doctrine.

PHB: Why didn't you mention doctrine?

Expastor: Well, for one thing, I thought if I state doctrinal reasons, I'm not going to get any assistance, financial assistance [to shift] back home. That's what I thought. Knowing what the president had said, and from the way he worked, I thought he would probably wipe me off the slate. I was trying to hedge my bets, in other words. I wanted to get what I could, particularly when I had heard and knew that there were some men who were being kicked out with nothing. I wanted to be sure we'd be able to get back home. However, if they came back and said to me that they weren't going to give me any support with the transportation, I was going to take them to court. And I actually went to a solicitor and sought legal opinion as to where I stand if I follow such a move. [The solicitors] told me that because the Handbook is couched in such general terms then it would be difficult to mount a civil damages claim in court. . . . So that was another reason why I didn't go doctrinally. I had to be careful, so I put it in terms of my family life and just wanting to get out.

For most expastors the letter of resignation was a symbolic act signifying a permanent end to painful struggles in ministry. In this sense the lengthy and detailed criticisms of Adventist theology "sealed" exit and gave it permanence. These letters were a form of "bridge burning" (Hine 1970; Gerlach and Hine 1970) which, as one expastor explains, "made the exit irrevocable . . . there was no turning back."

RESPONSE OF OFFICIALS

With the exception of two expastors who report that Conference officials "at first did not believe" them and a third who notes that his president puzzled over his desire to leave ministry and told him to have "a break" instead, a majority reported that officials were not surprised by the announcement and did not contest their exit. Two Conference presidents visited the expastors at their homes but did not discuss exit. Three others were visited by the Union Conference ministerial secretary, but it would appear that exit was a difficult subject on which to dialogue. One recalls, "We talked about the dog, we talked about how the kids were doing at school and a multitude of other totally unimportant things, and then he looked at his watch and said, oh, it must be time to go." The fact that no attempt was made to dissuade expastors from leaving confirms Hirschman's (1970) observation that some organizations prefer that "trouble-makers" exit rather than deal with their complaints. An expastor was surprised and "saddened . . . with the ease with which my resignation went through," adding that it took four years full-time study for him to enter ministry, but his career had terminated "in minutes." "What frustrated me most, and put this on record," states another, "was that the administration couldn't give a shit" about expastors. Two report that their Conference presidents prayed with them, one adding, the president "prayed . . . that God would forgive me."

The letter of resignation set in motion formal organizational procedures for terminating employment. Conference and Union officials formalized the termination and notified the expastor in writing of loss of ascribed status and terms of settlement. Official Conference minutes often distinguish between *real* and *stated reasons* for exit. Concerning four expastors who gave "personal and family reasons" for leaving, the Conference minutes record, respectively, that "there are some doctrinal uncertainties in the background of the decision," that exit was "due to doctrinal problems," and that the named expastors showed an "inability to remain loyal to the fundamental beliefs of the Church." Where the expastor focused exclusively on theology, the minutes record that doctrine was used to conceal personal and relational factors. Concerning one expastor who attributed his exit to problems with Adventist theology, the minutes record that "home and moral problems . . . contributed to his resignation." What expastors wrote in their letters of resignation was less critical than the fact that the letter mobilized institutional processes for managing deviating pastors.

Two different wordings were used to record exits in official minutes depending on the background of the leaver and his stated reasons for exit. Only five of the forty-seven expastors whose entries I noted in Conference minutes contain expressions of thanks: two are thanked "for their faithful service," two are commended for their "fine work" and "satisfactory work," and one is thanked for his contribution to "public evangelism." In addition to such comments, in the case of expastors who left "for personal reasons" which were not contested by Conference officers, the minutes additionally record that efforts were being made by the authorities to find them alternative employment within the organization:

We look forward to the time when he is able to apply to re-enter denominational employment.

He was a fine minister . . . and the committee has agreed to defer settlement to see if he wishes to return to denominational employment.

The president is endeavoring to arrange a transfer to another section of the denominational employment for him.

Expressions of appreciation, *in every case*, were in relation to expastors who were born Adventists; two were sons of continuing Adventist pastors. In the official records *no convert is thanked for his work in ministry*. Expastors express dismay that their ministry was terminated with not so much as a word of appreciation for their efforts in ministry and their contributions to the movement over the years:

I am annoyed that after eleven years of ministry I didn't even get a handshake. Not a comment, like, "You have done really well." . . . Nothing, except a bill from the Conference treasurer for what I still owed.

It's a very uncaring setup. I devoted fifteen years of my life as a minister and even many years before that doing all I could to promote and uphold and further the aims of the church, and as soon as I exit they couldn't even be bothered to continue my subscription to the *Ministry* magazine. They send that to ministers of other churches, you know, but as soon as . . . I left the ministry, choof, cut off like that, you know, which is ridiculous. I mean if anybody should still be receiving the *Ministry* magazine [it] should surely be ex-Adventist ministers. Oh, it's quite crazy though. They have never tried again to approach me in any way whatsoever. They just write you off, throw you away like a wrung-out rag and that's it. It's a funny set-up.

No matter what you contributed in the past, there's no letter of thanks for what you did for twenty-six years, or to say, we're sorry you've left the church, we believe you've done a wonderful contribution. None of that counts anymore. Furthermore, you have nothing to contribute to us in the future. Putting aside the egotistical things, it cannot be that every person who leaves ministry has nothing to contribute. That doesn't make any sense. Let's forget about me, and let's think of all the others who left. Are we saying, these people have nothing to contribute anymore? To my mind that is an impossible situation. But that is exactly the position. The church now denies you social equality, you're always a second class citizen, a backslider or whatever. It denies you any opportunity to contribute anything to the organization. So you can have no achievement needs met at all. You have nothing to offer us.

Expastors critical of sect doctrines and converts were additionally remonstrated in the official minutes. Concerning one expastor the minutes record that the "Conference will not assume responsibility for returning him and his family to his home town." Concerning a second, the minutes read that "Conference has not only withdrawn [his] credentials . . . but also annulled his ordination," thereby highlighting the committee's double displeasure. Variations in the way exits were recorded in official minutes are indicative of a social divide that pervades Adventist ministry. The division is evident also in the way final settlement was calculated.

FINAL SETTLEMENT

The matter of settlement was the last formal exchange expastors had with Adventist authorities, and not surprisingly, this too encapsulates themes and attitudes that recur in expastors' accounts. Discussions over payment to which expastors were not privy, were strictly between key Conference and Union personnel. Without exception, expastors had little or no idea how to calculate final settlement or what their entitlements were until settlement payments arrived in the mail. Both the process and outcome of settlement further embittered expastors who felt they were "run over" by the Adventist bureaucratic juggernaut.

All expastors were informed that settlement would be "according to policy." However, there are inconsistencies and some significant variations between expastors in how the authorities calculated settlement payments. Some expastors claim they received no reimbursement at all. Four expastors in this category had been in ministry for between one and three years, and a fifth who was a minister for seven years claims that he was told he was not eligible for "settlement" because he arranged an "independent transfer." A group of six expastors received no cash settlement but had relocation costs paid by the Conference, although there are variations in the way this concession was applied. Most had the costs paid or received cash equivalent for relocating to their "home town." Others received only a minimal sum to cover the costs of being relocated to Sydney. New Zealanders working in Australia, and Australians working in New Zealand and who had been in ministry for a short time, were affected by this. The majority of expastors received cash payments for their years of service and had their transportation costs paid as well. However, once again there are some important variations in the remuneration paid to leavers. Most received the equivalent of one week's pay for each year in ministry, thereby prompting one expastor to remark that "God is generous with forgiveness but stingy with money." Four expastors were reimbursed two weeks pay for each year in ministry. The discrepancy in settlement entitlements is highlighted by the fact that one expastor who had been in ministry for eleven years received the same amount in settlement as an expastor who served the church for twenty-six years.

Conference minutes reveal that administrators were well aware of irregularities in how policy was applied to ministers who left. Between 1982 and 1983 the subject of pastor fallout and terms of settlement was regularly debated by Conference and Union leaders. Fallout from the Adventist ministry had reached epidemic proportions, and administrators were under pressure to standardize procedures and maintain consistency with regard to settlement. In November 1984, the Union Conferences passed the most comprehensive policy statement on final settlement with employees. For the first time, an attempt was made to bring church policy in line with government/state provisions and to accept responsibility for returning former ministers "to the place from which he/she originally entered [ministry]." The policy did not increase the entitlements of expastors, although the expanded statement ensures that licensed ministers and converts do receive something.

An expastor who claims that his settlement amount was "about nine thousand dollars" short of what he should have been paid for his sixteen years of service is one of fourteen expastors who believe they were "cheated by the system." Six sought legal advice, and two actually planned to contest their amount in court but abandoned the idea because of legal costs. The Adventist Church is "a greedy institution," according to one expastor, a criticism that echoes Coser's (1974) description of organizations that consume the whole human personality. In expastor narratives three things are consistent in their descriptions of separation from ministry and settlement procedures: expastor belief of inconsistency; the amount received was less than what they expected; and the fact that they were paid an amount less 10 percent of tithe. Four expastors commented that they were first crushed by the organization before being robbed by it. However, even more painful for most expastors was their marginalization by former friends and church members.

RESPONSE OF CHURCH MEMBERS

With the exception of five expastors whose ministry was terminated abruptly by Conference and eight others whose departures culminated in public "brawls" with members and the authorities, 71 percent of expastors remained pastorally sensitive and announced their exits in a manner designed not to undermine the faith of parishioners. Seventeen expastors told their parishioners that they were planning to do "further study," although only four did so. For these expastors study leave was a way of softening the blow. Three did not give any reasons for leaving ministry. One expastor claims he had an opportunity to "really kick up a fuss" by "exposing the authorities" but for the sake of the members kept his concerns to himself. A second explains that he deliberately "lied" because he did not want to hurt the members: "I was fairly certain that I would never go back to church once I left but what I told . . . all my members . . . was that I'm leaving the ministry and going back to my home town. I said, I think ministry is not for me. Maybe I could do some good as a layman. . . . I actually lied because I wasn't sure that I wanted to tell them that I was going to run away. I mean, how do you tell someone that you've just baptised that you're about to leave what they've just joined." Expastors believe they had opportunity to harm the church in how they separated from ministry. One reported that the local church elder informed him that the local church "would disband if Conference did anything" to him. A second states that church members were planning to redirect tithe to him if he were forced out by Conference. In the end no church closed its doors because the pastor left ministry, and no expastor interviewed reports receiving tithe directly from church members. Nevertheless, the narratives reflect a belief that expastors had an opportunity to make their exit even more painful for the organization but chose to maintain their pastoral integrity instead—something one expastor believes cannot be said of the authorities.

Unlike Catholic priests, most of whom do not abandon their church when they leave the priesthood (Rice 1990), one out of every three expastors (32 percent) who exited ministry also separated from the Adventist community. As one expastor explains, "I wanted to escape from the Adventist community. I didn't want to meet anybody who had thought of me as a minister. . . . I didn't want to teach anybody. I didn't want to be upheld in any respect. I wanted to be just ordinary . . . and for these reasons, I didn't want to have contact with them. . . . I didn't want Adventists as friends." At the same time, 23 percent of interviewed expastors continued to attend church unaffected by their changed status. Two claim that involvement in Adventist programs was more satisfying once they were freed from the bureaucratic constraints and that they now participate in the church's programs because they want to and not because they have to. Approximately half (45 percent) of the interviewed expastors planned to continue to maintain social contact with the church. However, each of these expastors reports that members experienced difficulty relating to an ex and claim they were marginalized and excluded from the church's program. How one left ministry and for what reasons apparently mattered little to church members, who looked upon all former pastors as "apostates" and "heretics." "Exministers are placed in the apostate group and ignored," according to one expastor. A second states that he was "treated as a non-Christian going to church." A third recalls that the leading elder of the Adventist church he was attending told his wife that her husband was "a fallen angel from Satan." These expastors were labelled "trouble makers" and derided as "wolves in sheep's clothing." Notwithstanding the stories of congregation support, there is a perception among leavers that pastors were reconstituted into "instant outsiders" once they left ministry (Richardson 1975:140).

Berger (1963:80) states that "in small communities" ridicule and gossip are "subtle" but "powerful" mechanisms of social control and are particularly effective against individuals who formerly enjoyed "a high degree of social visibility." An expastor hoped his relocation some thousands of kilometers from his previous parish would enable him to make a new start but discovered that rumors exaggerating the circumstances of his exit were communicated to his new parish, warning members and the local pastor to be wary of him. A more cruel form of social censure was opprobrium or shunning. A former pastor states that people "shook their heads" when he walked into church and heard them say, "Poor old Pastor G. He'd lost his way." Berger argues:

[One] of the most devastating means of punishment at the disposal of a human community is to subject one of its members to systematic opprobrium and ostracism. . . . An individual who breaks one of the principal taboos of the group . . . is "shunned." This means that, while permitted to continue to work and live in the community, not a single person will speak to him ever. It is hard to imagine a more cruel punishment. (Berger 1963:88)

Unlike Amish Mennonites who, according to Berger, make effective use of shunning to punish deviating members, no such formal regulation is observed by Adventists. However, from what expastors reported during interview, marginalization if carried out informally is an equally effective form of censure. An expastor who for eight years attended an Adventist church regularly after leaving ministry explains that "they were lonely years. . . . There's been a measure of good will and fellowship, but there also has been an aloofness." Expastors discovered that friends lost interest in them once they left ministry and they were treated as "strangers" and "lepers" by former colleagues. An expastor recalls that he was desperate for work after leaving ministry and managed to get a part-time job as a landscape gardener but that "as soon as my Adventist boss got wind that I was an expastor, he didn't want me any more."

Some established friendships with church members but report that the matter of leaving ministry and Adventist theology were not discussed. One former pastor "was dying to talk with someone about leaving ministry," and explains:

I guess the issue of not being able to talk about religious questions is a big factor that I didn't handle very well. I remember going out to a meal, to a party where there was a group of Adventists. Now they weren't conservatives, they were fairly open-minded but still loyal Adventist people who didn't know, or who hadn't been exposed to a lot of the issues. I can remember holding forth, you know, this is my chance (whispers), you know, to try to discuss the issues with them (laughs), and going home I remember saying to my wife, I am going to shut up or we won't be invited out any more. That was painful.

An expastor who hoped to maintain links with the church as "a normal lay person" discovered that marginalization and exclusion are the new norms for leavers. Four expastors hoped to contribute to the Sabbath program by preaching occasionally, and two were granted access to local pulpits only after being formally approved by the Conference president and the Executive Committee. One reports that for more than a year he had to negotiate with Conference officials before being allowed to preach and showed me a folder of correspondence as proof. Ironically, these expastors preached one sermon each and were stopped from taking any more because the parishioners had complained. The willingness of former pastors to preach would have eased some of the burden of finding competent and willing preachers. However, the fact that their expertise was rejected suggests that local members preferred the sermons of inexperienced but "loyal" Adventist laymen to better presented but "suspect" messages of former pastors. As one of these expastors recalls:

Pastor B. saw me at church and said to me, look, I'm sorry I can't give you another sermon because I know that there would be maybe as many as ten people who would just get up and walk out if you stood up there in the front of the church to preach. I was horrified by that. I just couldn't believe it. Here were people who were prejudging me, who wouldn't give me a go. My one sermon had been inoffensive enough; it was a gospel centered pastoral sermon, but a spiritually challenging sermon. It had nothing to do with doctrine; it was just gospel centered. . . . I was just horrified, and I hated Pastor B. for saying it and despised his bloody gutlessness. I thought that if people thought that, then let them walk out.

In a number of instances the marginalization of expastors initiated by Conference administrators was reinforced by church members with "blatant signals" (Shaffir and Rockaway 1987:106) announcing the altered identity of the former pastors. Parents and parents-in-law of expastors who were born Adventists reacted harshly to the exit.

PARENTS AND PARENTS-IN-LAW

Skonovd (1981:58–59) observed that family supports often facilitate disaffection from new religious movements. Jacobs (1989:121) found that families also aid reintegration of former members into mainstream secular society. According to Beckford (1985:162–164), some former members of new religious movements actually returned to live with parents following exit. Nine expastors (two converts and seven who were born Adventists) described in some detail the reactions of their parents to their leaving ministry. Wright (1987:85) made the observation that following exit some leavers reestablish family bonds that deteriorated following conversion. The two expastors who were converts explained that they now have more respect and appreciation for the beliefs of their non-Adventist fathers, and one in particular went to great lengths to describe his newly established affection for his father. The reactions of parents of expastors who were born Adventists made exit and post-exit "recovery" particularly painful for some. In the following three responses expastors recall painful moments after telling parents and family members of their decisions to leave ministry. Two expastors recalled bitter altercations with parents-in-law who accused them of leading their daughters astray:

When the in-laws came to visit us, they talked to us about our views and, you know, father said, well, son, if you believe like that I don't think that I could ever have you in my home again. . . . I was a bit blown by that and so was my wife. They were in tears when we told them where we were theologically. . . . This was symbolic of the tensions and pressures felt by us from within the family.

We visited my wife's parents but did [not] discuss the issue of leaving ministry till the very last. It was a very painful thing and something which we were totally surprised by how severe it was. It was taken very severely. That shocked us both, and it was actually very traumatic. It was very very painful and very sad. . . . Worst of all is that we thought her father has always come over as being sort of with an enlightened mind even though the mother has been always traditional, you know, straight up and down, you do it this way, ask no questions. She accepted what we were saying much better. . . . He just could not accept it, he refused to accept it even when we were telling him. It was very sad. It got nasty, very nasty. I really haven't got over it. . . . He criticised me. . . . It was really awful. At two o'clock in the morning . . . this wreck of a man crawled into our room and begs, actually woke us out of sleep and begged us not to do what we're doing (whispers). "Don't desert the truth. Don't desert the truth. You're doing the wrong thing." It was just so traumatic. This guy just could not accept it. . . . To him, basically, we were lost. His thinking is just very clear that we are lost people. We argued for hours, debated for hours and hours, and when . . . he realized the situation, you know, "You are the one who's misled my daughter" (laughs). It came down to that. "You've misled my daughter, you've made my daughter a lost soul" (whispers). I just can't forget it. It got very personal. It got very bitter. It was very terrible. We really felt that we shouldn't have even said anything. We felt so bad.

These two responses illustrate the expastors' tense relations with family members. Both expastors no longer identify with the Adventist movement. The latter explains that he had "put up with it for six months" and then stopped attending church because "it was becoming a real effort just to turn up." Only four of the eighteen expastors who attended Adventist services following exit continue to do so. Their experiences of marginalization and alienation may account for their falling away.

The son of an Adventist pastor explains that his parents' acceptance of exit was the precursor to his post-exit emotional recovery:

Dad was more accepting than mum, because mum felt that once God had called you, He doesn't go back on the call. She found it very hard to accept where I am now.... [The issue of parents] came up in a counselling course I was doing.... I discovered that the non-acceptance of my parents of where I am at now ... was hampering who I was as a person. ... So I went back to confront mum and dad and tell them that I wanted to be accepted for who I was, not who they'd still like me to be ... I finally got that out of them and that was a real relief for me.

SYMBOLIC MARKERS

Expastors marked exit from ministry with actions signalling their changed occupational status. A number ceremoniously burnt the sermons they had amassed from years of preaching. One expastor explains, "When I burnt all my sermons ... that was the end of Adventism." Others systematically culled from their filing cabinets and bookshelves and gave away or destroyed articles and books they associate with ministry. Most also discarded their correspondence; only a handful of expastors interviewed were able to produce copies of their letters of resignation but wish they kept their correspondence as proof for people who apparently find their stories too incredible to believe. By discarding their "tools of trade" expastors signalled the termination of that line of work. Expastors reported a variety of other activities which in their retrospective retelling are imbued with special meaning.

Whereas shaving one's beard is a symbolic act of "final separation" among orthodox Jews (Shaffir and Rockaway 1987:102), two Adventist expastors grew beards to signal their exit from ministry. One of these expastors explained, "When I preached my last sermon, I didn't shave from that day till this. That was symbolic, you know, we weren't encouraged to have beards in the ministry, and for me that was proof that I was born again, I was setting out, I had come of age. It was all those things." For a second expastor, the beard was "a visual symbol of my freedom ... and the fact that now I could look rough for the job and it didn't matter." An expastor who converted to Adventism as a youth and who had not drunk alcohol for two decades since becoming an Adventist says that after delivering his letter of resignation he

went to the bottle shop and got some summer wine, which was just disgusting, but it was a symbolic gesture. I parked beside the road and drank the whole lot, but it felt so good just to be able to be an adult again, just to ... be able to choose what I wanted and choose my own morality. ... There was no struggle. I loved it and felt young again. I felt I had taken up where I left off. I was now nineteen again ... and I was just now living, and, you know, I was old enough to drink and to do as I pleased.

Six other expastors point to drinking alcohol as their symbol of post-ministry life. One of these expastors recalled that "at one stage [following exit] we were on barbecue and drinking terms with all of our neighbours at the back of our house and the front side. I really threw myself into it." Five expastors, including one third generation Adventist, who were vegetarians and believed that pork is an "unclean food" deliberately ordered salad sandwiches with ham. Still others went to the movies and dances, activities sect authorities condemn as "worldly" and unacceptable Adventist behavior. Several expastors explained that the interview itself marked the final stage in their rite of passage. Four used the occasion of my visit to remove the remnants of their past careers by donating to my research their collection of "Adventistana." "This stuff has been in that box for nearly four years," remarked one expastor. "Now I can finally tie it up and have it removed." Another said his carton of material was obstructing his post-ministry recovery and therefore felt obliged to "get it out . . . to make room for the Holy Spirit to come in." To an observer not familiar with Adventist culture the events are neither spectacular nor unique and may even appear trivial, but to the expastors the actions are symbolic and charged with meaning.

The point being emphasized here is that the rituals cited by expastors are intentional indicators of attitudinal and behavioral change. In the same way that separating couples redefine objects that symbolise their previous coupled identity, the symbolic gestures of expastors point to a "negative redefinition" (Vaughan 1986:134) of norms of behavior which Adventists associate with ministry. Cohen (1985:58–69) argues that "symbolic reversal" is a "ubiquitous phenomenon of symbolism in community life" by means of which members define community boundaries. In the case of expastors symbolic inversion declares the termination of ministry and "transgression" of Adventist conventional boundaries. These symbolic rituals are "bridge-burning acts" (Hine 1970; Gerlach and Hine 1968, 1970) by means of which expastors signal discontinuity with the past and affirm commitment to the present course of action and the irreversibility of their intentions. The symbolic actions reflect expastor release from the organizational constraints of ministry.

POST-EXIT EMOTIONS

The interviews with expastors abound with "emotionality" (Denzin 1989:29). Expastors shout to convey displeasure and at times are barely audible as they recount hurts. On occasions they bang their fists on the table for emphasis or walk around the room in frustration, while at other times they sit almost motionless, staring at some invisible object in the distance as they recount painful moments in their experience of leaving ministry. For the most part the language of expastors is carefully selected. Their words are precise, and they only occasionally resort to using expletives. Eleven expastors swore during their interviews when describing local Conference administrators. All expastors, at one time or another during interview, communicated their emotions with laughter. Seventeen cried. One expastor explained that his were "tears of joy rather than sorrow"; a majority cried as they *relived* their exits.

Wright (1987) argues that emotions differentiate voluntary from coerced or "deprogrammed" defectors. Wright found that the overwhelming majority of voluntary defectors from religious organizations he surveyed were better adjusted emotionally and thus spoke positively of their past associations in contrast to individuals who had undergone "deprogramming." Jacobs (1989) used the variety of emotions recounted to her by the defectors she had interviewed to construct a typology of "stages" of adjustment leavers go through in the process of reestablishing social and emotional life. Emotionality features centrally also in Skonovd's (1981) study of apostasy, where it is argued that negative emotions are more pronounced among persons leaving "totalist" organizations and that negativity toward the past is therapeutic and integral to adjusting to normality. Recent studies in sociology emphasize that emotions are shaped by and mirror their social-institutional contexts. Thoits (1989), for example, argues that emotions are not independent bio-physiological phenomena but dependent variables and products of social influences. Zurcher (1982) and Lofland (1985) believe that emotions are socially shaped and "scripted" by particular structural and interactional contexts. In the retrospective narratives of expastors, however, emotions are incidental and triggered by the specific experiences they recounted during interview. Thus the emotions of expastors witnessed during interview were neither "withdrawal reactions" (Skonovd 1981:129) nor expressions of adjustment (Jacobs 1989) but indicators of how expastors currently feel about particular aspects of their past.

Freedom and Elation

Whereas ex-Moonies found the period immediately following exit difficult and trying (Beckford 1985:168), SanGiovanni (1978) states that former nuns were full of "heady pleasures and emotional exhilaration" during their first six weeks after leaving. Jacobs (1989:120) reports that defectors whom she had surveyed similarly "savor the privileges of nonrestricted life." The experience of freedom following exit is a universal phenomenon and certainly not restricted to defectors from religious associations. In his *Asylums* (1961:70) Goffman writes that "immediately upon release the inmate is likely to be marvellously alive to the liberties and pleasures of civil status." Regardless of whether they resigned or were dismissed, expastors similarly recalled feeling elated and relieved when they finished with ministry. The following selection of responses illustrate the emotions of expastors at the time of exit.

As a minister I felt I had submitted to the controls of the organization and surrendered my personal freedom. . . . When I left I felt the controls of the church no longer. It was great to be free again.

It was liberating.

I just wanted to be independent emotionally. When I resigned they had no more claim over me, my life, my time or anything, and it's really what I wanted to do.

A weight was lifted off my shoulders.

It felt great. I felt that I was walking on air.

I sort of felt a sense of release. This was as soon as I had taken the decision to resign. . . . It was like a great burden was lifted off my shoulders. I had been working under pressure for so long.

I was fed up to the teeth with the church trying to control my life and curtail my freedom. . . . It's lovely to be able to make your own decisions. Instead of the church saying go thence, you make up your own mind and say, well, I'd like to do that and off you go and do it. I like being in control of my life again. . . . Now I really value that freedom—the freedom to believe what I want to believe and the fact that my personal life makes no impact on my job. . . . I can swear and tell dirty jokes and I'm not going to lose my job . . . and the fact that now I have work life and private life and social life, whereas in ministry it was all one, and the only social life you had was with the church, [and] the fact that now you've rejoined the human race. . . . I like my freedom. I like the independence I now have. I couldn't stand to lose that again.

It was a release, and I was happy, very happy about that.

Relief, that's what I felt. I always had been fighting the ministry. . . . There were just some things that weren't me about ministry. So there was release. . . . I now have the chance to be myself and call my own shots.

I broke down and cried because of this enormous sense of relief (laughter). . . . There was this enormous sense of relief. This tension that we had been living under for years, now, suddenly was gone. That was enormous relief.

The sense of a weight being lifted or a great burden removed that five expastors used to describe their post-exit feelings has rich biblical and religious connotations. Christ, for example, promised to remove the burden from those who choose to follow him (Matthew 11:28–30). In his *Pilgrim's Progress*, John Bunyan writes that when "Christian came up [to] the cross, his burden loosed from off his shoulders, and fell from off his back, and began to tumble . . . till it came up to . . . the Sepulchre . . . [and] he saw it no more." Expastor recollections of feeling released capitalize on imagery that is central to the Christian faith and thus carries a retrospective criticism of the devotee's former life. Indirectly, it conveys a criticism of the very organization whose claim to legitimacy is founded on freedom; Adventist expastors felt liberated only after they left.

However, there is a discernible difference between how expastors born Adventists and converts describe their freedom. For the latter, freedom entails the negation and rejection of the whole sectarian system. As one states, "The things which I was taught by Adventists as being wrong, are not wrong." For converts, "this freedom is felt in all aspects of the devotee's life, including freedom from the religious discipline, freedom from the pressure to conform, freedom from the emotional demands of devotion, and freedom from the constraints of a narrowly defined sense of self" (Jacobs 1989:121). By contrast, the descriptions of those born and raised Adventists are more circumspect and restrained. Two expastors from an Adventist background state that their exit has "stripped away legalism" from their Adventism. Another explains that he is now free to be friends also with church administrators, and adds, "The Conference president is more of a friend to me now than he ever was. . . . I can relate to him easier now than I did in ministry." For all expastors, the initial feelings of elation were short-lived and gave way to a range of emotions and experiences best described as personal anomie.

Personal Anomie

The post-exit grief experienced was "beyond what I had ever imagined," states one expastor. A second describes it as "the biggest trauma of my life." The adjectives expastors use to describe their change of mood are similar: it was a "traumatic experience," "very stressful," "very painful," "cruel" and "emotionally devastating." One expastor claims that he came close to having "a nervous breakdown." A second explains that his "life was in tatters," while "the bottom had fallen out of everything," acording to another. An expastor who was a second generation Adventist states that once the initial elation of leaving ministry had subsided, it had "dawned" on him that leaving ministry was like having "turned away from the shore into the sea . . . in a little raft . . . and I didn't know where I was going." Wright (1987:75), Skonovd (1981:120–133), and Beckford (1978a:249–250, 1985:167–173) employ the concept of "floating" to describe the post-elation outlook of exiters. Skonovd (1981:133) argues that "floating" is a relatively common occurrence and compares it to "reality vertigo" or "a type of flashback similar to the common experience of waking up from a deep sleep thinking one is somewhere else." According to Wright (1987:75), floating is the response of "individuals [who] have not yet firmly relocated in new plausibility structures, that can provide support for redefinition of identity and objective reality." Descriptions of the experience resemble what has been traditionally described in sociology as "anomie."

There is considerable disagreement as to the usefulness of the concept of anomie as an analytical tool. "Pure sociologists" (Hart 1976:194) like Durkheim (1952, 1976) and Merton (1938) interpret anomie in macro terms as a condition that is derived from the society as a whole. In their terms anomie is endemic to societies undergoing radical social change. As a result of the extent and rate of change, traditional structures, values, and norms are shaken, according to these authors, and individuals are left to grope alone in a social vacuum without fixed reference points. By contrast social psychologists, including Srole (1956) and McClosky and Schaar (1965), conceptualize anomie as an individual condition that emanates from changes in the individual's social and psychological circumstances. They equate anomie with cognitive, emotional, and personal factors that impede socialization. They define anomie as "a state of mind, a cluster of attitudes, beliefs and feelings in the minds of individuals" who feel that "the world and oneself are adrift, wandering, lacking clear rules and stable moorings" (McClosky and Schaar

1965:19). Beckford (1975:178) believes the concept of anomie carries a diversity of "interpretations" and "ideological connotations" and has become "embodied in a highly conventionalised type of explanation" of so-called deviant behavior, and argues that when used as a "blanket explanation" the concept lacks precision and analytical clarity and obfuscates "the total range of meanings" of a situation. For these reasons Beckford prefers not to use the concept at all. In the present context, anomie is used as a general descriptive term similar to the way that Hart (1976:194–195) uses it, to describe the experiences of individuals whose normative world has been suddenly overturned following a personal crisis. Almost everyone of Hart's (1976:195) respondents who reported marriage breakdown reported feelings and attitudes the author equates with personal anomie or normlessness. Hart contends that the abrupt dismantling of marriage sends shock waves into every sphere of an individual's life and generates feelings of confusion, loss of motivation, and loss of personal identity. In the following passages expastors employ imagery that is reminiscent of Hart's respondents as they reflect on their ministries.

I had become quite emotional. . . . I guess I was heading toward a nervous breakdown. . . . With the kind of trauma I had gone through . . . my life had become just a cloud, a bewilderment for me, and I wondered where on earth I could turn for help. . . . It took a while for me, you know, to come to terms with it. . . . I think that it's only recently that I've begun to feel at ease with who I am. . . . I think having my parents accept [the new me] . . . has been the final part of adjusting.

I was pretty low. It was a low time for me. . . . I can remember quite distinctly saying to myself, I have no church family, I have no immediate family, I have no vocation, I have no education. All I've got is a calling. I can recall distinctly thinking these things. . . . I recall going out on a walk and wanting to cry . . . because I felt that my whole status, my place in society had gone.

No one in my sample of expastors was prepared for the cataclysmic changes necessitated by exit, not even the nine expastors who for almost three years had been contemplating and planning their departures. Expastors state that the initial exhilaration of disengaging quickly subsided. Within weeks of leaving ministry, expastors vacated their Conference-owned home and relocated to a different city or town and left friends and established social networks behind. With career in shambles, no regular income, marginalized by church members, and in many instances also abandoned by their Adventist relatives, many expastors felt isolated and alone. Leaving ministry had a "spill over effect" (Hart 1976:195) that touched every aspect of the expastor's life and personal identity. Beckford (1985:159) points out that among Moonie defectors "nobody made plans for leaving" and consequently experienced great difficulties coping with changes following exit. Adventist expastors thought much and for a long time about their exit. Even so, two wish they planned their exits more carefully. A third thinks he would have remained in ministry had he known the level of emotional anguish he would have to endure and the enormity of the changes his exit necessitated.

Hart (1976:195) indicates that "personal anomie is a relatively short-term phenomenon." It is difficult to estimate with accuracy the duration of the experience. However, from the interview data one may generalize that personal anomie is accentuated by particular social circumstances. The experience of normlessness is more pronounced, for example, among the three senior expastors who were unemployed for between eighteen months and two years, the two expastors who additionally experienced marriage failure following exit, and three others whose career change coincided with major personal and family crises. Normlessness was less pronounced among younger expastors who had time and energy to reestablish alternative careers.

Anger

In general terms expastors are not angry people. They are not bitter and twisted with hatred either toward the organization they believe has let them down or for the administrators whose actions, in their opinions, fell short of the Christian ideals they espouse. Researchers disagree over the level of importance they should assign to negative emotions in the experience of individuals making transitions. Skonovd (1981:163) argues that negative emotions toward the previous group, including "anti-cult activism," are necessary precursors to adjustment among religious defectors. Jacobs (1989:119–120) equates anger with "intense rage" and "feelings of resentment" and claims it is an emotion defectors experience during the "adjustment period" of exit. Jacobs notes that 55 percent of the forty former members she surveyed reported feeling angry and resentful after leaving their sect and concludes that anger is a mechanism that serves to establish "emotional distance" from the previous religious community. Wright's (1987:89) findings do not support these claims. He found that only 7 percent of his sample of religious defectors are angry and that the majority (67 percent) look back upon their past with a degree of social and emotional distance, claiming that they are "wiser for the experience." Wright (1987:90) attributes the difference in orientation between his and Jacobs's findings to the fact that his subjects were voluntary defectors and thus contends that "the voluntary defector . . . has had more time to weigh the decision [of leaving], to consider alternatives, and to build an entirely different rationale for living." All expastors express disappointment or resentment toward one or more aspects of their time in ministry, process of exit, and post-exit lives. On the basis of the interview data Adventist expastors may be placed into three general groupings which represent the different ways they have dealt with their anger.

While disappointed and hurt by the circumstances that culminated with their exit from ministry and with the way they were treated by members and administrators, twenty-three expastors stated that they either had "forgotten" past hurts or claim the hurts no longer intrude into or affect their post-ministry lives. These expastors parallel Wright's defectors who are "philosophical" about the past. A second group of expastors internalized the anger. The nine expastors in this category, eight of whom are converts, blame themselves for entering ministry in the first place and for allowing themselves to be dominated by the sectarian system. The one expastor in this category with an Adventist background is angry at himself for being angry with his wife while in ministry. A third group of eleven expastors who were at the time of interview between four to seven years out of ministry continue to harbor anger and resentment about their past, and this is contrary to Jacobs's (1989:119) observation that the feelings of anger reported by 90 percent of her sample immediately following exit dissipated over time. Four expastors are angry at the rumors circulated about them by members and administrators accusing them of moral indiscretion, and about the fact that they have no way of contesting them. Three expastors continue to be angry at the fact that they have been marginalized by the Adventist community and labelled heretics and apostates. Two resent the fact that their ordination credentials were annulled. Two expastors continue to be pained by their economic circumstances because of their time in ministry. There is strong correlation between the emotional well-being of expastors and their present social and economic circumstances.

SUMMARY

Final separation was neither a passive drift out of ministry nor the outcome of unanticipated or unusual circumstances. Exit was more the culmination of a host of tension-producing experiences punctuated with clashes and confrontations with administrators and church members than the result of a single decisive encounter. The final break with ministry was not at all the predictable unfolding transition depicted in the theorizing. The process of disengaging from the Adventist ministry was both more complex and less orderly than what is depicted in models such as status passage, while the timing of exit, writing the letter of resignation, and informing the relevant parties reflect organizational processes and denominational routines. The chapter also noted that the post-exit emotions of expastors are situationally conditioned and linked with particular social circumstances. While it may be true that for some expastors negative attitudes (or the absence thereof) toward the sectarian organization are indicative of post-exit recovery, the evidence presented in this chapter suggests that expastors' attitudes and emotions witnessed during interview do not automatically correspond with degrees of emotional recovery, but reflect present social, relational, and employment circumstances, as well as the interview itself, which called on expastors to recall and reflect on their past.

Chapter 11 _____

Adventist Crossroads

During the 1980s the Seventh-day Adventist Church in Australia and New Zealand experienced a fallout from the ministry in proportions never before witnessed. The controversies in the Adventist community, which often centered on the teachings and influence of Australian theologian Des Ford, and culminated with his dismissal, exploded in the community with a ferocity and intensity that shattered the peacefulness of the sect and threatened to destroy it. Adventist churches were polarized: family disagreements were transposed into doctrinal feuds, sons turned against fathers, and daughters against mothers. The issues evoked feelings rarely witnessed in a Christian community. In this climate of hostility that left no room for neutrality even the most disinterested minister took a stand. More than 180 pastors exited from the Adventist ministry during the eight-year period of the study, a loss equivalent to four large Conferences of pastors or 40 percent of the present ministerial work force in these two countries. A decade later the issues continue to haunt the Adventist organization, and while exit has subsided to a constant irritating flow and the administration has tightened its grip over all areas of operation, there is a sense that Adventism has been permanently affected.

Hirschman (1970:68) cites the maxim that "a model is never defeated by facts, however damaging, but only by another model." In the present study I set out neither to defeat any one of the models of exiting discussed in Chapter 2 nor to arrive at a prime cause of exit. Rather, the sociological problem was to identify and examine micro-social processes—"the build-up to the actual breaking of contact," "the nature of the social interactions" and "intensive questioning" (Beckford 1978b:108–109)—to elucidate how personal experiences, social relationships, and organizational processes interacted with and were reinforced by religious convictions so as to erode commitment and generate exit. Detailed analysis of expastors' narratives revealed that the depiction of exit as an orderly movement from one status/role to another does not correspond with the indeterminate character of the phenomenon evident in the accounts of expastors. My analysis of the interview data showed that processes associated with exit were subtle, confused, and difficult. Often expastors were not aware of the outcomes of their actions, nor, did they possess complete understanding of what was happening in their lives. What is often "very clear" (Ebaugh 1988a:181) to researcher observers remained obscure and confusing to the actors involved in the experience. Moreover, any patterns discernible in the narratives are retrospective and secondary to the experience. If there was a single model that could fit the patterns observed in expastors' accounts, it would be one which connected *what expastors said* with *what they did*. Hirschman's (1970) discussion of the ways organizations respond to criticism and member/customer loss is insightful for understanding what happened in the Adventist community that culminated with the unprecedented fallout from its ministry. The exit-voice framework ties together the many strands identified in the earlier chapters regarding expastors' experiences of exiting.

EXIT AND VOICE IN MINISTRY

Hirschman's interest on how institutions react to criticism and membership loss grew out of his research on the railway system in Nigeria. Hirschman observed that although the state-run railway was abysmally inefficient, few people ever complained. He also noted that merchants of any power and importance preferred to send their goods by the considerably more expensive but efficient road transport rather than protest the railway's inefficiency. The minority critical of the railway system was content to use the alternative mode of transport, thereby leaving the railways to care for the passive majority who could not afford road transport. Because of this arrangement the Nigerian railway system was under no pressure to improve its services, provided that its management continued to accept the loss of some customers in preference to changing the system (Hirschman 1970:44–45). The combination of exit and voice took a particularly noxious form in Nigeria's railway system—"exit did not have its usual attention focusing effect because the loss of revenue was not a matter of the utmost gravity for management, while voice did not work as long as the most aroused and therefore the potentially most vocal customers were the first ones to abandon the railroads for the trucks" (Hirschman 1970:45). Hirschman expected that criticism of the organization's inefficiency and loss of customers would prompt management to reassess its operations and take appropriate measures to rectify the problems. The fact that neither voice nor exit generated the anticipated organizational responses led him to speculate about "the elusive mix" of exit and voice and to postulate the conditions under which the exit option is preferred to voice, and to explore the factors facilitating voice and the relative effectiveness of voice and exit in organizations.

Hirschman used the absence and/or presence of exit and voice to construct a typology classifying organizations into four "ideal types." According to Hirschman (1970:77), organizations where both exit and voice play important roles are few and far between. He cites voluntary associations and competitive political parties among these "rare birds." At the opposite extreme totalitarian one-party systems respond neither to exit, which is equated with treason, nor voice, which is considered mutiny; members in totalitarian systems are obliged to keep their mouths shut or lose their heads. Competitive business enterprises, by contrast, are more responsive to exit because even though customers can and often do protest at the deterioration in the quality of the products or services provided, most take the easy route and choose another product or call on the services of a competitor. The economic consequences of loss of sales force businesses to make the necessary changes to reclaim lost customers. In Hirschman's model churches are typical of the fourth type of organization which takes the complaints and protests of members seriously but from which exit is not a common occurrence. What is of relevance to this study of expastors is not the typology itself but Hirschman's preoccupation with "voice" and his discussion of "perverse" or "pathological" organizations that are equipped with reaction mechanisms to which they do not respond (Hirschman 1970:122). Exit and voice, Hirschman argues, are unavoidable and necessary processes even of "healthy" organizations. "Every organization . . . navigates between the Scylla of disintegration-disruption and the Charybdis of deterioration due to lack of feedback," according to Hirschman (1981:224). The critical point is not whether members criticize the system or leave, but how the organization responds to negative feed-back. His discussion of the exit-voice duality provides some useful insights for understanding fallout from the Seventh-day Adventist ministry.

Hirschman (1970:33–36) argues that voice is a residual of exit; whoever does not exit is a candidate for voice, or better still, dissatisfied individuals activate voice and complain whenever the exit option is not available to them. In other words, one could argue that pastors who complained were less likely to exit. Conversely, voice can be an initial response and exit the "reaction of last resort" after voice has failed. In other words, decisions of whether or not to exit are taken in the light of the prospects for the effective use of voice. Members in organizations will postpone exit if they believe they can do something about the problem or if in the past they have had success with using voice (Hirschman 1970:38, 43). Hirschman (1970:33) argues that "it is difficult to conceive of a situation in which there would be too much . . . voice" but concedes that individual choice alone does not guarantee success of free and open discussion and identifies a multiplicity of ways voice is muted, distorted, corrupted, exploited, and negated in organizations. Some organizations, for instance, stifle voice by penalizing critics or threatening them with retaliation and reprisals (Hirschman 1981:240), and there is evidence in expastors' accounts that some Adventist leaders did this. Other organizations welcome open discussion and encourage members to get problems off their chest so that discussion becomes an end in itself and does not generate change. The expastors also detail examples of this. According to Hirschman, organizations that do value input from their members also establish mechanisms that make voice "retaliation proof." These include "the secret vote, the Ombudsman institution which make[s] it possible for individuals in bureaucratic organizations to complain outside of hierarchical channels, and trade union bargaining" (Hirschman 1981:388). From what the exapstors had to say, none of these "safety valves" were available to Adventist pastors. The Seventh-day Adventist organization as depicted by expastors approximates Hirschman's description of "lazy monopolies" or organizations where "laziness, flabbiness, and decay" have set in and prefer exit to voice. "Those who hold power in the lazy monopoly may actually have an interest in creating some limited opportunities for exit on the part of those whose voice might be uncomfortable" (Hirschman 1970:59–60). The "good riddance" reaction permits the lazy monopoly to persist with mediocrity "by unburdening it of its more troublesome customers."

The ideology of ministry as a career that requires sacrifice, self-denial, and a degree of hardship mitigates against open rebellion and limits the possible avenues of protest available to clergy. Ministers can be seen taking part in public demonstrations and campaigning on important social issues, although one does not see or hear of ministers, even from mainline denominations, going on strike in protest against work conditions, and the very idea of the minister or priest engaging in destruction of church property in protest is also rejected as a contradiction of terms (Seidler 1974a). One of the few avenues of protest available to Adventist pastors was voice, and its most potent expression was criticism of the doctrines.

The intricacies of the exiting phenomena I observed in expastors' narratives can be understood when we recognize the symbiotic relationship between exit and voice. As a form of protest, the questioning of the doctrines was powerful because it is the principal means critics use to attack Adventism. It is powerful also because doctrine is the language Adventist members and leaders understand and to which they respond. Expastors adopted the voice of theology because the Seventh-day Adventist administration in Australia and New Zealand did not hear other voices. The theological focus became a potent tool in the hands of leavers by empowering them to confront systems of domination and social control which they believed were instrumental in the collapse of their ministries. Criticism of the doctrines reversed expastors' previous subordinate status by forcing Church authorities into adopting a posture of defense. The accounts of expastors from this point of view are a form of revenge (Yankelovich 1982:5, 6, 71) attacking the sect system at those points where former pastors saw it as being most vulnerable and at a time they perceived it to be down. Expastors' antipathy toward Adventist theology invariably focused on key Seventh-day Adventist doctrines, those teachings that differentiated Adventists from their denominational competitors. Rejection of the doctrines became for the expastors the most certain way of confirming exit.

By the time of exit many expastors repudiated the foundational Adventist doctrines of the sanctuary, the investigative judgement, and the interpretation of the prophecies, rejected the idea that Ellen G. White was an inspired interpreter of the Bible, relativized the Sabbath as one of personal choice, and dismissed the Adventist movement as a "historical mistake." It was as if in protest former pastors thrust the knife at the very heart of the Adventist system. In this sense voice was an expression of exit. However, Adventist theology and bureaucracy are so intertwined that rejection of one involved a simultaneous rejection of the other, and criticism of the doctrines was at the same time an attack on the "system of ordered procedures for the production, regulation, distribution, circulation and operation" (Foucault 1980:133) of those doctrines.

ADVENTISM AS LAZY MONOPOLY

In their accounts of leaving ministry expastors describe an organization in crisis and exit as one manifestation of a movement uncertain of its status and role in society. Seventh-day Adventism is depicted as a system that promotes the professionalization of its pastors but demands their laicization, preaches denominational inclusiveness but practices sectarian exclusiveness, aspires for a denominational future but is committed to its sectarian past. Expastors condemn the administration's apparent tolerance of exit as a mechanism for maintaining traditional bureaucratic sect boundaries. The picture that emerges in expastors' accounts is of a community that does not value its pastors. Hirschman's notion of lazy monopoly, which Seidler (1979) used to describe the Roman Catholic Church in the United States, approximates what expastors have to say about Adventism in Australia and New Zealand during the 1980s. Lazy monopolies have singular control over decision making, are slow to make essential changes, and allow personnel who are critical of the system to exit rather than deal with their criticisms. Labor turnover is used to secure the continuation of mediocre leadership and traditional authority structures. It is worth noting that the findings of this study support the views of two Conference presidents who during their interviews stressed that I should make it clear that the reason why expastors leave is only partly theological. Ironically, however, administrators themselves feature as a significant cause. Expastors' accounts highlight lack of freedom or trust in ministry, inadequate or inappropriate support structures, antiquated management styles, the abuse of power, the absence of impartial review agencies, and lack of leadership accountability as areas of concern. If these perceptions are correct and if similar conditions continue to exist, it could be expected that pastors will continue to grow disillusioned with their work, fallout from the ministry will persist, and expastors will continue to construct accounts pointing out the weaknesses of the Adventist system.

Two aspects of the study previously presented as strengths—reliance on the testimony of leavers and my own status as "insider" and expastor—may be interpreted by others as limitations. In defence of the first I argue that caution is required when using expastors' critiques of organizational processes and Adventist theology, and that their judgements will need to be evaluated alongside the constructions of continuing pastors. However, any study of exiting ultimately will rely on the retrospective reports of leavers, and while the narratives of expastors do not reveal everything one would wish to know about Seventh-day Adventist ministry and the sectarian theology, they do present a vital and often neglected perspective on how experiences and perceptions blend to produce exit and accounts of exiting. In respect to my status as an insider, I reiterate that my firsthand knowledge of the Adventist organization, ministry, and exit benefited my insights and aided my interpretation of the data and theorizing about exit. It is for the reader to judge the limitations of my account and to decide whether an outsider would have read the interview data differently and identified a different set of processes in expastors' narratives than the ones I have noted.

Will this exodus of pastors mean the eventual demise of the Adventist system? Pearson (1990:278) thinks not. He argues that "a discerning public will always create a demand for a reliable product, whatever the price." Pearson believes the future of Adventism is guaranteed by virtue of the fact that there will always be a section of the community attracted to a sect movement such as Adventism. Branson (1982:2) is less certain and acknowledges that while the movement has been successful at resisting fragmentation, the controversies and exits have left pastors and members with "little energy to undertake bold, new tasks—or ignite the enthusiasm of the next generation." According to this view, there is every possibility that Adventism could die from exhaustion. Bull and Lockhart (1989:266) adopt a more cynical outlook and employ the image of a revolving door to argue that the future of this organization is the same as its past, as the "outs" are balanced by the "ins." Bull and Lockhart contend that "the constant flow through both entrance and exit" of converts and revisionists, respectively, helps to preserve the movement's sectarian ethos and thus frustrate its transformation into a denomination.

The study does not preclude any of these projections of how change affects a community. What the research does tell us is that the future of Adventism is in the hands of a bureaucracy that is self-appointed, maintains a tight fist over organizational processes and theological interpretation, and has the power to crush insubordinates and expel nonconformists. The evidence of expastors indicates that the key to Seventh-day Adventism's future is not only in market forces (Pearson), the psychological frame of mind of its pastors and members (Branson), and sociological processes (Bull and Lockhart), but also in the power that Adventist authorities have to push the movement—"with the blessing of God"—in whatever direction they deem appropriate.

Bibliography

Adams, R. 1993. *The Sanctuary: Understanding the Heart of Adventist Theology*. Hagerstown, Md.: Review and Herald.

Ahlstrom, S. 1972. *A Religious History of the American People*. New Haven: Yale University Press.

Albrecht, S. L., and H. M. Bahr. 1983. "Patterns of Religious Disaffiliation: A Study of Lifelong Mormons, Mormon Converts, and Former Mormons." *Journal for the Scientific Study of Religion* 22:366–379.

Anders, M. E. 1973. "Review of 'Sect Ideologies and Social Status' by G. Schwartz." *Review of Religious Research* 14:287.

Anderson, G. T. 1969. "The Christian Scholar and the Church." *Spectrum* 1, Winter: 7-14.

———. 1986. "Sectarianism and Organization, 1846–1864." In *Adventism in America: A History*, edited by G. Land, 36–65. Grand Rapids, Mich.: William B. Eerdmans.

Anderson, E., J. Butler, M. Couperus, and A. Zytkoskee. 1981. "Must the Crisis Continue?" *Spectrum* 11: 44–52.

Annual Council Resolution. 1976. "Evangelism and Finishing God's Work." *Spectrum* 8, no. 2:54.

Anti-Discrimination Board. 1984. *Discrimination and Religious Conviction: A Report of the Anti-Discrimination Board in Accordance with Section 119 (a) of the Anti-Discrimination Act 1977*. New South Wales: Anti-Discrimination Board.

Arthur, D. T. 1974. "Millerism." In *The Rise of Adventism: A Commentary on the Social and Religious Ferment of Mid-Nineteenth Century America*, edited by E. R. Gaustad, 154–172. New York: Harper and Row.

Atkinson, D., and P. Shakespeare. 1993. Introduction to *Reflecting on Research Practice: Issues in Health and Social Welfare*, edited by D. Atkinson, P. Shakespeare, and S. French. Buckingham: Open University Press.

Atkinson, J., and P. Drew. 1979. *Order in Court: The Organisation of Verbal Interaction in Judicial Settings*. London: Macmillan.

Austin, J. 1961. "A Plea for Excuses." In *Philosophical Papers,* edited by J. P. Urmson and G. Warnock. Oxford: Clarendon Press.

Ballis, P. H., ed. 1985. *In and Out of the World: Seventh-day Adventists in New Zealand.* Palmerston North, New Zealand: Dunmore Press.

_____. 1991. "Adventists, Compulsory Unionism and the Division of Labour." In *Journey of Hope: Seventh-day Adventist History in the South Pacific,* edited by A. J. Ferch, 45–60. Wahroonga, New South Wales: South Pacific Division of Seventh-day Adventists.

_____. 1992. "Wounded Healers." *Adventist Professional* 4: 28–32.

_____, and P. Richardson. 1997. "Roads to Damascus: Conversion Stories and their Implications for Literacy Educators." *English in Australia* 119–20:110–119.

Becker, H. S. 1960. "Notes on the Concept of Commitment." *American Journal of Sociology* 66:32–40.

_____, and A. L. Strauss. 1956. "Careers, Personality, and Adult Socialization." *American Journal of Sociology* 62:253–263.

_____, and B. Geer. 1958. "The Fate of Idealism in Medical School." *American Sociological Review* 23:50–56.

_____, B. Geer, et al. 1961. *Boys in White: Student Culture in Medical School.* Chicago: University of Chicago Press.

Beckford, J. A. 1975. *The Trumpet of Prophecy: A Sociological Study of Jehovah's Witnesses.* Oxford: Basil Blackwell.

_____. 1978a. "Accounting for Conversion." *British Journal of Sociology* 29, no. 2:249–262.

_____. 1978b. "Through the Looking-Glass and Out the Other Side: Withdrawal from Reverend Moon's Unification Church." *Archives de Sciences Sociales des Religion* 45:95–116.

_____. 1983. "Talking of Apostasy: Telling Tales and 'Telling Tales.'" In *Accounting for Conversion,* edited by M. Mulkay and N. Gilbert. London: Greenwood Press.

_____. 1985. *Cult Controversies: The Societal Response to New Religious Movements.* London: Tavistock Publications.

Bell, R. W., and J. P. Koval. 1972. "Collegiality and Occupational Change in the Priesthood." *Kansas Journal of Sociology* 7:47–61.

Berger, P. 1963. *Invitation to Sociology: A Humanistic Perspective.* Harmondsworth, Middlesex: Penguin Books.

_____. 1969. *The Sacred Canopy: Elements of a Sociological Theory of Religion.* Garden City, N. Y.: Anchor Books.

_____. 1980. *The Heretical Imperative: Contemporary Possibilities of Religious Affirmation.* Garden City, N. Y.: Anchor Books.

_____, and B. Berger. 1972. *Sociology: A Biographical Approach.* Harmondsworth, Middlesex: Penguin Books.

_____, and T. Luckmann. 1966. *The Social Construction of Reality.* New York: Doubleday.

Berry, D. 1974. *Central Ideas in Sociology: An Introduction.* London: Constable.

Bird, van. S. 1976. "An Examination of Clergy Discontent and One Response to It: Further Professionalization of the Episcopal Church." Ph.D. thesis, Temple University.

Blaikie, N.W.H. 1979. *The Plight of the Australian Clergy: To Convert, Care or Challenge?* St. Lucia, Queensland: University of Queensland Press.

Blanchard, D. A. 1973. "Some Social and Orientative Correlates of Career Change and Continuity as Revealed Among United Methodist Pastors of the Alabama-West Florida Conference, 1960–1970." Ph.D. thesis, Boston University.

Blau, Z. S. 1973. *Old Age in a Changing Society*. New York: Franklin Press.

Blizzard, S. W. 1956a. "Role Conflicts of the Urban Protestant Parish Minister." *City Church* 7:13.

_____ . 1956b. "The Minister's Dilemma." *Christian Century* 73:508–510.

_____ . 1958a. "The Parish Minister's Self Image of His Master Role." *Pastoral Psychology* 89:25–32.

_____ . 1958b. "The Protestant Minister's Integrating Roles." *Religious Education* 89:374–380.

_____ . 1959. "The Parish Minister's Self-Image in Community Culture." *Pastoral Psychology* 90.

Blombery, T. 1989. *God Through Human Eyes: Report from the Combined Churches Survey for Faith and Mission*. Hawthorn, Victoria: Christian Research Association.

Bloom, H. 1993. *The American Religion: The Emergence of a Post-Christian Nation*. New York: Simon and Schuster.

Bodycomb, J. 1978. *The Naked Churchman: A Protestant Profile—A Study of Protestant Beliefs and Attitudes in South Australia*. Melbourne: Joint Board of Christian Education of Australia and New Zealand.

Borhek, J. T. 1960. "Social Bases of Participation in the Seventh-day Adventist Church." Master's thesis, University of California.

Bott, E. 1971. *Family and Social Network: Roles, Norms, and External Relationships in Ordinary Urban Families*. 2d ed. London: Tavistock Publications.

Bottomley, M. 1977. "And What Does Your Husband Do? How Do Ministers' Wives Try to Be Themselves?" B.A. Honours thesis, La Trobe University, Melbourne.

Bouma, G. 1992. *Religion: Meaning, Transcendence and Community in Australia*. Melbourne: Longman Cheshire.

Bouma, M. La G. 1981. "Ministers' Wives: The Walking Wounded." *Leadership* 2:30–38.

_____ . 1979. *Divorce in the Parsonage: Why It Happens, Ways to Prevent It*. Minneapolis: Bethany Fellowship.

Boyer, P. 1992. *When Time Shall Be No More: Prophecy Belief in Modern American Culture*. Cambridge, Mass.: Belknap Press.

Branson, R. 1982. "A Time for Healing." *Spectrum* 13:2–3.

Brinkerhoff, M. B., and K. L. Burke. 1980. "Disaffiliation: Some Notes on Falling from the Faith." *Sociological Analysis* 41:41–54.

Brinsmead, R. 1979. *1844 Re-examined*. Fallbrook, Calif.: Verdict Publications.

_____ . 1980. *Judged by the Gospel: A Review of Adventism*. Fallbrook, Calif.: Verdict Publications.

_____ . 1983. "Interview by Robert Wolfgramm." In R. Wolfgramm, "Charismatic Delegitimation in a Sect: Ellen White and Her Critics," 346–357. Master's thesis, Chisholm Institute of Technology, Melbourne.

Bromley, D. G., A. D. Shupe, and J. C. Ventimiglia. 1979. "Atrocity Tales, the Unification Church, and the Social Construction of Evil." *Journal of Communication* 29, no. 3:42–53.

_____ . 1983. "The Role of Anecdotal Atrocities in the Social Construction of Evil." In *The Brainwashing/Deprogramming Controversy: Sociological, Psychological,*

Legal and Historical Perspectives, edited by D. G. Bromley and J. T. Richardson, 139–160. New York: Edwin Mellen Press.

Brown, G. W. 1983. "Accounts, Meaning and Causality." In *Accounts and Action: Surrey Conferences on Sociological Theory and Method,* edited by G. N. Gilbert and M. Abell, 35–68. Aldershot, Hampshire: Gower.

Bruce, S., and R. Wallis. 1985. "'Rescuing Motives' Rescued: A reply to Sharrock and Watson." *British Journal of Sociology* 36, no. 3:467–470.

Bull, M., and K. Lockhart. 1989. *Seeking a Sanctuary: Seventh-day Adventism and the American Dream.* San Francisco: Harper and Row.

Burton, R., S. Johnson, and J. Tamney. 1989. "Education and Fundamentalism." *Review of Religious Research* 30, no. 3:344–359.

Butler, J. 1974. "Adventism and the American Experience." In *The Rise of Adventism: A Commentary on the Social and Religious Ferment of Mid-Nineteenth Century America,* edited by E. S. Gaustad, 173–206. New York: Harper and Row.

_____. 1980. "General Conference Arouses Constituency: Ford Firing Ignites Criticism." *Criterion* (Loma Linda University), 17 October.

_____. 1987. "The Making of a New Order: Millerism and the Origins of Seventh-day Adventism." In *The Disappointed: Millerism and Millenarianism in the Nineteenth Century,* edited by R. L. Numbers and J. M. Butler, 189–208. Bloomington: Indiana University Press.

_____. 1992. "Introduction: The Historian as Heretic." In R. L. Numbers, *Prophetess of Health: Ellen G. White and the Origins of the Seventh-day Adventist Health Reform,* xxv–lxviii. Knoxville: University of Tennessee Press.

_____, and R. Numbers. 1987. "Seventh-day Adventism." In *The Encyclopedia of Religion,* edited by M. Eliade, 179–183. NewYork: Macmillan.

Campbell, E. G., and T. F. Pettigrew. 1959. "Racial and Moral Crisis: The Role of Little Rock Ministers." *American Journal of Sociology* 64:509–516.

Campiche, R. J., and C. Bovay. 1979. "Priests, Pastors, Rabbis: A Change of Role? Thematic Bibliography." *Archives de Sciences Sociales des Religions* 24:133–183.

Caplovitz, D., and F. Sherrow. 1977. *The Religious Drop-outs: Apostasy Among College Graduates.* Beverly Hills: Sage Publications.

Cardwell, S. W., and R. A. Hunt. 1979. "Persistence in Seminary and in Ministry." *Pastoral Psychology* 28:119–131.

Chalfant, H. P., R. E. Beckley, and C. E. Palmer. 1981. *Religion in Contemporary Society.* Sherman Oaks, Calif.: Alfred Publishing.

Chapman, M. G. 1980. Letter to A. H. Tolhurst, 11 September (in my possession).

Cherniss, C. 1980. *Staff Burnout: Jobstress in the Human Services.* Beverly Hills: Sage Publications.

Clapham, N., ed. 1985. *Seventh-day Adventists in the South Pacific, 1885–1985: Australia, New Zealand, South-Sea Islands.* Warburton, Victoria: Signs Publishing.

Clark, E. T. 1949. *The Small Sects in America.* Rev. ed. New York: Abingdon Press.

Clifford, J. A., and R. R Standish. 1976. *Conflicting Concepts of Righteousness by Faith in the Seventh-day Adventist Church—Australasian Division.* Biblical Research Institute Paper.

Cohen, A. P. 1985. *The Symbolic Construction of Community.* London: Tavistock Publications.

Committee of Six. 1980. "Statement on Desmond Ford Document." *Ministry,* October:20–

22.

Comprehensive Index to the Writings of Ellen G. White. 1962. Mountain View, Calif.: Pacific Press Publishing Association.

Coser, L. A. 1974. *Greedy Institutions: Patterns of Undivided Commitment.* New York: Free Press.

Cottrell, R. F. 1980. "The Sanctuary Review Committee and Its New Consensus." *Spectrum* 11:2–26.

Cryns, A. G. 1970. "Dogmatism of Catholic Clergy and Exclergy: A Study of Ministerial Role Perseverance and Open-Mindedness." *Journal for the Scientific Study of Religion* 9:239–243.

Damsteegt, P. G. 1977. *Foundations of the Seventh-day Adventist Message and Mission.* Grand Rapids, Mich.: William B. Eerdmans.

Dann, Y. 1980. "The Clergy Wife: A Stereotype Crumbles." *St Mark's Review* 104:16–25.

Darroch, M. 1984. *Everything You Ever Wanted to Know About Protestants.* Wellington: Catholic Supplies.

Della Cava, F. A. 1975. "Becoming an Ex-Priest: The Process of Leaving a High Commitment Status." *Sociological Inquiry* 45:41–49.

Dempsey, K. 1969a. "Conflict and Harmony in Minister-Lay Relationships in an Australian Methodist Community." Ph.D. thesis, University of New England, Armidale.

———. 1969b. "Conflict in Minister/Lay Relations." In *A Sociological Yearbook of Religion in Britain*, edited by D. Martin, Vol. 2. London: S.C.M. Press.

———. 1973a. "Lay Power and Ministerial Careers." In *Social Change in Australia: Readings in Sociology*, edited by D. E. Edgar, 427–440. Melbourne: Cheshire.

———. 1973b. "Secularisation and the Protestant Minister." *Australian and New Zealand Journal of Sociology* 9:46–50.

———. 1983. *Conflict and Decline: Ministers and Laymen in an Australian Country Town.* North Ryde: Methuen Australia.

———. 1985. *The Fate of Ministers' Wives.* Sociology Papers No. 15. Melbourne: La Trobe University.

Denton, G. W. 1961. "Role Attitudes of the Minister's Wife." *Pastoral Psychology* 12:17–23.

———. 1962. *The Role of the Minister's Wife.* Philadelphia: Westminster.

Denzin, N. K. 1989. *Interpretive Interactionism.* Newbury Park, Calif.: Sage Publications.

De Vaus, D. A. 1994. *Letting Go: Relationships Between Adults and Their Parents.* Melbourne: Oxford University Press.

Dick, E. N. 1977. "Advent Camp Meeting of the 1840's." *Adventist Heritage* 4, no. 2:3–10.

Douglas, W. G. T. 1961. "Minister's Wives: A Tentative Typology." *Pastoral Psychology* 12:10–16.

Dudley, R. L., and D. Cummings. 1982. "Factors Related to Pastoral Morale in the Seventh-day Adventist Church." *Review of Religious Research* 24:127–137.

———. 1983. "A Study of Factors Relating to Church Growth in the North American Division of Seventh-day Adventists." *Review of Religious Research.* 24:322–335.

———, and G. Clark. 1981. "The Pastor as Person and Husband: A Study of Pastoral Morale." Unpublished research study. Berrien Springs, Mich.: Andrews University.

———. 1981. *The Pastor as Person and Husband: A Study of Pastoral Morale.* Andrews University, Institute of Church Ministry.

Durkheim, E. 1952. *Suicide: A Study in Sociology.* London: Routledge and Kegan Paul.

———. 1976. *The Elementary Forms of the Religious Life.* 2d ed. London: George Allen and Unwin.

Eastman, K. 1980. Letter to K. S. Parmenter, 26 September (in my possession).

Ebaugh, H.R.F. 1977. *Out of the Cloister: A Study of Organisational Dilemmas*. Austin: University of Texas Press.

———. 1984. "Leaving the Convent: The Experience of Role Exit and Self-Transformation." In *The Existential Self in Society*, edited by J. A. Kotabara and A. Fontana, 156–176. Chicago: University of Chicago Press.

———. 1988a. *Becoming an Ex: The Process of Role Exit*. Chicago: University of Chicago Press.

———. 1988b. "Leaving Catholic Convents: Toward a Theory of Disengagement." In *Falling from the Faith: Causes and Consequences of Religious Apostasy*, edited by D. G. Bromley, 100–121. Newbury Park, Calif.: Sage Publications.

———, K. Richman, and J. S. Chafetz. 1984. "Life Crises Among the Religiously Committed: Do Sectarian Differences Matter?" *Journal for the Scientific Study of Religion* 23, no. 1:19–31.

———, and P. Ritterband. 1978. "Education and the Exodus from Convents." *Sociological Analysis* 39, no. 3:257–264.

Etzioni, A. 1961. *A Comparative Analysis of Complex Organizations on Power, Involvement and Their Correlates*. New York: Free Press.

Feeney, D. 1980. "The Changing Role of the Clergy." In *The Shape of Belief: Christianity in Australia Today*, edited by D. Harris, D. Hynd, and D. Millikan, 123–131. Homebush West, N.S.W.: Lancer.

Ference, T. P., F. H. Goldner, and R. R. Ritti. 1971. "Priests and Church: The Professionalization of an Organization." *American Behavioral Scientist* 14:507–524.

Festinger, L., H. W. Riecken, and S. Schachter. 1956. *When Prophecy Fails: A Social and Psychological Study of a Modern Group that Predicted the Destruction of the World*. New York: Harper and Row.

Fichter, J. H. 1961. *Religion as an Occupation: A Study in the Sociology of Professions*. Notre Dame: University of Notre Dame Press.

———. 1963. "A Comparative View of Priests." *Archives de Sociologie des Religions* 8:44–48.

———. 1970. "Catholic Church Professionals." *Annals of the American Academy of Political and Social Science* January:77–85.

———. 1984. "The Myth of Clergy Burnout." *Sociological Analysis* 45:373–382.

Finch, J. 1980. "Devising Conventional Performances: The Case of Clergymen's Wives." *Sociological Review* 28, no. 4:851–870.

———. 1983. *Married to the Job: Wives' Incorporation in Men's Work*. London: George Allen and Unwin.

Ford, D. 1977. *Daniel*. Nashville: Southern Publishing Association.

———. 1978. "The Truth of Paxton's Thesis." *Spectrum* 9:37–45.

———. 1980a. *Daniel 8:14, the Day of Atonement, and the Investigative Judgement*. Casselberry, Fl.: Euangelion Press.

———. 1980b. "Daniel 8:14 and the Day of Atonement." *Spectrum* 11:30–36.

———. 1985. *Good News For Adventists*. Auburn, Calif.: Good News Unlimited.

———. 1988. Interview by P. H. Ballis. Croydon, Melbourne, 23 April.

———, and G. Ford. 1982. *The Adventist Crisis of Spiritual Identity*. Newcastle, Calif.: Desmond Ford Publications.

Foucault, M. 1980. *Power/Knowledge: Selected Interviews and Other Writings 1972–1977*. Edited by C. Brown. New York: Pantheon Books.

Frame, J. 1983. *To the Is-land: An Autobiography*. Vol. 1. London: Women's Press.

———. 1988. *The Carpathians*. Auckland: Century Hutchinson.

Freudenberger, H. J. 1974. "Staff Burn-Out." *Journal of Social Issues* 30, no. 1:59–165.

Froom, L. E. 1953. "Seventh-day Adventists." In *The American Church of the Protestant Heritage*, edited by V. Ferm, 371–386. New York: Philosophical Library.

Fulcher, T. O. 1971. "Factors Related to Attrition of Parish Ministers in the North Carolina Conference of the United Methodist Church, 1966–1970." Ed.D. thesis, North Carolina State University.

Galanter, M. 1983. "Unification Church ('Moonie') Dropouts: Psychological Readjustment After Leaving A Charismatic Religious Group." *American Journal of Psychiatry* 140:984–989.

Garfinkel, H. 1956. "Conditions of Successful Degradation Ceremonies." *American Journal of Sociology* 61:420–424.

———. 1967. *Studies in Ethnomethodology*. Englewood Cliffs: Prentice-Hall.

Gaustad, E. S. 1976. *Historical Atlas of Religion in America*. Rev. ed. New York: Harper.

Gee, M. 1978. *Plumb*. Wellington: Oxford University Press.

General Conference of Seventh-day Adventists. 1957. *General Conference of Seventh-day Adventists Answer Questions on Doctrine*. Washington, D.C.: Review and Herald.

———. 1975. *The Work of the Pastor*. Washington, D.C.: Review and Herald.

General Conference of Seventh-day Adventists Ministerial Association. 1988. *Seventh-day Adventists Believe: A Biblical Exposition of 27 Fundamental Doctrines*. Washington, D.C.: Review and Herald.

Gerlach, L. P., and V. H. Hine. 1968. "Five Factors Crucial to the Growth and Spread of Modern Religious Movements." *Journal for the Scientific Study of Religion* 7:23–40.

———. 1970. *People, Power, Change, Movements of Social Transformation*. Indianapolis: Bobbs-Merrill.

Giddens, A. 1991. *The Consequences of Modernity*. Cambridge: Polity Press.

Gladson, J. A. 1992. *The Crime of Dissent: My Search for Integrity*. Atlanta, Ga.: Psychology Studies Institute.

Glaser, B. G., and A. L. Strauss. 1965. "Temporal Aspects of Dying as a Non-scheduled Status Passage." *American Journal of Sociology* 71:48–59.

———. 1967. *The Discovery of Grounded Theory: Strategies for Qualitative Research*. Chicago: Aldine.

Goffman, E. 1961. *Asylums: Essays on the Social Situation of Mental Patients and Other Inmates*. Garden City. N.Y.: Doubleday.

———. 1962. "On Cooling Out the Mark: Some Aspects of Adaption to Failure." In *Human Behaviour and Social Processes: An Interactionist Approach*, edited by A. M. Rose, 482–505. London: Routledge and Kegan Paul.

———. 1967. *Interaction Ritual*. New York: Doubleday Anchor.

———. 1974. *Frame Analysis: An Essay on the Organisation of Experience*. Harmondsworth, Middlesex: Penguin Books.

Goldner, F. H., R. R. Ritti, and T. P. Ference. 1977. "The Production of Cynical Knowledge in Organizations." *American Sociological Review* 42:459–551.

———, T. P. Ference, and R. R. Ritti. 1973. "Priests and Laity: A Profession in Transition." *Sociological Review Monograph* 20:119–137.

Goldschmidt, W. R. 1959. "Class Denominationalism in Rural Californian Churches." *American Journal of Sociology* 44:348–355.

Goldstone, S. R. 1980. *The Angel Said Australia.* Warburton, Victoria: Signs Publishing.

———. 1983. *Nothing to Fear: Stories of the Seventh-day Adventist Church in New Zealand.* Napier, New Zealand: Max Printing.

Goode, W. J. 1960. "A Theory of Role Strain." *American Sociological Review* 25:483–496.

Goodling, R. A., and C. Smith. 1983. "Clergy Divorce: A Survey of Issues and Emerging Ecclesiastical Structures." *Journal of Pastoral Care* 37:277.

Goodrich, C. I. 1975. *The Frontier of Control: A Study of British Workshop Politics.* London: Pluto Press.

Gowler, D., and K. Legge. 1975. "Stress and External Relationships—The Hidden Contract." In *Managerial Stress,* edited by D. Gowler and K. Legge. Epping: Gower Press.

Graham, W. L. 1985. "The Psychological Experience of Resigned Catholic Priests." Ph.D. thesis, University Without Walls and Union Graduate School.

Grant, L. H. 1980. "Bureaucratic Theology?" *Spectrum* 11:62–63.

Graybill, R. 1979. "Millenarians and Money: Adventist Wealth and Adventist Beliefs." *Spectrum* 10:31–32.

———. 1983. "The Power of Prophecy: Ellen G. White and the Women Religious Founders of the Nineteenth Century." Ph.D. thesis, Johns Hopkins University.

Greeley, A. M. 1982. *Religion: A Secular Theory.* New York: Free Press.

Grosso, J. B. 1974. "Former Episcopal Clergymen: Why they Left and What Happened to Them." Ph.D. thesis, United States International University.

Gusfield, J. F. 1960. "Field Work Reciprocities in Studying a Social Movement." In *Human Organization Research: Field Relations and Techniques,* edited by R. N. Adams and J. J. Preiss, 99–108. Homewood, Ill.: Dorsey Press.

Gustafson, J. M. 1954. "An Analysis of the Problem of the Role of the Minister." *Journal of Religion* 34:187–191.

———. 1963. "The Clergy in the United States." *Daedalus* 92:724–744.

Hack, A. L. 1993. "The Clergyman's Spouse: Predictors of Satisfaction in the Spousal Role." Ph.D. thesis, University of Kentucky.

Hadaway, C. K. 1989. "Identifying American Apostates: A Cluster Analysis." *Journal for the Scientific Study of Religion* 28:201–215.

———, and W. C. Roof. 1979. "Those Who Stay Religious 'Nones' and Those Who Don't: A Research Note." *Journal for the Scientific Study of Religion* 18:194–200.

Hadden, J. K. 1965. "A Study of the Protestant Ministry of America." *Journal for the Sociological Study of Religion* 5:10–23.

———. 1968a. "Ideological Conflict Between Protestant Clergy and Laity on Civil Rights." *Social Science Quarterly* 49:923–925.

———. 1968b "Role Conflicts and the Crises in the Churches." *Ministry Studies* 2:16–29.

———. 1969. *The Gathering Storm in the Churches.* Garden City, N.Y.: Doubleday.

Hammill, R. 1990. "Reflections on the Adventist Typological Interpretation of the Mosaic Tabernacle and its Cultus." Manuscript.

———. 1992. *Pilgrimage: Memoirs of an Adventist Administrator.* Berien Springs, Mich.: Andrews University Press.

Hammond, P. E., and R. E. Mitchell. 1965. "Segmentation of Radicalism—The Case of the Protestant Campus Minister." *American Journal of Sociology* 71, no. 2:133–143.

Harstock, N.C.M. 1983, "The Feminist Standpoint: Developing the Ground for a Specifically Feminist Historical Materialism." In *Discovering Reality*, edited by S. Harding and M. B. Hintikka, 283–310. Dordrecht: Reidel.

Hart, N. 1976. *When Marriage Ends: A Study in Status Passage.* London: Tavistock Publications.

Hartley, S. F. 1978. "Marital Satisfaction Among Clergy Wives." *Review of Religious Research* 19:178–191.

_____ , and M. G. Taylor. 1977. "Religious Beliefs of Clergy Wives." *Review of Religious Research* 19:63–73.

Heritage, J. 1983. "Accounts in Action." In *Accounts and Action: Surrey Conferences on Sociological Theory and Method*, edited by G. N. Gilbert and M. Abell, 117–131. Aldershot, Hampshire: Gower.

_____ . 1984. *Garfinkel and Ethnomethodology.* Oxford: Polity Press.

Heynen, R. 1973. "Dropouts from the Pastorate." *The Banner* 28 (September).

Hill, M. 1973. *A Sociology of Religion.* London: Heinemann.

Hine, V. 1970. "Bridge-Burners: Commitment and Participation in a Religious Movement." *Sociological Analysis* 31:61–66.

Hirschman, A. O. 1970. *Exit, Voice and Loyalty: Responses to Decline in Firms, Organizations and States.* Cambridge, Mass.: Harvard University Press.

_____ . 1981. *Essays in Trespassing: Economics to Politics and Beyond.* Cambridge: Cambridge University Press.

Hoge, D. R., J. E. Dyble, and D. T. Polk. 1981. "Organizational and Situational Influences on Vocational Commitment of Protestant Ministers." *Review of Religious Research* 23:133–149.

Hunsberger, B. E. 1980. "A Reexamination of the Antecedents of Apostasy." *Review of Religious Research* 21:158–170.

_____ . 1983. "Apostasy: A Social Learning Perspective." *Review of Religious Research* 25:21–38.

Hunt, S. A., and R. D. Benford. 1994. "Identity Talk in the Peace and Justice Movement." *Journal of Contemporary Ethnography* 22:488–517.

Jackson, L. F. 1985. "Seventh-day Adventists in New Zealand: Towards a Demographic History." In *In and Out of the World: Seventh-day Adventists in New Zealand*, edited by P. H. Ballis, 131–151. Palmerston North, New Zealand: Dunmore Press.

Jacobs, J. L. 1984. "The Economy of Love in Religious Commitment: The Deconversion of Women from Nontraditional Religions." *Journal for the Scientific Study of Religion* 23, no. 2:155–171.

_____ . 1987. "Deconversion from Religious Movements." *Journal for the Scientific Study of Religion* 26, no. 3:294–307.

_____ . 1989. *Divine Disenchantment: Deconverting from New Religions.* Bloomington: Indiana University Press.

Jehenson, R. B. 1969. "The Dynamics of Role Leaving: A Role Theoretical Approach to the Leaving of Religious Organisations." *The Journal of Applied Behavioral Science* 5:287–308.

Johnsson, W. G. 1980. "Overview of a Historic Meeting." *Australasian Record*, 8 September.

Johnston, R. 1981. "Omega: A Theological View." *Spectrum* 12:53–57.

Jud, G. J., E. W. Mills, and G. Burch. 1970. *Ex-Pastors: Why Men Leave the Parish Ministry.* Philadelphia: Pilgrim Press.

Kanter, R. 1968. "Commitment and Social Organization: A Study of Commitment

Mechanisms in Utopian Communities." *American Sociological Review* 33:499–517.

Kapitzke, C. 1995. *Literacy and Religion: The Textual Politics and Practice of Seventh-day Adventism*. Philadelphia: John Benjamins.

Kelly, H. E. 1971. "Role Satisfaction of the Catholic Priest." *Social Forces* 50:75–84.

Klink, T. W. 1969. "The Ministry as Career and Crisis." *Pastoral Psychology* June:13–19.

Knight, G. R. 1985. *Myths in Adventism: An Interpretive Study of Ellen White, Education and Related Issues*. Washington, D.C.: Review and Herald.

_____. 1987. *From 1888 to Apostasy: The Case of A. T. Jones*. Washington, D.C.: Review and Herald.

Knight, J. 1977. "The World Not Turned Upside Down—Case-study in Sociocultural Change." Ph.D. thesis, University of Queensland.

Krackhardt, D., and L. W. Porter 1985. "When Friends Leave: A Structural Analysis of the Relationship Between Turnover and Stayer's Attitudes." *Administrative Science Quarterly* 30:242–261.

Krause, E. A. 1971. *The Sociology of Occupations*. Boston: Little, Brown.

Kurtz, L. R. 1983. "The Politics of Heresy." *American Journal of Sociology* 88:1085–1115.

Lamp, H. C. 1980. Letter to W. R. Lesher, 20 February (in my possession).

Land, G., ed. 1986a. *Adventism in America: A History*. Grand Rapids, Mich.: William B. Eerdmans.

_____. 1986b. "Coping with Change, 1961–1990." In *Adventism in America: A History*, edited by G. Land, 208–230. Grand Rapids, Mich.: William B. Eerdmans.

Larson, R. n.d. "My Reply to Dr Desmond Ford's Opinions About the Sanctuary." Unpublished manuscript.

Lawson, R., and M. Lockwood Carden. n.d. "Ghettoization and the Erosion of a Distinct Way of Life: The Seventh-day Adventist Experience." Unpublished manuscript.

Lee, G. A. 1980/1981. "President's Letter to All Conference Employees, 14 November 1980." *Logos—Western Australian Adventist Forum Magazine* 1, no. 5 and 6, December/January.

Lester, D. and A. J. P. Butler. 1980. "Job Satisfaction and Cynicism in Police: A Cross-National Comparison." *Police Studies* 2, no. 4:44–45.

Levine, S. V. 1984. *Radical Departures: Desperate Detours to Growing Up*. San Diego: Harcourt Brace Jovanovich.

Lewis, J. R. 1989. "Apostates and the Legitimation of Repression: Some Historical and Empirical Perspectives on the Cult Controversy." *Sociological Analysis* 49, no. 4:386–396.

Lim, D. 1981. "Victory or Fiasco?" Unpublished manuscript.

Linden, I. 1978. *The Last Trump: An Historical-Genetical Study of Some Important Chapters in the Making and Developments of the Seventh-day Adventist Church*. Frankfurt am Main: Peter Lang.

_____. 1982. *1844 and the Shut Door Problem*. Uppsala: Libertryck Stockholm.

Llewellyn, K. 1986. "Eve." In *The Penguin Book of Australian Women Poets*, edited by S. Hampton and K. Llewellyn, 159–160. Ringwood, Victoria: Penguin Books Australia.

Lofland, L. H. 1985. "The Social Shaping of Emotion: The Case of Grief." *Symbolic Interaction* 8:171–190.

London, H., and K. R. Allen. 1986. "Family Versus Career Responsibilities." In *Men's Changing Roles in the Family*, edited by R. A. Lewis and M. B. Sussman, 199–

208. New York: Haworth Press.

Ludowici, T. 1986. "Interview by P. H. Ballis." Longburn Adventist College, Palmerston North, New Zealand, 23 April.

MacDonald, G. 1980. "Dear Church, I Quit." *Christianity Today* 27 June:16–19.

Macionis, J. J. 1991. *Sociology.* Englewood Cliffs, N.J.: Prentice-Hall.

Magnusson, E. 1991. "Hierarchical Episcopacy and the DUCs." *Adventist Professional* 3, no. 3:22–23.

Manual for Ministers. 1977. Takoma Park, Washington, D.C.: Review and Herald.

Marks, R. R. D. N.d. *A Protest Against the Dissemination of Heresy in the Church.* Tract.

Marshall, J., and C. L. Cooper. 1979. *Executives Under Pressure: A Psychological Study.* London: Macmillan.

Martin, D. A. 1978. *A General Theory of Secularisation.* Oxford: Blackwell.

Mauss, A. L. 1969. "Dimensions of Religious Defection." *Review of Religious Research* 10:128–135.

Maxwell, M. C. 1981a. "Sanctuary and Atonement in SDA Theology: An Historical Survey." In *The Sanctuary and the Atonement: Biblical, Historical, and Theological,* edited by A. V. Wallenkampf and W. R. Lesher, 516–544. Washington, D.C.: Review and Herald.

————. 1981b. "The Investigative Judgement: Its Early Development." In *The Sanctuary and the Atonement: Biblical, Historical, and Theological,* edited by A. V. Wallenkampf and W. R. Lesher, 545–581. Washington, D.C.: Review and Herald.

McAdams, D. 1985. "Free the College Boards: Toward a Pluralism of Excellence." *Spectrum* 16, no. 4:28–31.

McCall, G. J., and J. L. Simmons. 1966. *Identities and Interactions: An Examination of Human Association in Everyday Life.* New York: Free Press.

McClosky, H., and J. Schaar. 1965. "Psychological Dimensions of Anomy." *American Sociological Review* 30:14–40.

McMahon, D. P. 1979. *Ellet Joseph Waggoner: The Myth and the Man.* Fallbrook, Calif.: Verdict Publications.

Merrill, D. 1985. *Clergy Couples in Crisis: The Impact of Stress on Pastoral Marriages.* Carol Stream, Ill.: Word Books.

Merton, R. K. 1938. "Social Structure and Anomie." *American Sociological Review* 3:672–682.

————. 1968. *Social Theory and Social Structure.* Enlarged edition. New York: Free Press.

————. 1972. "Insiders and Outsiders: A Chapter in the Sociology of Knowledge." *American Journal of Sociology* 78:9–47.

————. 1988. Foreword to *Becoming an Ex: The Process of Role Exit,* by H.R.F. Ebaugh, ix–xi. Chicago: University of Chicago Press.

Middleton, D., and D. Edwards. 1990. "Conversational Remembering: A Social Psychological Approach." In *Collective Remembering,* edited by D. Middleton and D. Edwards, 23–45. London: Sage Publications.

Mills, C. Wright. 1940. "Situated Actions as Vocabularies of Motive." *American Sociological Review* 5:904–913.

————. 1959. *The Sociological Imagination.* Harmondsworth, Middlesex: Penguin Books.

Mills, E. W. 1965. "Leaving the Pastorate: A Study in the Social Psychology of Career Change." Ph.D. thesis, Harvard University.

————. 1968. "Types of Role Conflicts Among Clergymen." *Ministry Studies* 2:13–15.

_____ . 1969. "Career Change in the Protestant Ministry." *Ministry Studies* 3:5–21.

_____ , and J. P. Koval. 1971. *Stress in the Ministry.* Washington, D.C.: Ministry Studies Board.

Minnery, T. 1980. "The Adventist Showdown: Will It Trigger a Rash of Defections?" *Christianity Today* 10 (October): 6–77.

Moberley, W. H., W. Griffith, H. H. Hand, and B. M. Meglino. 1979. "Review and Conceptual Analysis of the Employee Turnover Process." *Psychological Bulletin* 86:493–522.

Mol, H. 1976. *Identity and the Sacred: A Sketch for a New Social-Scientific Theory of Religion.* Oxford: Basil Blackwell.

Moore, A. Leroy 1980. *The Theology Crisis or Ellen G. White's Concept of Righteousness by Faith as it Relates to Contemporary SDA Issues.* Corpus Christi, Tex.: Life Seminars.

Morgan, G. W. 1980. "Memo from Morgan." Manuscript, 28 April.

Mowday, R. T. 1981. "Viewing Turnover from the Perspective of Those Who Remain: The Relationship of Job Attitudes to Attributions of the Causes of Turnover." *Journal of Applied Social Psychology* 66:120–123.

_____ , L. W. Porter, and R. M. Steers. 1982. *Employee Organisation Linkages: The Psychology of Commitment, Absenteeism and Turnover.* New York: Academic Press.

Neff, D., and L. Neff. 1985. "Pilgrims Share Their Stories." In *Evangelicals on the Canterbury Trail: Why Evangelicals Are Attracted to the Liturgical Church,* edited by P. E. Webber, 149–161. Waco, Tex.: Jarrell.

Neufeld, D. F., and J. Neuffer. 1966. *Seventh-day Adventist Encyclopedia.* Washington, D.C.: Review and Herald.

Newman, W. M. 1971. "Role Conflict in the Ministry and the Role of the Seminary: A Pilot Study." *Sociological Analysis* 32, no. 4:238–248.

Numbers, R. 1976. *Prophetess of Health: A Study of Ellen G. White.* New York: Harper and Row.

_____ . 1992. *Prophetess of Health: Ellen G. White and the Origins of the Seventh-day Adventist Health Reform.* Knoxville: University of Tennessee Press.

_____ , and J. M. Butler. 1987. *The Disappointed: Millerism and Millenarianism in the Nineteenth Century.* Bloomington: Indiana University Press.

Nyberg, K. N. 1979. "Whatever Happened to Ministers' Wives?" *Christian Century* 96:7–14, 151–154, 156–157.

O'Dea, T. 1957. *The Mormons.* Chicago: University of Chicago Press.

_____ . 1966. *The Sociology of Religion.* Englewood Cliffs, N.J.: Prentice-Hall.

Okely, J. 1992. "Anthropology and Autobiography: Participatory Experience and Embodied Knowledge." In *Anthropology and Autobiography,* edited by J. Okely and H. Callaway, Association of Social Anthropologists, Monograph 29, 1–28. London: Routledge.

Olson, R. W. 1978. "Who Decides What Adventists Believe: A Chronological Survey of the Sources." 15 March. Unpublished paper, White Estate (File DF 326), Washington, D.C.

Oosterwal, G. 1980. "The Seventh-day Adventist Church in the World Today." In *Servants of Christ: The Adventist Church Facing the '80s,* edited by G. Oosterwal, et al., 1–52. Berrien Springs, Mich.: Andrews University Press.

"Open Letter to President Wilson from Concerned Pastors and Scholars at Andrews

University Seminary and Graduate School, 10 September 1980." 1980. *Campus Chronicle,* 25 September.

Pahl, J. M., and R. E. Pahl. 1971. *Managers and Their Wives.* London: Allen Lane.

Parer, M., and T. Peterson. 1971. *Prophets and Losses in the Priesthood: In Quest of the Future Ministry.* Sydney: Alella Books.

Parmenter, K. S. 1980a. Letter to D. Ford, 25 August (in my possession).

_____. 1980b. "Ford Document on Sanctuary Reviewed: Variant Views Rejected." *Australasian Record,* 8 September:3.

Patrick, A. N. 1980a. "Beyond Colorado: A Tentative Interpretation." Unpublished manuscript.

_____. 1980b. "Memo." 22 October. EGW/SDA Research Centre, Cooranbong, N.S.W.

_____. 1980c. "Notes from A. N. Patrick's Telephone Call to W. Duncan Eva, Noon, September 12, 1980." Manuscript, EGW/SDA Research Centre, Cooranbong, N.S.W.

_____. 1983. "Interview by Robert Wolfgramm." In R. Wolfgramm, "Charismatic Delegitimation in a Sect: Ellen White and Her Critics," 358–374. Master's thesis, Chisholm Institute of Technology, Melbourne.

_____. 1987. "Interview by P. H. Ballis." 29 September. Cooranbong, N.S.W.

Paxton, G. J. 1978. *The Shaking of Adventism: A Documented Account of the Crisis Among Adventists Over the Doctrine of Justification by Faith.* Grand Rapids, Mich.: Baker Book House.

Pearson, M. 1990. *Millennial Dreams and Moral Dilemmas: Seventh-day Adventism and Contemporary Ethics.* Cambridge: Cambridge University Press.

Pierson, R. H. 1978. "An Earnest Appeal from the Retiring President of the General Conference." *Review and Herald* November 26:10-11.

Pines, A., E. Aronson, and D. Kafry. 1981. *Burnout: From Tedium to Personal Growth.* New York: Free Press.

_____, and D. Kafry. 1978. "Occupational Tedium in the Social Services." *Social Work* 23, no. 6:499–507.

_____, and C. Maslach. 1979. "Combating Staff Burnout in a Child Care Centre." *Child Care Quarterly* 9, no. 1:5–16.

Potter, J., and M. Wetherell. 1987. *Discourse and Social Psychology: Beyond Attitudes and Behaviour.* London: Sage Publications.

Potvin, R. H. 1976. "Role Uncertainty and Commitment Among Seminary Faculty." *Sociological Analysis* 37:45–52.

Price, J. L. 1977. *The Study of Turnover.* Ames: Iowa State University Press.

Pryor, R. J. 1986. *At Cross Purposes: Stress and Support in the Ministry of the Wounded Healer.* Kew: Commission on Continuing Education for Ministry, Uniting Church in Australia, Synod of Victoria.

Quinley, H. E. 1974. *The Prophetic Clergy: Social Activism Among Protestant Ministers.* New York: John Wiley and Sons.

Rankin, R. P. 1960. "The Ministerial Calling and the Minister's Wife." *Pastoral Psychology* 4:16–22.

Ratzlaff, D. 1981. "Crisis in Freedom." Manuscript, 12 September.

Rea, W. T. 1982. *The White Lie.* Turlock, Calif.: M and R Publications.

Reynolds, K. J. 1986. "The Church Under Stress, 1931–1960." In *Adventism in America: A History,* edited by G. Land, 170–207. Grand Rapids, Mich.: William B. Eerdmans.

Rice, D. 1990. *Shattered Vows: Exodus from the Priesthood.* London: Michael Joseph.

Richardson, J. T. 1975. "New Forms of Deviancy in a Fundamentalist Church: A Case Study." *Review of Religious Research* 16:134–141.

———. 1978. *Conversion Careers: In and Out of the New Religions.* Beverly Hills, Calif.: Sage Publications.

———, J. van der Lans, and F. Derks. 1986. "Leaving and Labelling: Voluntary and Coerced Disaffiliation from Religious Social Movements." *Research in Social Movements, Conflicts and Change* 9:97–126.

Ritti, R. R., T. P. Ferrence, and F. H. Goldner. 1974. "Professions and Their Plausibility: Priests, Work and Belief Systems." *Sociology of Work and Occupations* 1, no. 1:24–51.

Robbins, A., and J. Richardson. 1978. "Theory and Research on Today's 'New Religions.'" *Sociological Analysis* 39, no. 2:95–122.

Robbins, S. P. 1974. *Managing Organizational Conflict.* Englewood Cliffs, N.J.: Prentice-Hall.

Roof, W. C., and C. K. Hadaway. 1979. "Denominational Switching in the Seventies: Going Beyond Stark and Glock." *Journal for the Scientific Study of Religion* 18:363–379.

Rush, J. P. 1990. "The Relationship of Cynicism to Role Conflict, Worker Alienation, and Role Orientation Among Alabama Juvenile Probation Officers." D.P.A. thesis, University of Alabama (Ann Arbor, Mich.: University Microfilms International, 1992).

Salaman, G. 1979. *Work Organisations: Resistance and Control.* London: Longman.

Sanctuary Review Committee. 1980. "Christ in the Heavenly Sanctuary." *Ministry,* October:16–19.

SanGiovanni, L. F. 1978. *Ex-Nuns: A Study of Emergent Role Passage.* N.J.: Ablex.

Sarason, S. B. 1977. *Work, Aging, and Social Change : Professionals and the One Life–One Career Imperative.* New York: Free Press.

Scanzoni, J. 1965. "Resolution of Occupational Role Conflict in Clergy Marriages." *Journal of Marriage and Family.* August:396–402.

Schantz, B. 1983. "The Development of the Seventh-day Adventist Missionary Thought: Contemporary Appraisal." Ph.D. thesis, Fuller Theological Seminary.

Schneider, L., and L. Zurcher. 1970. "Toward Understanding the Catholic Crisis: Observations on Dissenting Priests in Texas." *Journal for the Scientific Study of Religion* 9, no. 3:197–207.

Schoenherr, R. A., and A. Sorensen. 1982. "Social Change in Religious Organizations: Consequences of Clergy Decline in the U.S. Catholic Church." *Sociological Analysis* 43, no. 1:23–52.

———, and L. A. Young. 1990. "Quitting the Clergy: Resignations in the Roman Catholic Priesthood." *Journal for the Scientific Study of Religion* 29, no. 4:463–481.

Schoun, B. D. 1982. *Helping Pastors Cope: A Psycho-social Support System for Pastors.* Berrien Springs, Mich.: Andrews University Press.

Schwartz, G. 1970. *Sect Ideologies and Social Status.* Chicago: University of Chicago Press.

Schwarz, R. W. 1979. *Light Bearers to the Remnant: Denominational History Textbook for Seventh-day Adventist College Classes.* Mountain View, Calif.: Pacific Press Publishing Association.

Scott, M. B., and S. Lyman. 1968. "Accounts." *American Sociological Review* 33:46–62.

Scott, R.B.Y. 1968. *The Relevance of the Prophets: An Introduction to the Old Testament Prophets and Their Message.* Rev. ed. New York: Macmillan.

Seidler, J. 1972. "Rebellion and Retreatism Among the American Catholic Clergy." Ph.D. thesis, University of North Carolina, Chapel Hill.

———. 1974a. "Priest-Protest in the Human Catholic Church." *National Catholic Reporter* 10 (May):6–9, 12–14.

———. 1974b. "Priest Resignations, Relocations and Passivity." *National Catholic Reporter* 10:6–9, 14–17.

———. 1979. "Priest Resignations in a Lazy Monopoly." *American Sociological Review* 44:763–783.

Selznick, P. 1952. "A Theory of Organizational Commitment." In *Reader in Bureaucracy*, edited by R. K. Merton et. al., 194–202. New York: Free Press.

Seventh-day Adventist Church Manual. 1971. Washington, D.C.: Review and Herald.

Seventh-day Adventist Yearbook. 1983. Washington, D.C.: Review and Herald.

Shaffir, W., and R. Rockaway. 1987. "Leaving the Ultra-Orthodox Fold: Haredi Jews Who Defected." *Jewish Journal of Sociology* 29:97–114.

Shea, W. H. 1980. "Daniel and the Judgement." *Spectrum* 11:37–43.

Shupe, A. D., and D. G. Bromley. 1980. "Walking a Tightrope: Dilemmas of Participant Observation of Groups in Conflict." *Qualitative Sociology* 2:3–21.

Skonovd, L. N. 1981. "Apostasy: The Process of Defection from Religious Totalism." Ph.D. thesis, University of California, Davis.

———. 1983. "Leaving the Cultic Religious Milieu." In *The Brainwashing/Deprogramming Controversy: Sociological, Psychological, Legal and Historical Perspectives*, edited by D. G. Bromley and J. T. Richardson, 91–105. New York: Edwin Mellen Press.

Sloper, D. W., and B. Hill. 1985. "Organisation Effectiveness: Some Observations from a Pacific College, Part II." *Journal of Christian Education* 82, part 2:10–20.

Smith, D. E. 1974. "Women's Perspective as a Radical Critique of Sociology." *Sociological Inquiry* 44:7–13.

———. 1988. *The Everyday World as Problematic: A Feminist Sociology.* New York: Open University Press.

Smythe, E.E.M. 1984. "Burn-out: From Caring to Apathy." In *Surviving Nursing*, edited by E.E.M. Smythe, 46–57. Menlo Park, Calif.: Addison-Wesley.

Snow, D. A., and R. Machalek. 1983. "The Convert as a Special Type." In *Sociological Theory 1983*, edited by R. Collins, 259–289. San Francisco: Jossey-Bass.

———, E. B. Rochford, Jr., J. K. Worden, and R. D. Benford. 1986. "Frame Alignment Process, Micromobilization and Movement Participation." *American Sociological Review* 45:464–481.

———, L. A. Zurcher, and S. Ekland-Olson. 1980. "Social Networks and Social Movements: A Microstructural Approach to Differential Recruitment." *American Sociological Review* 45:787–801.

Solomon, T. 1981. "Integrating the 'Moonie' Experience: A Survey of Ex-Members of the Unification Church." In *In Gods We Trust: New Patterns of Religious Pluralism in America*, edited by R. Robbins and D. Anthony, 275–294. New Brunswick, N.J.: Transaction Books.

Spalding, A. W. 1961. *The Origins of Seventh-day Adventists.* Vol. 1. Washington, D.C.: Review and Herald.

Spedding, J. 1975. "Wives of the Clergy: A Sociological Analysis of Wives of Ministers of Religion in Four Denominations." Ph.D. thesis, University of Bradford.

Srole, L. 1956. "'Social Integration and Certain Corollaries: An Explanatory Study."

American Sociological Review 21:709–716.

Standish, C. D., and R. R. Standish. 1988. *Keepers of the Faith.* Rapidan, Va.: Hartland.

Stark, R., and C. Y. Glock. 1968. "The Switchers: Changes in Denomination." In *American Piety: The Nature of Religious Commitment,* edited by R. Stark and C. Y. Glock. Berkeley: University of California Press.

Steeley, D. 1985. "The Adventist Package Deal: New Lives for Old." In *In and Out of the World: Seventh-day Adventists in New Zealand,* edited by P. H. Ballis, 152–171. Palmerston North, New Zealand: Dunmore Press.

Stone, G. P. 1962. "Appearance of the Self." In *Human Behaviour and Social Processes, an Interactionist Approach,* edited by A. M. Rose, 68–118. London: Routledge and Kegan Paul.

Strauss, A. 1959. *Mirrors and Masks: The Search for Identity.* Glencoe, Ill.: Free Press.

Suessenbach, Heinz. 1980/1981. "Letter of Resignation." *Logos* 1, nos. 5 and 6, December/January.

Sweet, L. I. 1983. *The Minister's Wife: Her Role in Nineteenth-Century American Evangelicalism.* Philadelphia: Temple University Press.

Tarling, L. 1981. *The Edges of Seventh-day Adventism.* Barragga Bay, Bermagui South, N.S.W.: Galilee.

Taylor, B. 1976. "Conversion and Cognition: An Area for Empirical Study in the Microsociology of Religious Knowledge." *Social Compass* 23:5–22.

Taylor, M. G., and S. F. Hartley. 1975. "The Two-Person Career: A Classic Example." *Sociology of Work and Occupations* 2:354–372.

Teel, C. Jr. 1980. "Withdrawing Sect, Accommodating Church, Prophesying Remnant: Dilemmas in the Institutionalization of Adventism." Unpublished paper, Loma Linda University.

Theobald, R. 1979. "The Seventh-day Adventist Movement: A Sociological Study with Particular Reference to Great Britain." Ph.D. thesis, London School of Economics.

―――――― . 1978. "A Charisma Too Versatile?" *Archives Europeennes de Sociologie* 19:192–198.

Thoits, P. A. 1989. "The Sociology of Emotions." *Annual Review of Sociology* 15:317–342.

Thompson, K. 1980. Letter to Members of the Australasian Division Committee, 14 September (in my possession).

Tolhurst, A. H. "Telephone Call from John Carter re Meeting Des Ford Had in Sydney with 16 Ministers (on 13 March 1983)." Manuscript, Trans-Tasman Union Conference, Sydney.

Towler, R. 1969. "The Social Status of the Anglican Minister." In *Sociology of Religion,* edited by R. Robertson, 443–450. Harmondsworth: Penguin.

―――――― , and A.P.M. Coxon. 1979. *The Fate of the Anglican Clergy: A Sociological Study.* London: Macmillan.

Townend, C. A. "Discussion Paper on North New Zealand Tithe, Income for 1983." Paper presented at North New Zealand Conference of Seventh-day Adventists, Manukau City, Auckland.

Tramonte, M. R. 1986. "A Study of the Resigned Priests from the Perspective of Levinson's Psychological Theory of Adult Development." Ed.D. thesis, Boston University.

Travisano, R. 1981. "Alternation and Conversion as Qualitatively Different Transformations." In *Social Psychology Through Symbolic Interactionism,* edited by G. P. Stone and H. A. Farberman, 237–248. New York: John Wiley and Sons.

Trenchard, W. C. 1980. "In the Shadow of the Sanctuary: The 1980 Theological

Consultation." *Spectrum* 11:26–30.

Truman, R. 1974. *Underground Manual for Ministers Wives (and Other Bewildered Women)*. Nashville, Tenn.: Abingdon.

Unruh, T. E. 1977. "The Seventh-day Adventist Evangelical Conferences of 1955–1956." *Adventist Heritage* 4:35–46.

Utt, W. 1980a. "Desmond Ford Raises the Sanctuary Question." *Spectrum* 10:3–8.

———. 1980b "Journalistic Fairness?" *Spectrum* 11:63–64.

———. 1981. "Omega: An Historical View." *Spectrum* 12:57–62.

Vande Vere, E. K. 1972. *The Wisdom Seekers: The Intriguing Story of the Men and Women Who Made the First Institution for Higher Learning Among Seventh-day Adventists*. Nashville, Tenn.: Southern Publishing Association.

Vaughan, D. 1986. *Uncoupling: Turning Points in Intimate Relationships*. New York: Oxford University Press.

Vecchio, R. P., G. Hearn, and G. Southey. 1992. *Organisational Behaviour: Life at Work in Australia*. Australian ed. Sydney: Harcourt Brace Jovanovich.

Wallenkampf, A. V. 1981. "A Brief Review of Some of the Internal and External Challengers to the SDA Teachings on the Sanctuary and the Atonement." In *The Sanctuary and the Atonement: Biblical, Historical, and Theological*, edited by A. V. Wallenkampf and W. R. Lesher, 582–603. Washington, D.C.: Review and Herald.

Walsh, E. J. 1981. "Resource Mobilization and Citizen Protest in Communities Around Three Mile Island." *Social Problems* 29:1-21.

Walton, L. R. 1981. *Omega*. Washington, D.C.: Review and Herald.

Weber, M. 1948. *From Max Weber: Essays in Sociology*, translated and edited by H. H. Gerth and C. Wright Mills. London: Routledge and Kegan Paul.

———. 1968. *Economy and Society: An Outline of Interpretive Sociology*, edited by G. Roth and C. Wittich. New York: Bedminster Press.

Wetherell, M., and J. Potter. 1992. *Mapping the Language of Racism: Discourse and the Legitimation of Exploitation*. Hemel Hempstead: Harvester Wheatsheaf.

White, E. G. 1911. *The Great Controversy*. Washington, D.C.: Review and Herald.

———. 1941. *Gospel Workers*. Washington, D.C.: Review and Herald.

———. 1946. *Evangelism as Set Forth in the Writings of Ellen G. White*. Washington, D.C.: Review and Herald.

———. 1948. *Testimonies to the Church*. 9 vols. Mountain View, Calif.: Pacific Press Publishing Association.

———. 1952. *The Adventist Home: Counsels to Seventh-day Adventist Families as Set Forth in the Writings of Ellen G. White*. Nashville, Tenn.: Southern Publishing Association.

———. 1962. *Testimonies to Ministers and Gospel Workers*. Mountain View, Calif.: Pacific Press.

———. 1963. *Medical Ministry: A Treatise on Medical Missionary Work in the Gospel*. Mountain View, Calif.: Pacific Press Publishing Association.

Wilson, B. R. 1966. *Religion in Secular Society: A Sociological Comment*. London: C. A. Watts and Co.

———. 1975. "Sect or Denomination: Can Adventism Maintain Its Identity?" *Spectrum* 15:34–43.

———. 1978. "Becoming a Sectarian: Motivation and Commitment." In *Religious Motivation: Biographical and Sociological Problems for the Church Historian*, edited by D. Baker, 481–506. Oxford: Basil Blackwell.

_____. 1982. *Religion in Sociological Perspective.* Oxford: Oxford University Press.

_____. 1990. *The Social Dimensions of Sectarianism: Sects and New Religious Movements in Contemporary Society.* Oxford: Clarendon Press.

Wilson, N. C. 1980. "This I Believe About Ellen G. White." *Adventist Review* 20 (March):8–10.

Winter, E. 1983. "Ministers in Conflict: A Study of Role Conflicts Experienced by the Pastoral Leadership of the Seventh-day Adventist Church." Master's thesis, Avondale College, Cooranbong, N.S.W.

Wolfgramm, R. 1983. "Charismatic Delegitimation in a Sect: Ellen White and Her Critics." Master's thesis, Chisholm Institute of Technology, Melbourne.

Wooffitt, R. 1992. *Telling Tales of the Unexpected: The Organisation of Factual Discourse.* Hemel Hempstead: Harvester Wheatsheaf.

Working Policy of the South Pacific Division. 1986. Wahroonga, N.S.W.: Australasian Conference Association Ltd.

World Council of Churches. 1973. *So Much in Common.* Geneva: WCC.

Wright, S. A. 1984. "Post-Involvement Attitudes of Voluntary Defectors from Controversial New Religious Movements." *Journal for the Scientific Study of Religion* 23:171–182.

_____. 1986. "Dyadic Intimacy and Social Control in Three Cult Movements." *Sociological Analysis* 44, 2:137–150.

_____. 1987. *Leaving Cults: The Dynamics of Defection.* Monograph 7. Washington, D.C.: Society for the Scientific Study of Religion.

Wuthnow, R. 1976. "Recent Pattern of Secularization: A Problem of Generations." *American Sociological Review* 41:850–867.

Yankelovich, D. 1982. "Lying Well is Best Revenge." *Psychology Today*, August:5–6, 71.

Yinger, J. M. 1970. *The Scientific Study of Religion.* London: Routledge.

Yob, I. M. 1988. *The Church and Feminism: An Exploration of Common Ground.* Englewood, Colo.: Winsen Publications.

Young, N. H. 1989. *Innocence regained: the fight to free Lindy Chamberlain.* Annandale, N.S.W. : Federation Press.

Zelan, J. 1968. "Religious Apostasy, Higher Education and Occupational Choice." *Sociology of Education* 41:370–379.

Zelus, P. R. 1975. "Structural Determinants of Clergy Resignation." Ph.D. thesis, Northwest University.

Zurcher, L. A. 1982. "The Staging of Emotions: A Dramaturgical Analysis." *Symbolic Interaction* 5:1–22.

Zygmunt, J. F. 1960. "The Role and Interrelationship of Symbolic and Structured Processes in the Development of a Sectarian Movement." Ph.D. thesis, University of Chicago.

Zytkoskee, A. 1980. "Interview with Desmond Ford." *Spectrum* 11:53–61.

Index

About the Author

PETER H. BALLIS is Senior Lecturer and Head of Sociology and Social Research in the School of Humanities and Social Sciences at Monash University, Gippsland Campus. He is the editor of *In and Out of the World: Seventh-Day Adventists in New Zealand* (1985) and the author of numerous journal articles and book chapters on Adventist history.

ISBN 0-275-96229-6

90000

EAN

9 780275 962296

HARDCOVER BAR CODE